D1579703

LONDON
THE
Executioner's
CITY

DAVID BRANDON & ALAN BROOKE

SUTTON PUBLISHING

First published in the United Kingdom in 2006 by
Sutton Publishing Limited

This paperback edition first published in 2007 by
Sutton Publishing, an imprint of NPI Media Group Limited
Cirencester Road · Chalford · Stroud · Gloucestershire · GL6 8PE

British Library Cataloguing in Publication Data
A catalogue record for this book is available from the British
Library.

ISBN 978-0-7509-4024-5

Typeset in Sabon.
Typesetting and origination by
NPI Media Group Limited.
Printed and bound in England.

Contents

Acknowledgements

We would like to acknowledge the generous support and assistance of the staff at the Guildhall Library in the City of London. We also wish to thank Christopher Feeney at Sutton Publishing for his light-handed guidance and support, Anne Bennett for her sense of humour and the other members of the Sutton team for their efficient work.

David Brandon and
Alan Brooke

ONE

Introduction

In 1998, under Section 36 of the Crime and Disorder Act, the death sentence was abolished for the last two offences which had retained the capital sanction – piracy with violence and treason. This brought to an end a practice that had existed as a common punishment in Britain for over a thousand years. The death penalty for murder had been effectively ended under the Murder (Abolition of the Death Penalty) Act in 1965.

Since the abolition of public executions in 1868 the death penalty had been carried out within the privacy of prison walls with only a small number of witnesses in attendance. Peter Anthony Allen and Gwynne Owen Evans, the last two people to be executed in Britain, both in 1964, stayed in their condemned cells (Allen in Walton, Liverpool, and Evans in Strangeways, Manchester) for the last few weeks of their lives, never alone, but always in the company of two prison officers. Two days before their execution the Home Secretary made it clear that there would be no reprieve although nobody had really expected one. This was evident from the fact that the majority of the media hardly thought it a worthy item of news. None the less these hangings yet again provoked calls for the total abolition of the death penalty as crowds gathered outside both prisons to make their feelings known.

The rituals leading up to their deaths were significantly different from those in the days of public executions, which were frequently attended by large crowds. The walk to the scaffold in 1964 was not greeted by abuse and insults from the crowd. It was an event held in camera, as it were. But there were similarities. The prisoners waited in the condemned cell still harbouring slender hopes of a last-minute reprieve; they walked, albeit a much shorter distance, to the scaffold; and the method of execution, hanging by the neck until dead, was familiar. A doctor examined the bodies of the executed men at intervals until no heartbeat or other signs of life could be detected. We cannot know what pain they felt once the door beneath the gallows opened and they plummeted to their deaths. Although they were left to hang for one hour, they were at least spared the longer and more painful strangulation suffered by their predecessors, whose friends pulled their legs to hasten death; and their families escaped the fights over the corpse with surgeons' agents that were so commonplace in earlier days.

This book looks at the history of execution in London, which ended at the gallows in Wandsworth Prison in September 1961 when the 49-year-old murderer Hendrick Neimasz was hanged. By then, the issue of capital punishment was rarely absent from the public agenda. The debate reached fever pitch when Ruth Ellis, at 28 years of age, gained the dubious distinction of being the last woman to be executed in Britain. This took place at Holloway Prison in London on 13 July 1955. The cause of her death was recorded as 'injuries to the central nervous system consequent upon judicial hanging'. Crowds assembled outside Holloway on the evening before and the morning of her execution and their numbers led the Governor to call for police reinforcements. However, this crowd was very different from those which had gathered in the days of public executions. At Holloway that day in 1955 around a thousand people stood silently as the sentence of the court was carried out. Some were praying for her soul, others were merely curious onlookers, but many among them were campaigners for the total abolition of the death penalty.

The subject of execution has long been and remains a controversial subject. Public executions attracted large, sometimes vast, crowds. Morbid though this may sound, execution represents an important aspect of history which affected thousands of people: the condemned, their families and friends, officials, observers and what we now might call the 'chattering classes'. It was etched deeply into popular culture. Public executions were a regular feature of London life. The sixteenth-century diarist Henry Machyn recorded that he attended two and sometimes three executions per day. In one month in 1557 he saw 8 felons hanged at Tyburn, 3 men and 2 women burned at Smithfield and 7 pirates hanged at Wapping. Machyn, like many Londoners, witnessed such executions as a matter of course, as part of the popular calendar.

The history of execution and of the scaffold crowd was an area of study once largely ignored by historians but in recent years new research has contributed significantly to our understanding of the subject. Interest in the history of crime is evident from the proliferation of books, courses, museums, films and Internet sites over the past few years. The excellent 'Old Bailey Online' is an important addition to our knowledge of the history of crime, with over 100,000 documented cases between 1674 and 1834 now being available for the researcher. There is a rich seam of records in the National Archives (formerly the Public Record Office), as well as in other archives and libraries, particularly the Guildhall, the prime source for material on the history of London.

By the early seventeenth century there was a thriving market in tabloid-style journalism. Cheap literature such as broadsheets fed the apparently insatiable popular appetite for sensation and titillation. This material is early evidence of a genre consisting of tales of sex, blood and gore and the supernatural. Crime, criminals and criminality, both real and fictional, fascinate us – but they also repel us. While enjoying stories of murder and suspense, people in almost every period have expressed their fear that crime is getting out of hand. The issue has always featured in general elections. London, with its huge population and wealth, has understandably had more than its share of crime throughout the centuries. The most important seats of justice in the country, the Royal Courts, have long been based in London and have witnessed many high-profile and important cases. More executions, both in public and behind closed doors, have taken place in London than anywhere else in the United Kingdom. It is truly the execution capital of Britain.

In the late eighteenth and early nineteenth centuries there were over 200 offences which carried the death penalty. Methods of execution over the centuries have ranged from burning, hanging, boiling, shooting, drowning and beheading to hanging, drawing and quartering. The latter was reserved for traitors, whose remains were subsequently put on public view, their heads placed on poles and displayed on Old London Bridge while their body parts likewise adorned the city gates. Later, in an age of expanding medical knowledge, surgeons would sometimes legally claim the bodies of the condemned for the purpose of anatomical teaching.

The rationale for inflicting such severe punishment was retribution and deterrence. However, by the late eighteenth century questions were increasingly being asked about the effectiveness of public execution as a deterrent. The belief was growing that the crowds were simply treating the spectacle as entertainment. Crowds flocked to the different sites of execution around London but they responded to the condemned and indeed to the whole occasion in ways that were not always consistent with what the authorities intended. If the purpose of the gruesome spectacle was deterrence then the exercise largely failed. Executions may well have served the function of summoning the people to witness the might and power of the monarch or the state, but the crowds all too often responded by displaying irreverence and mockery of that power. The reformer Henry Fielding (1707–54) recognised this when he wrote that public executions inspired the 'vulgar with a contempt of the gallows rather than a fear of it'.

In an earlier book, *Tyburn, London's Fatal Tree* (Sutton, 2004), we made the point that Tyburn was a significant place in the popular culture of London and it loomed large in the minds of the populace for six centuries or more. People visited the sites of executions, they talked about them constantly and the stories often developed into legends as they were retold, frequently being distorted or exaggerated in the process. In this book we have gone beyond Tyburn, although we still devote a chapter to it, to look at other places of execution in London. Some of these are well known, such as the Tower and Smithfield, but others are less familiar. Smithfield and

Tyburn, for example, witnessed thousands of victims going to their deaths but across London there were many other places where executions were carried out, although some only infrequently or sometimes on no more than one occasion. We have tried to cover the best-known places of execution. We know that there were many other places where executions took place less often, and some of these are mentioned. We are only too aware that there may be other locations which have gone unrecorded or which our researches have not located. While we do not pretend to have achieved a comprehensive coverage of all execution sites, we hope that this book adds to an understanding of the importance and significance of the role that execution has played in the wider history of London.

TWO

Evolving Penal Policy

A day in prison on which one does not weep is a day on which one's heart is hard, not a day on which one's heart is happy.

Oscar Wilde (1854–1900)

Ever since humans have been able to produce more than they needed for immediate consumption, a minority of society has appropriated the bulk of wealth for itself and established mechanisms for preserving the privileges and power which go with that wealth. Through government institutions and the machinery of the law, supported if necessary by force, they have devised methods to seek out and punish those whose behaviour they deem unacceptable. The actions or activities considered legal or illegal and the nature of the punishments inflicted have varied with changing social and economic circumstances over the centuries. Throughout, punishment has been intended to have both deterrent and retributive effects. In more modern times it has also sometimes been associated with the concept of rehabilitation of the offender.

In the seventh century an elaborate system of fines was established and executions were exceptional in the case of men because it was felt that every single man potentially had a role to play in the defence of the kingdom. Women, however, were regarded as dispensable. Their punishment for theft, for example, was likely to be drowning. The Danes, who first arrived in the eighth century, relied mainly on the payment by the offender of compensation to the victim's family in the case of a murder. Compensation was on a sliding scale according to the perceived status of the victim. In the tenth century financial penalties began to be superseded by punishment involving physical violence, which was considered to be a more effective deterrent. For this reason whipping and mutilation were extensively employed. Executions for the most serious offences took the form of drowning or stoning.

Executioners were kept busy during the reign of Canute, who came to the throne in 1016. Capital punishment was infrequent but wrongdoers might be mutilated or scalped or have their eyes put out. Under William I executions were also exceptionally rare but mutilations, eye-extractions and the removal of testicles were all common punishments. All of these were, of course, inflicted without any form of anaesthesia. During the reigns of the Conqueror's sons William II and Henry I capital punishment returned for those whose guilt had been established, usually after ordeal by fire or boiling water. Murder, treason, burglary, arson, robbery and theft carried the death penalty. By contrast Henry II (r. 1154–89) favoured amputation of hands or feet rather than execution for such crimes as robbery, murder and coining.

In the thirteenth century serious offenders were likely to find themselves being outlawed rather than executed, but this was not because of any merciful instinct on the part of the authorities. In practice outlawing subjected the offender to a living death. He was literally an outcast, and both he and his family lost their property. No one was allowed to give him succour and for some time at least he could be killed with impunity by any citizen. No legitimate way of making a living was open to an outlaw.

In 1241 hanging, drawing and quartering was employed for the first time in England. The victim was placed on a hurdle or sledge and dragged by horses to the place of execution. He was then hanged by a rope until nearly dead, whereupon he was cut open and drawn (or disembowelled) – his entrails being burned at the scene in front of him, preferably while he was still alive – whereupon he was then dismembered. Those subjected to this frightful death had been found guilty of treason – of waging war against the king – and only an aggravated form of execution was regarded as sufficient for such a heinous crime.

An important element in execution was that it took place in public and was intended to act as a deterrent to those who observed it. Punishment for lesser offenders also took place in public. The stocks and the pillory, for example, probably came into use for the first time in the late fourteenth century, generally for various petty offences. They were an economical form of punishment, easy to set up and requiring little or no supervision for the victim, who was exposed to public humiliation while suffering considerable physical discomfort. Additionally the crowd could express their abhorrence by showering the miscreant with various kinds of unsavoury filth. If the occupant was particularly disliked, the crowd, although it was against the law to do so, might assail him or her with harder missiles such as rocks. This could have fatal effects. In 1731 Mother Needham, the most notorious London procuress of her time, was stoned in this way, receiving fatal injuries. In 1732 John Waller, a known informer and false witness, was pelted severely until a member of the crowd calmly removed him from the pillory while the beadles and constables stood by and watched. Waller was then knocked down, kicked, beaten and trodden on until he was dead. Such excesses were, thankfully, rare.

Exposure to public ridicule and shame were for centuries of pivotal importance in penal practice. Reputation and standing in the community could be permanently damaged by a spell in the pillory, especially for such people as dishonest traders or those found guilty of unnatural or odd sexual offences. From early times, however, much to the chagrin of the authorities, a sense developed that entertainment and enjoyment were to be had from watching punishments and executions. This obviously detracted from the official intention that such spectacles would overawe observers with the majesty of the law and act as effective deterrents to criminal activity.

Another intended way to discourage serious crime was the impaling on spikes in prominent places of the boiled or pickled heads of executed traitors. For many years the gatehouse of London Bridge was adorned with these grisly exhibits. London Bridge was the main route into the city for those who had arrived from the continent at Dover. It was always busy with English and foreign travellers who could not but be impressed, favourably or otherwise, by this stark evidence of the Crown's success at rooting out sedition. The most heads ever noted in place at any one time was thirty-four. London Bridge even had an official Keeper of the Heads, whose responsibility it was to place each new arrival on a sharp spike where it could be seen by all passers-by. If there was any danger that some of the rotting heads were becoming old hat, as it were, he casually took them off their spikes and threw them down into the Thames. A viewing of the latest heads decorating London Bridge was one of the joys of a pleasant Sunday afternoon family stroll for those who lived in the city or in Southwark. Among the most illustrious figures whose heads ended up on London Bridge were (probably) William Wallace; Jack Cade, the rebel leader in 1450; Bishop Fisher and Sir Thomas More in 1535; Thomas Cromwell in 1540; some of the regicides in 1661; and in 1684 William Staley, a wealthy Catholic framed by that evil and mendacious little toad, Titus Oates. The only female head known to have adorned the bridge was that of Elizabeth Barton, a religious visionary who came to be regarded as a political subversive and was executed in 1534.

An extremely odd story concerning the heads on London Bridge dates back to the sixteenth century. A number of German workers who were employed at the Mint fell seriously ill, apparently from the poisonous fumes given off by the molten metal with which they were working. In accordance with a hoary old folk-belief that drinking out of a cup made from a human skull could have miraculously therapeutic effects, permission was given to remove some of the heads at that time adorning the bridge and fashion from them a number of drinking vessels. The German workers, whose skills must have been highly valued to merit such preferential treatment, then drank from these cups. The outcome was something of a curate's egg, only being excellent in parts. Some of the men recovered but most died.

From 1684 Temple Bar, which marked the western boundary of the city where Fleet Street met the Strand, also displayed the heads or other body parts of traitors. A formal gate here seems to have dated back to the fourteenth century but in the early 1670s it was rebuilt in a state-of-the-art fashion by Wren. The heads of the Rye House Plotters and some other traitors were stuck on spikes atop the bar. The Jacobite Francis Towneley, in 1746, may have had the dubious privilege of being the last person whose head was exhibited on Temple Bar, although some accounts state that the last heads were put on show there in 1776. Spyglasses could be hired for closer examination of the gruesome trophies posted up on Temple Bar. In 1772 two of the heads on Temple Bar fell off during a violent storm and then rolled with apparent determination some distance down the street, watched by knots of horrified bystanders. In 1878 Temple Bar was removed because it was causing traffic congestion. It has recently been re-erected close to St Paul's Cathedral. Near Temple Bar there stood a pillory, whose most notable occupants were probably Titus Oates in 1685 and Daniel Defoe in 1703.

Hanging became the most common method of execution, although people of noble blood were entitled to the 'privilege' of decapitation with a sword or axe. Heretics were punished by burning. It is clear that crime was coming to be regarded as a more serious problem from the late fifteenth century with the emergence of stricter punishments attempting to keep it within bounds. Henry VIII (1509–47) was the first monarch to allow executions on Sundays. He also inaugurated boiling to death as a form of execution. Whipping was employed against vagrants, whose very existence was seen as a major source of criminality. Henry's reign was an extremely busy one for the executioners of London and elsewhere. As many as 70,000 people may have met their death at the executioners' hands during that time. Fines, public and painful humiliation and spells in prison were used to punish minor offenders. Punishment became more barbaric. Someone consigned to the pillory might also have his ears nailed to the woodwork or perhaps a hole bored in his tongue. Interestingly in view of future developments, it was Henry who inaugurated the system whereby barber-surgeons were given the bodies of executed felons for research and demonstration purposes. In 1540 they were provided with four corpses annually. As will be seen later, this number was to increase in the eighteenth century amid considerable controversy.

Elizabeth – 'Good Queen Bess' – ascended the throne in 1558 but did not allow her much-vaunted femininity to soften penal policy. The number of executions rose significantly during her reign but she also made considerable use of banishment to the European continent. While this might appear humane by comparison with capital punishment, its effect on the recipient was not unlike outlawing, compounded by the fact that the victim was likely to find himself penniless, powerless and probably friendless in a foreign country. The idea of banishment lies behind the later extensive use of transportation as a punishment for criminal activity. Hanging was by now far and away the most common form of execution and indeed the English became notorious in Europe for the number of hangings they carried out.

The Tudor monarchs Henry VIII, Mary I and Elizabeth all unleashed ferocious punitive action against heretics, a practice that continued into the seventeenth century. Huge numbers were strangled, disembowelled and burned, often after having been tortured. The hangman was also kept exceptionally busy during the Protectorate under Oliver Cromwell. However, as those in power have found before and since, ideas can have a force and potency that cannot be expunged simply by punishing or executing all those who utter them.

The Tudor monarchs wanted to strengthen the power of the Crown and the ability of the law to protect and encourage the business activities of the developing merchant and financier classes on whom they leant. They were also determined to clip the wings of those nobles who had survived the Wars of the Roses and who hankered after a return to the power their ancestors had enjoyed in feudal days. Likewise those in power were concerned about what they saw as the threat posed by the increasingly restive common people and particularly by 'sturdy vagabonds': menacing gangs of rootless, itinerant men who terrorised the countryside, robbing with impunity. The rudimentary law-enforcement agencies that existed were almost powerless to stem the growing tide of lawlessness and violence in sixteenth-, seventeenth- and eighteenth-century England.

The standard punishments for vagrancy and a range of other misdemeanours were whipping and sometimes branding. Even more barbaric were the practices of removing the ears of those who uttered seditious words and amputating the hands of those who wrote seditious material. In 1579 a Puritan named John Stubbes wrote a book criticising the proposed marriage of Elizabeth and the Duke of Anjou, a match that was exceedingly unpopular in England. Stubbes and the publisher of the book were condemned to lose their right hands.

Immediately after his hand had been severed, Stubbes waved the stump in the air crying, 'God save the Queen!' In 1630 Dr Leighton was foolish enough to publish a book lampooning royalty, the peerage and the Church of England. He was whipped severely and placed in the pillory after his ears had been ripped off. The septum of his nose was broken and he was branded with the letters SS to indicate that he had stirred up sedition.

From the early eighteenth century a wide variety of petty offenders were placed in houses of correction or bridewells, where they underwent usually short sentences involving hard labour. It was hoped that such work would have a reforming effect on those concerned who were feckless or wayward but not hopelessly criminalised. The principle of hard labour underpinned penal practice until well into the Victorian era. The prescribed punishment for felonies, these being the most serious offences, was death.

It was in London that the threat of escalating crime seemed worst. London offered a unique range of opportunities for criminal activity, both professional and opportunistic. Its population was growing steadily and many of those who migrated inwards were rootless, volatile, and unskilled, very much at the mercy of economic slumps. All around them was evidence of the stark contrast between the affluence of the few and the grinding poverty and squalor that was the everyday experience of the majority of the population. The labyrinthine layout of London offered numerous 'Alsatias', criminal ghettos offering anonymity and support networks for criminals. The agencies for law enforcement were feeble and certainly ineffective in coping with the rising levels of criminal and anti-social behaviour, much of which was highly organised.

Suggestions that an official and professional police force be established, however, met with very little support in eighteenth-century England.

The number of capital offences greatly increased during the eighteenth century as successive governments attempted to tackle the apparently inexorable rise in the incidence of crime. The new laws were particularly designed to protect the property of the increasingly important bourgeoisie – the merchants, industrialists and financiers who were busily enriching themselves as Britain was transformed into an urbanised and industrialised society – despite the lack of an effective police force. What became known as the 'Waltham Black Act' of 1722 was aimed ostensibly at poachers but was also used as a Trojan horse to bring in the death penalty for a host of other 'rural' crimes. As Sir Leon Radzinowicz, an expert in criminal jurisprudence, commented: 'The Act constituted in itself a complete and extremely severe criminal code which indiscriminately punished with death a great many offences, without taking into account either the personality of the offender or the particular circumstances of each offence.' These and various other legal enactments were evidence of a hardening of the attitude of the governing classes towards the common people, whom they saw as increasingly irreligious, disrespectful, truculent and criminally inclined. A few hard-liners muttered darkly that hanging was too good for common criminals and some even suggested that they should be broken on the wheel instead!

Public hanging continued to be the ultimate penal sanction and it was unashamedly intended to be a deterrent: terrifying evidence of the power of the state and its ability to bring those who broke the law to account for their crimes. The supposed solemnity and awfulness of public hanging was, however, appropriated by the populace and frequently turned into a mockery of the law, a form of free mass entertainment attracting vast crowds. Unpopular felons were subjected to verbal and, on occasions, physical abuse. Those felons who were liked by the crowd were cheered and often showered with flowers or fruit. The most popular of all were those who exchanged quips with the crowd, swaggered around with a devil-may-care hauteur and launched bitter diatribes against the executioner, informants, judges and corruption in high places. The hangman, the chaplain or Ordinary and other officials were the target of scornful, even scathing abuse. The vendors of refreshments and of so-called 'Last Dying Confessions' found a ready market for their wares while thieves enjoyed rich pickings, frequently oblivious to the felon kicking out in his death agonies, possibly sent to the gallows for the self-same crime of picking pockets! No wonder London was known as the 'City of the Gallows'. As Clive Emsley said,

> Public punishment was theatre. In as much as the ruling class or the state had devised such punishment it was didactic theatre: the gallows and the pillory were to provide lessons and warnings for other would-be transgressors of the law. But for the crowds, drawn from all social groups, the proceedings appear to have been rather melodrama of the rudest sort; there were villains who might be abused and unfortunate heroes who might be cheered and cherished.

From 1752 the death sentence for murder could, at the judge's discretion, be placed on an aggravated basis when

'An Act for the Better Preventing the Horrid Crime of Murder' was passed. Now the corpses of hanged felons were systematically made available for the surgeons as object lessons in the teaching of anatomy. Humiliation was further heaped on the deceased by this dissection taking place in public, with an audience of aspiring surgeons and physicians and anyone else who cared to come along. The same Act gave judges discretionary powers to order the bodies of hanged felons to be gibbeted and put on public display in prominent places. The phrase commonly used was 'hung in chains' but in reality the cadavers were placed within a cage of iron bars.

In 1688 there were about fifty capital offences. Between 1660 and 1819 no fewer than 187 additional offences came to carry a capital sentence. These included cutting hop-bines, setting fire to coal mines, concealing the death of an illegitimate child, sending threatening letters, damaging a fish pond, bigamy and stealing a shroud from a grave. This collection of laws was known as the 'Bloody Code' and pathetic stories have often been related of how children aged 12 or under were hanged for stealing items worth just a few pence. The actuality was more complex. On paper the law was indeed savagely punitive but in practice it could be applied with humanity and pragmatism. Courts were often reluctant to convict where the penalty seemed disproportionate to the crime committed. Increasingly they imposed non-capital punishments on convicted felons. These could involve detention with hard labour or transportation. Penal policy in the eighteenth century was characterised by a flexible although capricious balance between the deterrent of terror and practical humanitarianism. J.M. Beattie summed it up:

An overriding pattern is clear, despite fluctuations over time and differences from place. The stern imperative of a criminal code in which, under the Tudors, execution became mandatory for a wide range of property crimes gave way in practice to a more moderate regime, the harsh sanctions of the law being blunted by judges and jurors alike. More acquittals and partial verdicts . . . resulted in falling rates of hanging and the elaboration of a number of alternative, non-capital punishments.

Before the creation of police forces in the nineteenth century only small numbers of offenders were apprehended and brought to justice. Those who were caught risked being made an example of and could be dealt with ferociously. However, the courts frequently practised what was called 'pious perjury'. This meant, for example, that where capital offences involving theft were being tried, juries might deliberately undervalue what had been stolen to render the offence a misdemeanour, thus attracting a lesser penalty than a felony. Judges sometimes dismissed cases on their own initiative and reprieves, even on the day set for the hanging, were by no means uncommon. Many pregnant women convicted of capital offences avoided the death sentence by pleading 'benefit of belly'. This allowed them a stay of execution until the baby was born, after which most were pardoned anyway. People of good character or those who could convince the court of extenuating circumstances might be treated leniently. Before 1706 it had been possible for clergy and other lettered persons to elude the death penalty for a number of offences by pleading 'benefit of clergy', an ancient and increasingly anomalous form of privilege resulting from the existence of ecclesiastical courts alongside secular ones. Those claiming benefit of clergy merely had to recite a brief passage from the Bible. This passage could easily be learned by the most ignorant and illiterate of offenders, who then used it to escape the gallows. In an increasingly secular society this was clearly an anomaly and it gradually dropped out of use. The new capital offences that came on to the statute book in the eighteenth century were made 'non-clergyable' and benefit was finally abolished in 1827.

The unpredictable, even capricious, mixture of terror with humanity and clemency by the courts added powerfully to their mystique. Bewigged judges in ermine-tipped scarlet robes donned the black cloth when death sentences were to be pronounced, thereby emphasising the majesty of the law and overawing those who offended against it. The fact that the court's decision might be unclear until the very last minute added enormously to the tension. Such flexibility in applying the law, however, meant that it was frequently both inconsistent and inequitable.

The first known reference to the idea of transportation is believed to be that by the geographer and historian Richard Hakluyt, who in 1584 recommended the sending of criminals to the American colonies where they could be usefully employed in sawing and felling trees and planting sugar cane. Small numbers of felons and political prisoners were dispatched to the North American colonies of Virginia and Maryland and to plantations in the Caribbean during the seventeenth century. However, it was in the eighteenth and nineteenth centuries that Britain systematically transported large numbers of felons convicted of serious crimes, including many who previously would have been hanged and for whom transportation was a reprieve from or commutation of the death sentence.

Between 1718 and 1775 at least 30,000 convicts were transported to the Americas. The Transportation Act of 1718 made it clear that transportation was considered to be not only a punishment and a deterrent to crime, but also a means of supplying the colonies with the labour force they needed for their economic expansion to proceed. Transportation was also employed in cases where for a variety of reasons, such as the prisoner's youthfulness or previous good character, it was decided to commute the death sentence. After the American colonies won their independence and refused to receive any more convicts, there was a somewhat panicky search for alternative destinations before Australia was agreed upon. As a temporary expedient it was decided that convicts whose capital sentences had been commuted would be housed in superannuated wooden warships that had been stripped of their armament, running rigging and other fittings. These notorious prison 'hulks' were moored on the River Thames and elsewhere. The convicts were mostly employed in public building, dockyard labour or maintenance works. The conditions in these hulks quickly became even worse than in the foulest prisons on land and their existence was widely regarded as scandalous.

Whether transportation to the New World was an effective form of punishment was the subject of vigorous debate. Notable prison reformers such as Sir John Fielding and John Howard believed that transportation taught felons the benefits of hard work and took them away from the criminal networks and rookeries which were such a feature of London especially. The lawyer Sir William Eden disagreed. He believed that some people offended simply so that they could enjoy the 'cushy' conditions of a term of transportation with the possibility of a fresh start in the New World at the end of it. He further suggested that the most dangerous felons, instead of being transported, should be exchanged for Christians who had been enslaved and were eking out miserable existences in parts of North Africa, sometimes as galley slaves.

The concept of hard labour in the colonies or in the houses of correction in England can now be seen as a significant development in the process whereby punishment changed from being a physical and public spectacle to one carried out away from the public gaze and defined in terms of labour and time. Hard labour was believed to combine elements of punishment for the criminal and retribution for society with the possibility of reforming the criminal's character. The ferment of debate around penal issues stands alongside efforts to supervise alehouses and other drinking places more effectively and to abolish sports such as cockfighting, pugilism and bull-baiting, which attracted potentially riotous crowds. An arsenal of draconian legal sanctions was drawn up to clamp down on poaching, which was seen as another example of the reprehensible and growing lack of deference to authority among the so-called 'lower orders'.

Among those who influenced public policy, attitudes were contradictory. Some called for harsher punishment. The apparent severity of the law, however, frequently led judges and juries down the paths of clemency and humanity. The voices of many were raised against conditions in the country's prisons and on board the hulks. Transportation, too, had its critics. Some argued that it was too harsh, others that it was too lenient, while some believed it was not cost-effective. As the debate continued to rage, the number of executions declined. Between 1819 and 1825 only 597 out of 7,770 people sentenced to death were actually hanged. In London in 1829 only 24 hangings for offences other than murder took place. From 1832 hangings for crimes other than murder had virtually ended. However, between 1787 and 1868 about 160,000 convicts were transported to Australia, Van Diemen's Land and Norfolk Island.

The eighteenth century saw the beginning of serious criticism of the penal system. Henry Fielding, the Westminster and Middlesex JP and co-founder with his brother Sir John of the Bow Street Runners, deplored the exhibitionist nature of public hangings and the way in which they either made serious miscreants into swaggering popular heroes or highlighted the pathetic behaviour and lack of dignity of those unable to hide their terror. He argued that 'the executions of criminals . . . serve . . . a purpose diametrically opposite to that for which they were designed; and tend to inspire the vulgar with a contempt for the gallows rather than a fear of it'. In 1778 Sir William Meredith MP argued that barbarous laws and their inconsistent application did little to deter crime. Most offences went undetected and only a small proportion of those convicted of felony were hanged. The criminal could therefore go about his activities knowing that he had a good chance of evading arrest and conviction, let alone a premature death on the scaffold. Those convicted of forgery and coining were very rarely pardoned, but the frequency with which these crimes continued to be committed strongly suggested that hanging was not an effective deterrent.

Critics of penal practice varied enormously in their explanations of why crime was apparently such a serious problem. Some, for example, blamed it on the growing irreligiousness of society while others argued that material and environmental factors needed to be addressed. The question of how to deal with rising levels of crime likewise elicited proposals that varied from increasing the number of capital offences and greater employment of corporal punishment to the use of alternatives such as custodial sentences involving reform and rehabilitation. Jeremy Bentham (1748–1832) was among those who believed that punishments should be made to fit specific offences. Enlightenment thinkers on the European continent, including Charles-Louis Montesquieu and Cesare Beccaria, argued that crime was a social problem that could not be solved simply by creating more severe punishments. Sir Samuel Romilly (1757–1818) thought that brutal punishments such as hanging were merely retributive, had little deterrent effect and should be reduced in number. He also argued that the savagery of the penal code often led the courts, for humanitarian reasons, to be inconsistent in the way in which they applied the law. Romilly was tireless in his campaigning for a reduction in capital offences but the received opinion continued to be that hanging was essential if public order was to be maintained and so his success was limited. Like others at the time, Romilly was opposed to the idea of establishing a professional police force in spite of the possibility that effective policing might deter criminal activity.

Romilly was a man ahead of his time, the advance guard of reform as it were, and there is no doubt that by the time he died there were signs that public opinion was changing and new ideas emerging. As Robert Shoemaker said, 'instead of injuring their bodies and damaging their reputations, the new punishments sought to reform convicts from the inside out by changing their frame of mind.' In 1819 the House of Commons appointed a Committee of Inquiry into the Criminal Laws. In 1822 Sir Robert Peel (1788–1850) became Home Secretary and between 1823 and 1827 initiated the modification and clarification of the criminal justice system, substantially reducing the number of capital offences. By this time some people were criticising him for moving too cautiously but he had his heart set on the establishment of a police force in London. Bravely flying in the face of enormous hostility from powerful sources, he pushed through his Metropolitan Police Act in 1829. There were many teething problems and considerable initial hostility to the new 'Peelers' or 'Bobbies', but they proved effective in combating crime and a few years later new legislation came into force allowing paid police forces to be raised and equipped in the provinces.

When Queen Victoria came to the throne in 1837 the number of hanging offences had come down from well over 200 to just 15. These included murder, arson, rioting, robbery with violence, piracy, wrecking, serious sexual crimes and the theft of government money or securities. Two decades later the number of capital offences was reduced to just four. The number of hangings in London was falling significantly. This was evidence of a greater sense of security in homes and workplaces and on the streets of the metropolis, and this had much to do with the existence of the police. In 1834 one of London's executioners had to be laid off because there was insufficient work for him. Branding ended in

1829, gibbeting was abolished in 1834 and the pillory in 1837. Public hangings continued in Britain until 1868. Transportation ended in the same year. Increasing use was made of custodial sentences for serious offenders, all prisons coming under Home Office control in 1877.

All this may have been evidence of a more enlightened and rational approach to penal matters but one area of the hangman's work still smacked of superstition and witchcraft. The bodies of suicides were not usually permitted burial on consecrated ground. Instead they were interred at a crossroads as dawn broke, with a stake driven through them by the hangman. It was thought that the stake pinned the spirit of the departed to the ground and thus stopped it haunting those left behind. There may also have been some symbolic significance in the crucifix shape of the crossroads. If nothing else, some believed that the number of possible routes at a crossroads confused the suicide's ghost, who thus found it difficult to decide in which direction to go in order to wreak revenge on the living. In 1823 Parliament ended crossroad burials and allowed suicides to be buried on consecrated ground. However, such burials were still normally confined to the disfavoured northern side of the churchyard and were conducted between nine in the evening and midnight and without religious ceremony. For another fifty years the bodies of suicides continued to be subjected to dissection in medical schools.

Two of the last traditional burials of suicides in London took place in 1823 and 1825 respectively. The first was that of a man named Griffiths, who was buried near Sloane Square after having a stake driven through his heart by the hangman. The second interment was more bizarre and involved a prisoner in Newgate who successfully committed suicide by slitting his throat. His body was taken out in a cart accompanied by the hangman. Next to the body stood a miniature gallows with a razor hanging from it. This was held up by the hangman to indicate that the deceased had cheated the gallows. He then drove a stake through the body which was placed in a prepared hole. Finally lime was thrown over the body and the hole filled in.

A battery of arguments was used to counter the efforts of those wishing to abolish capital punishment. There was no realistic alternative to hanging for those who committed cold-blooded murder, it was asserted. Hanging was the ultimate deterrent and its abolition would lead to increased murder rates and to the more determined members of the criminal fraternity using guns as a matter of course. The public felt safer knowing that the capital sanction was still available. The existence of the abolition movement was cited as evidence of precisely those namby-pamby liberal attitudes which valued the murderer's welfare above that of his victim.

In the years following the Second World War a number of murder trials caught the public imagination in Britain, in particular the cases of Craig and Bentley in 1953, the hanging of Timothy John Evans in 1950, the execution of John Reginald Christie in 1953 and finally the trial and hanging of Ruth Ellis in 1955. All these threw up questions and concerns about capital punishment and ensured that the issue was prominent in the public agenda. In 1957 an Act was passed which formally distinguished between capital and non-capital murder and introduced the defence of 'diminished responsibility'. The penalty for all but the most serious types of murder was now to be life imprisonment. In 1965 a Labour government abolished hanging after a sequence of controversial judgments and miscarriages of justice had continued to keep the issue at the forefront of public debate. Despite many calls for the restoration of the death sentence for selected offences, such as the murder of on-duty police officers, successive governments have so far resisted a return to capital punishment in the United Kingdom.

THREE

The Tower of London

The Tower of London is probably the most
familiar symbol of the English state – of its power,
and also of a good deal of its history.

A.L. Rowse (1903–97)

The Tower of London is arguably the most famous
castle in the world. Work on building a fortress at
the eastern extremity of London began soon after William
of Normandy had established himself on the English
throne in 1066. From the start prisoners were kept there
and many died within its gloomy precincts. Today it teems
with tourists eager to be regaled with bloodcurdling
anecdotes about its past and they gaze raptly not only at
the buildings but also at the fascinating display of items
associated with the Tower's history. The word 'Tower' is
almost synonymous with ideas of human misery,
imprisonment, mutilation, torture and execution.

Over the centuries the Tower has been the scene of
bustling and sometimes frantic activity. There have always
been troops stationed there. Forges echoed to the sound
of armourers making and repairing weapons and arms;
coins were minted in enormous quantities; members of
royalty and their attendant households resided there;
exotic animals were kept in its menagerie and prisoners

whiled away interminable years of confinement or the few short days before execution clanking their chains in dark, vermin-ridden, insanitary cells and dungeons. In its early years few humble people found themselves confined within its walls. It was essentially a royal castle with the reputation of being sufficiently secure to allow monarchs to confine within its precincts those they regarded as a serious threat. They were almost always rich, powerful and high-born. There were plenty of other prisons and punishments available for offenders of more humble status. As a fortress, the Tower may have seen remarkably few shots fired in anger but throughout the centuries in which it has acted as a prison it has housed many thousands of miserable individuals, many of whom never left its portals alive. It is all too easy to forget that even today the Tower can still be used as a prison.

From its initial foundation in the eleventh century the Tower has always been intended to look forbidding. It intimidated and overawed those poor unfortunates about to be incarcerated within its precincts, and browbeat the common people of London who for centuries were regarded as truculent and potentially rebellious. It was built in the first place to provide visual evidence of the reality of William's rule over a hostile and resentful people and ever since it has continued to symbolise the power of the Crown and state. It still commands awe.

It was not just outspoken dissidents, seasoned plotters or hapless individuals caught in the wrong place at the wrong time who found themselves confined in the Tower with no apparent prospect either of release or of being brought to trial. And it was not just men, either. In 1531 a huge consignment of gold crowns being shipped to Henry VIII's treasury disappeared in transit. It took two years before investigations pinpointed a villain named Wolfe as the likely mastermind behind the robbery. In 1533 Wolfe was seized and placed in the Tower, where he was frequently visited by his common-law wife, Alice Tankerville. By all accounts she was an extremely toothsome young lady and she used her charms, maybe even her sexual favours, on several of the gaolers in order to be allowed to provide various comforts for Wolfe. The evidence against Wolfe being weak, he was released, but then new evidence was unearthed implicating both Wolfe and Alice and it was decided that both should stand trial. Wolfe himself had disappeared, but it was an easy matter to seize Alice because she was still an almost daily visitor to the Tower, meeting the men with whom she had become friendly. One of these was John Bawd. Thoroughly besotted with her, he concocted a plan to help her to escape, intending to flee with her to a lifetime of mutual happiness in the great blue yonder. Duplicate keys were made and suitable lengths of rope obtained. Everything went according to plan as they descended the outer walls of the precinct – but they had only reached Tower Hill before they were caught. Bawd soon had cause to regret his libidinous urges because he was thrown into the Tower's meanest, foulest dungeon, so small that any occupant was forced to adopt a foetal position. He was racked and then put on trial. Having little to offer in his own defence, he was hanged in chains to die of exposure and starvation. Wolfe was later recaptured and both he and the lovely Alice were sentenced to death. Securely chained, they were lowered into the Thames at low tide and subjected to a miserable and slow death by drowning in the stinking waters of the river as the tide rose.

For those with a taste for the grisly and the macabre, the White Tower contains a collection of executioner's and torturer's tools. An executioner's block can be seen and at least one headsman's axe. A gibbet is a prominent feature. Various torture instruments also catch the eye, including thumbscrews and a version of an especially loathsome device nicknamed the scavenger's daughter. Invented by Leonard Skeffington, the Lieutenant of the Tower in the 1530s, it was also known as Skeffington's Gyves; it compressed and contorted the body, inflicting agony even more excruciating than that produced by the rack. In many ways it was the ideal torture machine: it was light and easily transported, and the mere sight of it was often enough to persuade a prisoner to cooperate wholeheartedly with his inquisitors.

Given its gruesome history, it is hardly surprising that the Tower has the reputation of being England's most haunted building. The phenomena associated with these ghosts are many and varied but those most germane to execution include an unexplained and eerie glow in the Salt Tower, where many prisoners were tortured on the rack, a screaming phantom reckoned to be the ghost of Margaret Pole, Countess of Salisbury, who was hacked to death by the executioner in 1541 and still cries out in terror as she attempts to dodge the falling axe, and an apparition thought to be the ghost of Lady Jane Grey, who was executed within the precincts in 1554. This ghost appears on the anniversary of her execution and is said to consist of a shimmering and understandably morose-looking figure which floats silently and rather pointlessly around the Tower precincts. At the Queen's House a frightening headless figure dressed in white is considered by some to be the spectre of Anne Boleyn, who was beheaded in 1536. The silhouette of a gigantic axe is said to be visible on a wall close to Tower Green.

Other ghosts that have manifested themselves in the Tower include that of Thomas Wentworth, the hated Earl of Strafford, whose execution in 1641 was witnessed by one of the largest crowds ever to turn up at such an event. Soon after Strafford died, he is said to have adopted spectral form and visited Archbishop Laud, awaiting execution in his cell in the Tower. Perhaps in an attempt to fortify Laud, the ghost apparently told him not to fear his impending fate. We do not know whether this provided the archbishop with any much-needed succour. At least Strafford's death was quick; the unfortunate Laud had to wait for four years in a fetid cell before his execution. Strafford's appearance as a spectre in Laud's cell seems to have been both his debut and his swan song in this particular mode.

At Tower Green executions could be carried out away from public gaze. The first recorded victim of Tower Green appears to have been Lord Hastings, an immensely ambitious man who foolishly and fatally manoeuvred against Richard, Duke of Gloucester, later Richard III, when he was acting as guardian to the young Edward V. The duke ordered Hastings to be seized and beheaded, both actions being carried out with extraordinary speed and efficiency. This decisive move had the intended effect of temporarily discouraging opposition to Richard, who soon afterwards was proclaimed king. The year was 1483.

Henry VII may have won the Battle of Bosworth in 1485 and gained the throne of England by force, but he had by no means won the hearts of all the nobility. Henry was a firm believer in *realpolitik* and he soon set about implementing measures to consolidate his power and further reduce that of the nobles. This aroused widespread resentment and Sir William Stanley, whose support had been instrumental in securing the throne for the new king, began plotting against Henry with other disaffected men at home and abroad. Unfortunately, he failed to take into account the extensive spy network that Henry was developing. Acting on intelligence provided by his undercover agents, Henry had the dissident noble placed in the Tower early in 1495. Shortly afterwards Stanley was executed on Tower Green, well away from prying eyes.

Anne Boleyn, Henry's VIII's second wife, had a miscarriage in 1536. Although she had conceived three times only one baby had survived, the future Elizabeth I, but this did not count in Henry's eyes because he wanted a son. Angry and frustrated by the lack of a male heir, Henry turned against the woman after whom he had once so unashamedly lusted. He needed another wife to provide him with an heir – and quickly. Henry was determined to avoid the complicated rigmarole which had surrounded the casting-off of his first wife, Catherine of Aragon. With calculated callousness a plot was devised which framed Anne for adultery with not one but eventually five men, one of whom was her own brother, Lord Rochford, so the stigma of incest was added to the charge of extra-marital sex. One of the men, Mark Smeaton, was tortured, after which he confessed his own adultery and implicated the others. As a mere commoner Smeaton was hanged but Rochford, Sir Francis Weston and William Brereton, being of gentler birth, were allowed the dubious privilege of being beheaded. They all died at Tower Hill in May 1536, just two days before

Anne herself was executed. Henry Norris, who had at one time been one of Henry's favoured cronies, was also incriminated on the evidence that he had picked up and enthused over a handkerchief which Anne had dropped, accidentally or otherwise. His protestations of innocence were spurned by the king. No concrete evidence was provided at the trial which condemned these men to death.

Anne must have felt the net closing around her but she stoutly refused to admit to adultery. Henry was anxious to avoid any public outbursts of histrionics on the scaffold and so it was arranged that Anne would be put to death out of public view on Tower Green. She was to be executed with a sword. Apparently the necessary expertise for such a task was not to be found in this country and so an experienced headsman was summoned from Calais, then an English possession. Observers described this man as an extremely sinister figure. He was dressed in a tight-fitting black suit with the upper part of his face hidden by a mask surmounted by a black cap. The execution was carried out shortly after eight in the morning. Anne said her prayers and then, escorted by what seems a needlessly large number of guards, estimated at 200, she mounted the scaffold. She was blindfolded, whereupon she knelt upright. Fortunately the headsman did his work efficiently and severed her head with one blow. As was expected in such circumstances, he then held up her head as proof that execution had been completed successfully on the right person. It was said that the eyes in the severed head were still moving and her lips still mouthing last-minute devotions. Her attendants immediately moved to take possession of her remains, only to find that the authorities had forgotten to provide a coffin. A resourceful yeoman warder unearthed a large old wooden chest in the nearby armoury for use as a makeshift coffin and Anne's remains were then carefully placed inside and taken to the chapel of St Peter ad Vincula. The king's official mourning for Anne was somewhat perfunctory, lasting just twenty-four hours. This was the first time that the consort of a reigning English monarch had been executed.

Anne's body lay in the chapel for some time unburied and rumours began to circulate that her relations had arranged for her remains to be removed and laid to rest at a church in Norfolk close to Blickling Hall where she was born. No serious evidence exists to support this contention, nor another rumour that her heart was placed in a casket and buried surreptitiously in a church at Thetford. However, there are still unanswered questions. In 1876 the exhumation was ordered of all those buried in the Chapel Royal, the intention being that they were to be reburied with due reverence in the crypt. They included the purported remains of Anne, but there was no trace of the sixth finger she was supposed to have had, so perhaps she really was buried elsewhere and some other unfortunate was interred in her place.

Catherine Howard was the fifth wife of Henry VIII, marrying him in 1540. She was a high-spirited, vivacious young woman whose sensuality and sexual drive must have aroused Henry to a frenzy of passion which by this time he was quite incapable of transforming into effective action. Immensely flattered to be the centre of the king's attentions, Catherine quickly realised that she had married a gross, ill-tempered and largely impotent man whose legs with their suppurating sores were evidence that more likely than not he was pox-ridden. It was clear that the king was in decline and the various coteries in courtly circles now started vying with each other as to who would exercise most influence over the regency that would inevitably occur when Henry died. A group led by the Earl of Hertford, Viscount Lisle and Archbishop Cranmer moved against the Norfolk faction with whom Catherine was associated. The outcome was success for the former group, who managed to draw the ageing and increasingly grumpy king's attention to the fact that he was being cuckolded and that his wife was carrying on an adulterous affair with Thomas Culpepper, an attendant in the privy chamber. Culpepper and another of Catherine's lovers, with whom she had been intimate before her marriage, were executed at Tyburn. In February 1542 Catherine herself was executed on Tower Green, together with Lady Rochford, who had set up assignations between the queen and Culpepper. The privacy of the execution was in accordance with Catherine's wishes. The evening before her death, she had amazed observers by repeatedly approaching the executioner's block, kneeling down, praying and laying her head on it. Call it vanity, but she wanted to ensure that she went to her death with dignity. She was a brave young woman and she did not let herself down on the fatal day. She died after a single blow of the axe.

In 1541 the Countess of Salisbury was the unfortunate victim of one of the most bungled executions of all time. Accounts vary, giving her age as anything from 68 years of age to 80 at the time of her death. Her son, Cardinal Pole, had vociferously attacked Henry VIII's attempts to disentangle himself from his marriage to Catherine of Aragon, but he made these pronouncements from the safe distance of the European continent and by design or otherwise left his mother to pick up the rap. Henry rounded on her and she was condemned to die for little reason other than guilt by association and sheer vindictiveness on the king's part. The countess was a doughty and spirited woman, who absolutely refused to place her head on the block. Defying her age and by no means overawed by the situation in which she found herself, she capered about on the scaffold shouting defiance at all and sundry, and most especially the executioner. The latter was made to look extremely foolish as he pursued her round and round, hacking at her with his axe. When he caught up with her he inflicted awful wounds, and continued to do so until there was little left to hack off – whereupon she stopped capering around and succumbed. It is only to be expected that this gory spectacle is said by some to be re-enacted annually on its anniversary as the screaming phantom of this plucky beldame races around pursued by an equally spectral executioner. The story of this 'death by a thousand cuts' may well have grown in the telling.

After the untimely death of Edward VI on 6 July 1553 Lady Jane Grey was nominated as his successor. A slender, almost wisplike young woman of 16, she had not sought the role she found herself in and was simply the pawn of various factions of self-seeking nobles. She was determined, however, to take her duties seriously. Strong factions at court and the populace favoured Mary Tudor as Edward's successor and civil war seemed a real possibility until those around Lady Jane, making a sober assessment of the balance of forces, decided that it was expedient for her to give up any intention of being crowned. From that time she was effectively condemned to death. Leading lights among those associated with her also found themselves in the Tower.

Mary Tudor, Henry's first child, had been out of favour for many years but now found herself in the position that she had always regarded as her birthright. Astute in many ways, she had no intention of making a martyr out of Lady Jane, even though she knew she would continue to be the focus of oppositon as long as she lived. Instead Mary dealt peremptorily with three of Jane's most prominent supporters, the Duke of Northumberland and his associates Palmer and Gates. Northumberland claimed an eleventh-hour conversion to Roman Catholicism, a religion he had spent his life reviling, but the die was cast and the three men were executed at Tower Hill on 22 August 1554. In the autumn Lady Jane, her husband Lord Guildford Dudley, some of their relations and Archbishop Cranmer were tried and condemned for treason. It is likely that Mary would later have found reasons for securing their release but events began to move very quickly and with a horrid inevitability.

Mary's coronation was accompanied by general rejoicing, albeit muted in some quarters. However, in 1554 Mary's announcement that she was to marry the Catholic King Philip of Spain led to a series of rebellions, one of which, in Kent, was led by Sir Thomas Wyatt. He was caught and tortured. In the turmoil unleashed by these events, Jane and Dudley could not be seen as anything other than serious threats to the throne and so, with mixed feelings, Mary ordered their execution. They died on the same day in February 1554. Poor Jane watched Dudley being taken the short distance to Tower Hill for his execution and then saw his body returning on a cart with his severed head wrapped in a cloth, before she herself went out to be executed on Tower Green. Before her death, she made a short speech declaring that she had been cast in the role of cat's-paw to evil and ambitious men jockeying for power. How right she was! Her frail body trembled convulsively as she was brought out to Tower Green and few could have felt anything other than compassion when the blindfolded young woman stumbled around the scaffold attempting to locate the block.

Mary's reign was, perhaps thankfully, a short one and she was succeeded by Elizabeth in 1558. Elizabeth never married and the salaciously inclined derived great pleasure from speculating about whether she remained a virgin to her death. There was certainly no shortage of potential suitors, at least while she was young and attractive. Being the object of Elizabeth's affections was, however, rather like riding a tiger.

Robert Devereux, Earl of Essex, was just the kind of handsome, dashing young aristocrat whose apparent devotion and flattery could still bring a flush to the queen's cheeks in her later years. Well aware of this, for a while he exploited it to the full. His sheer egotism, however, blinded him to the fact that the price the queen demanded for the favours she was prepared to shower on him was unswerving loyalty and the monopoly of his attention. He yearned for the political power and perks that his vanity, quite mistakenly, led him to believe were his right. This self-same egotism ensured that he made enemies aplenty, and they inevitably set out to plot his downfall. He persuaded the queen to give him various important commissions to undertake but his many shortcomings inevitably let him down. Elizabeth slowly, probably reluctantly, became aware that her hero had feet of clay and she had cause on a number of occasions to berate him for his incompetence. Innately petulant and

essentially stupid, he greatly resented his gradual fall from
favour. He had entertained vague hopes that he might be
able to seize the throne itself when Elizabeth died. He
contacted various dissident elements and allowed himself
to be led into a trap which culminated in a pathetic
uprising in London in 1601. The queen dithered about
signing his death warrant but his involvement in treason
could not be gainsaid. Her last favour to Essex was to
accede to his request that he be executed privately and so
on 25 February 1601 he was dispatched by the headsman
at Tower Green.

There was something of a lull in executions within the
Tower in the seventeenth century. On 12 July 1743 three
soldiers of the 43rd Highland Regiment (later the Black
Watch) were shot by firing squad on Tower Green. The
Highlanders had genuine grievances concerning pay,
conditions, the general contempt in which they were held
by the English authorities, a broken promise that they
would be reviewed by the king and fears that they would
be sent to serve in the Caribbean, a dreaded place because
so many soldiers there died from infectious disease.
Disaffection had been evident for some time and
eventually a substantial number of the Highlanders who
were in transit in the London area decided to desert and
make their way back home. Their intentions were
understandable, if hopeless. Despite their peaceful
intentions, they nevertheless found everyone's hand
against them as they made their way northwards through
the Home Counties. Troops were sent to intercept them
and bring them back by force if necessary. The main body
of Highlanders, about a hundred in number, got no
further than the Oundle area of Northamptonshire, where
they dug in defensively in a moated enclosure near the

bizarre and never completed structure known as Lyveden New Bield. A few wanted to fight on but they were demoralised and outnumbered and there was little alternative to surrender. They were all marched southwards and placed in the Tower. The plight of these proud men began to arouse some sympathy, especially in London. They were court-martialled and found guilty of mutiny. The death sentence was obligatory but the authorities knew that realistically they could not execute a hundred men so it was decided to exercise 'clemency'. All but four (who were regarded as the ringleaders) were dispatched to the American colonies and refused permission ever to return to Scotland. Of the ringleaders, one was sentenced to receive 1,000 lashes while the other three were executed, shot, ironically, by soldiers of the Scots Guards. They died bravely, well away from the public gaze, and were buried nearby.

In the run-up to the First World War the Germans were rightly concerned about Britain's naval power and the authorities there decided to establish a spy network to gather vital intelligence and information, particularly about the Royal Navy. Counter-espionage activity by the British quickly revealed the existence of these spies. Soon all those of German or Austrian origin living in Britain came under suspicion. Two of them, Carl Hans Lody and Carl Frederick Muller, were executed out of sight of the public at the Tower in 1914 and 1915 respectively. During the war about a dozen spies were executed in a miniature rifle range on the east side of the inner wall, in an area now used for car-parking. Official statements said that they were buried within the precincts of the Tower but in fact their bodies were surreptitiously removed and interred in the East London cemetery at Plaistow.

The last person to be executed within the precincts of the Tower was Josef Jakobs. He was shot by firing squad on 15 August 1941 on Tower Green in a rather uninspiring brick and asbestos shed, which was used as a makeshift rifle range by the contingent of Scots Guards stationed in the Tower at the time. Jakobs was a German spy. Hitler's plan was to subject Britain to saturation aerial bombardment as a necessary preliminary to an invasion and the vagaries of the British climate made it essential that he had agents on hand in Britain to provide up-to-date information on weather conditions so that bombing sorties would only be launched in suitable conditions. To achieve this, spies were smuggled into Britain equipped with radio transmitters, code books and a smattering of meteorological knowledge. This tactic somewhat belied the German reputation for efficiency, at least in the case of Jakobs. Espionage on enemy soil was exceptionally hazardous, but Jakobs seems to have been especially vulnerable given that he apparently had no training on how to survive in a hostile country without attracting attention. He was already in his 40s and a dentist by profession. With no previous experience of parachuting, he jumped out of an aircraft over the Fens in Huntingdonshire and broke his left ankle as he landed. It was winter and icy winds were blowing from the east. Unable to move and in severe pain, he fired several shots with his Mauser pistol to summon help. He was quickly found, seized, questioned – and sentenced to be hanged as an enemy spy. However, his shattered ankle meant that he could not stand so the military court that condemned him to death decided that he should be executed by firing squad while sitting down. The firing squad had eight members. Eight rifles were issued, one of which had a blank cartridge. No member of the firing squad could therefore be sure that it was he who had fired the fatal shot. People had been executed in the Tower for about 900 years. It was to fall to this man, curiously ill-equipped for the role of spy and far from home, to be the very last.

TOWER HILL

Tower Hill is a slightly elevated site close to the Tower of London. In all, 125 people are recorded as having been executed there between the fourteenth and the eighteenth century. This is not a large number but since most of them were from the ranks of the high-born, their deaths have perhaps received undue attention and so Tower Hill is disproportionately well known as a place of execution. Many of those who died there were executed for what was construed as treasonable activity. While this did indeed apply to many of them, others died simply because the authorities decided that their continued existence constituted a threat.

The first recorded executions there were unofficial and date from 1381 when Wat Tyler's rebels entered the city. They seized the hated Archbishop of Canterbury, Simon of Sudbury and three others, beheading them on Tower Hill on a makeshift block consisting of a large log. Sudbury's head was later taken to London Bridge and put on display. Two of the others were Lord Treasurer Hales, the man responsible for the hated poll tax, and a notorious tax collector named Legge, but the third was a luckless physician who died because he had attended the greatly disliked John of Gaunt. Sudbury, despite the execrations of the crowd, went to his death with courage, his sufferings being compounded because of the headsman's incompetence. Eight strokes with the axe were required to complete the job. The Peasants' Revolt failed and Tyler himself was struck down treacherously while parleying was still taking place and his head soon adorned London Bridge. Around 150 rebels were executed at various other sites.

Later in the same decade Richard II was under threat from a group of disaffected nobles known as the Lords Appellant, who had considerable support among the populace. To buy time the king perfidiously agreed to the execution of the unpopular Sir Simon Burley, his former revered tutor and counsellor. Burley died on Tower Hill but this concession to the rebels was something that Richard could not forgive. He waited nearly ten years until he was in a much stronger position and got his revenge when Arundel, one of the ringleaders, was executed at exactly the spot where Burley had died. So it was that Tower Hill came to be seen as a place where vengeance was extracted for treasonable acts.

In 1440 Richard Wyche, a priest from Essex and a Lollard, was condemned to death for his beliefs and practices. He was due to be executed at Smithfield, as was usual for such offenders at that time. However, it was thought that attempts might be made to rescue him and so it was decided to put him to death at Tower Hill. He came to be seen by many as a martyr, and as a result a cross and a stone cairn were erected in his memory. A local priest-cum-wideboy rather enterprisingly sold the martyr's ashes – and miraculously, no matter how much of the ashes he sold, there was always plenty more available for gullible purchasers. Many admirers of Wyche and his works were attracted to Tower Hill. The authorities had no truck with martyrs of this sort and so they removed the cairn and the attendant vendor of Wyche's ashes. With vindictive relish they then ploughed up the site and put a dungheap in its place.

It was in the reign of Edward IV (1461–83) that a permanent scaffold was erected at Tower Hill for the first time. The king had fallen out with the city authorities who, while recognising that Tower Hill was part of the Tower Liberties and therefore out of their immediate jurisdiction, resented that fact because it meant that they could not derive any income from the often very large crowds who turned up there to witness beheadings or hangings. Edward was circumspect in his dealings with the city burghers, knowing that he needed their goodwill, and so a compromise was reached. The city was given the monopoly of executions on Tower Hill and henceforth, when prisoners were led out of the Tower for execution there, they were symbolically handed over to the sheriffs of the city, who gave the Lieutenant of the Tower a receipt as a token of the official handover.

In 1497 Lord Audley, who had led an unsuccessful rebellion largely composed of Cornishmen, was executed. The authorities were concerned that this event might be made the subject of a popular demonstration and so they marched Audley to his execution on Tower Hill dressed in paper armour to make him the object of ridicule rather than admiration.

Sir James Tyrell was convicted of treason and executed on Tower Hill in May 1502. No sooner had his head plopped into the waiting basket than Henry VII's spin-doctors got to work. Just before Tyrell died, so it was averred, he had confessed to being responsible for the murder of the two princes in the Tower back in 1483, acting on the instructions of Richard, Duke of Gloucester. Leaving aside the controversies surrounding the boys' deaths, the circulation of this information was intended to discredit Richard and to justify and consolidate Henry's position on the throne. Additionally, by putting paid once and for all to the rumours that Edward IV's sons were still alive, it served to deter rivals and further pretenders to the throne.

Henry VIII came to the throne in 1509 amid scenes of rejoicing. The son quickly showed that he was every bit as much a master of *realpolitik* as his father had been. The late king's financial policies had been widely resented. In a quite unashamed attempt to gain popularity, Henry had Sir Richard Empson and John Dudley, who had been largely responsible for implementing these unwelcome policies, thrown into the Tower. In effect, the new king was telling his people that he was turning his back on his father's austere and niggardly policies. A trial was staged, at which Empson in particular skilfully made it clear that he had only been carrying out the late king's instructions, as any loyal subject should do. The king was infuriated; the last thing he wanted in such a situation was a jobsworth, and so he silenced the querulous Empson and Dudley once and for all when the two men were executed at Tower Hill in August 1510 on a trumped-up charge of conspiracy to treason. Henry wanted this episode closed as quickly as possible and the two men were quietly buried within the Tower, rather than continuing to be the object of attention by having their heads displayed in some prominent public place.

Henry clearly inherited his father's sense of insecurity and he set about imprisoning or executing those he considered to be a threat. Among them was the Duke of

Buckingham who seized on the assumption, mistakenly as it was to turn out, that the king would never have a male heir. A vainglorious young man, Buckingham was foolish enough to talk about his own claims to the throne and the changes he would bring about if and when he became king. He also publicly decried Cardinal Wolsey as a low-born upstart. The latter was a dangerous enemy, and he laid evidence before the king that Buckingham was plotting treason. Henry moved quickly and Buckingham last saw the light of day at Tower Hill in May 1520.

Thomas More, one of Henry's close friends, was unable to accept the king's assumption of supremacy over the Church and found himself being manoeuvred into what was virtually a position of treason by default. He and John Fisher, Bishop of Rochester, could not be persuaded to change their minds and publicly endorse Henry's actions, and were duly condemned to be hanged, drawn and quartered at Tyburn. This sentence was commuted to beheading on Tower Hill. In response to this, More, not known for his levity, quipped, 'God forbid the King shall use any more such mercy on any of my friends.' So it was that Fisher died there bravely on 22 June 1535, followed by More on 6 July. He was physically weak by this time and the story is often told of how he made another of his rare jokes when he asked an attendant to help him up on to the scaffold, remarking, 'I pray you, Mr Lieutenant, to see me safe up, and for my coming down let me shift for myself.' More's new-found jocularity kept those within earshot avidly waiting for his next quip – and they were not to be disappointed. As More knelt down by the headsman's block, he pulled his beard aside, saying, 'Pity that should be cut that has not committed treason.' Hardly side-splitting stuff perhaps, but good gallows humour.

More's head was placed for public display on London Bridge but the story is told that his daughter somehow persuaded the custodian of the heads to take it down and allow her to remove it, probably to be buried in a chapel at Canterbury. Some people have argued that the rest of More was buried at All Saints, Chelsea (known as Chelsea Old Church), where there is a mural memorial to him and his first wife. However, it is more likely that he was buried in the Chapel of St Peter ad Vincula within the precincts of the Tower. For many years a nearby convent showed off a fragment of his hair-shirt and a neighbouring church claimed to possess a small piece of his skull. It was a revered and therefore lucrative relic.

Thomas Cromwell proved to be a mighty source of strength and support to his master, Henry VIII. He was an extremely able and astute statesman, but Machiavellian through and through. He masterminded the divorce of Henry and Catherine of Aragon, put into effect the Act of Supremacy in 1534 and supervised the dissolution of the monasteries between 1536 and 1539. He pushed through these immensely important Acts with consummate determination and efficiency but in the course of doing so made himself widely unpopular in the country at large. He only fell from favour when he persuaded Henry to marry Anne of Cleves, as a sort of mail-order bride. When the king set eyes on her for the first time he was appalled, and this initial impression showed no sign of moderating as time went by. He found the unfortunate woman plain to look at and dull of personality. Cromwell's enemies now found just the opportunity they had been looking for. Aware that Henry was already casting lascivious glances elsewhere, they stage-managed the wafting of an exceptionally vivacious and sexually attractive young woman named Catherine Howard in front of him. Predictably the concupiscent king swallowed the alluring bait. Anne's expectations disappeared in a puff of smoke and Cromwell found himself cast in the role of scapegoat. Henry realised he could gain instant popularity by obliging the hated Cromwell to answer for his perceived mistakes. This he duly did at Tower Green on 28 July 1540. It was not long before Henry realised that he had ordered the death of his most sagacious and competent adviser on little more than a whim.

Henry VIII died in 1547 and was succeeded by his young son as Edward VI. He was just 9 years old and so the country now faced the political turbulence that so often surrounded the reign of a minor. The king's uncle Edward Seymour, Earl of Hertford, was appointed Protector and shortly afterwards was created Duke of Somerset. However, his rise to prominence was strongly resented by his younger brother Thomas, an unscrupulous scapegrace who indiscreetly boasted of plotting to bring his brother down, flirted quite outrageously with the young Princess Elizabeth and tried to worm his way into the king's affections by showering him with gifts. Eventually he went too far, being implicated in a plot to seize the Bristol Mint in order to obtain money to finance a coup. Somerset was well aware of his brother's failings but was reluctant to move against him; he was, after all, a sibling. Eventually, though, Thomas was arrested and confined in the Tower, where his arrogance and general obnoxiousness only served to antagonise all those who had dealings with him. He soon paid the price, being executed on 20 March 1549. Two blows of the axe were needed to sever his head from his body.

Somerset himself was soon to follow his brother to the block. A man of radical political and religious views, his power over the king was widely resented and many courtiers were looking to exploit any weakness on his part. He was regarded as irresolute when dealing with rebellions in East Anglia and the West Country. Although autocratic and arrogant in bearing, he had managed to lose control of the Scottish borders and his foreign and economic policies were proving disastrous. His enemies soon moved against him, led by John Dudley, Earl of Warwick, later to become Duke of Northumberland and Somerset's successor as Protector. Somerset was still popular with the common people but his enemies outmanoeuvred him and in January 1552 he died at Tower Hill. The authorities had decreed that no one was to leave their homes that morning until after the time scheduled for the execution but thousands of citizens disregarded the order and flocked to Tower Hill to offer the duke their moral support in his last moments.

In 1553 the Duke of Northumberland, who rapidly became extremely unpopular, made an ill-judged and foolhardy attempt to keep his family dynasty at the peak of political power by arranging the marriage of his son Lord Guildford Dudley to the king's cousin Lady Jane Grey, granddaughter of Henry VIII's sister and a possible claimant to the throne. He persuaded the young king, already dying of tuberculosis, to nominate Lady Jane as his successor instead of his half-sister, the Catholic Princess Mary. Edward was only too happy to do so as he loathed Mary's strongly held religious views. However, after his death it was obvious that the people preferred Mary, the recipient of much popular sympathy ever since her mother Catherine of Aragon had been abandoned by Henry in such an unprincipled fashion. It was also widely believed that Mary had a much more legitimate claim to the throne.

In 1554 Henry Grey, Duke of Suffolk, Lady Jane Grey's father and champion of her cause, was executed at Tower Hill. Unwittingly he, or at least part of him, was to become the source of one of London's many fascinating mysteries. In 1852 a severed head was discovered in a remarkable state of preservation in the vaults of the Church of Holy Trinity in the Minories in the city. The excellent condition of the head was ascribed to its being surrounded by sawdust and becoming largely mummified as a consequence. When Holy Trinity was closed in 1889, the head was transferred to St Botolph's, Aldgate. Enthusiastic amateur historians have argued ever since about the provenance of this head. Some have said that despite its antiquity it bears a remarkable resemblance to a portrait of the duke in the National Portrait Gallery, and it is known that he had property in the Minories. The opposing theory is more macabre and suggests that the head is nothing whatever to do with the Duke of Suffolk but was accidentally severed from the trunk of a cadaver by the sexton of Holy Trinity in 1786, when he was nefariously engaged in cutting up a number of coffins for timber to be used to repair the floorboards of his house.

Thomas Howard, Duke of Norfolk, was probably the richest nobleman in England in the 1560s. Despite his wealth he craved even greater power and was jealous of Queen Elizabeth's close counsellors. He hatched a scheme to marry Mary, Queen of Scots, which would enable him, he hoped, to rule Scotland jointly with Mary; furthermore, if Mary were to be nominated as Elizabeth's successor to the throne of England, he would have a dominating influence on affairs in that country as well.

A scion of a leading Catholic family, he was naturally a figurehead for those who supported Mary's claim to the throne of England; such people looked to him to use his position to reverse the discrimination that was already taking place against England's Catholic community. In this volatile situation it was all too easy for his machinations to be construed as subversive and for Norfolk himself to be seen as the focus of plots against Elizabeth. Foolishly he allowed himself to be implicated in the Ridolfi Plot to topple Elizabeth from the throne and he was convicted of high treason in January 1572. Elizabeth was extremely reluctant to have Norfolk executed because he was powerful and had considerable support. Four times she signed his death warrant only to rescind it, and four times Norfolk made the psychological and spiritual preparations for his execution. Elizabeth eventually succumbed to the pressure of Parliament and Norfolk went to his death on 2 June 1572, the first person for fourteen years to die at Tower Hill.

In May 1631 the Earl of Castlehaven was beheaded. He had set up and assisted in the raping of his own wife by two of his servants, including one named Brodway. Additionally, he had forced his wife to have sex with other servants while he watched, and also forced his stepdaughter, aged 12, to have sex with his servants. He himself buggered several of the servants who had had sex with his wife and stepdaughter. Brodway and another of Castlehaven's servants were also condemned to death for rape, but as mere commoners they were hanged at Tyburn.

Charles I, like his father James I, was given to having favourites. One of these was Thomas Wentworth, Earl of Strafford, who was widely loathed because his counsel was behind some of the king's most unpopular policies. In 1641 Parliament impeached him for treason and he was conveyed to the Tower through streets full of jeering crowds. Charles, who had only recently promised Strafford immunity, did what he could at first to prevent his execution going ahead but this only worsened his relations with Parliament and eventually the king rather churlishly signed Strafford's death warrant, encouraged no doubt by fears for his own and his family's safety at the hands of the London mob that was calling for blood. Strafford walked to the scaffold with his head held high. A jubilant crowd of at least a hundred thousand people turned up to watch his execution. A similarly popular execution was that of another of the king's advisers, William Laud, the unsaintly Archbishop of Canterbury. He followed Strafford to the scaffold at Tower Hill in 1645. He was widely hated for the barbaric punishments meted out, especially by the court of Star Chamber.

The monarchy was restored in 1660 amid much popular rejoicing. There was a growing sense of vindictiveness against those who had authorised the king's execution. In 1662 Sir Henry Vane was executed. He was associated with the regicides who had signed Charles I's death warrant. Earlier his possibly perjured evidence had been enough to secure the death of the Earl of Strafford. He was widely disliked as arrogant, overbearing and an intellectual bully. He could not bring himself to submit to Charles II and paid the price for his lack of humility, exciting little sympathy but some respect for the courage which he displayed.

James, Duke of Monmouth, the illegitimate son of Charles II, had innumerable gifts and privileges showered on him by his father but he strongly resented the fact that

Charles was succeeded on the throne by his brother James. Monmouth knew that his uncle was already unpopular but he overestimated his own public standing. He led an abortive uprising centred on the West Country but was soon captured and, despite grovelling for mercy from the king, was condemned to death. Large crowds, which were by no means totally unsympathetic to him, turned out for his execution on Tower Hill on 15 July 1685. With considerable insouciance, Monmouth asked the executioner, Jack Ketch, for reassurance that the axe was sharp enough for the job it had to do. He even ran his finger along the edge. His concerns were borne out. After the first blow, Monmouth was able partially to rise and cast a look of reproach at the quaking Ketch. The second blow also failed to remove Monmouth's head. Ketch was all set to run from the scene of his ignominy until he was told that he was going nowhere until he had completed the job. This he finally managed to do – but only with the aid of a knife.

Incompetence on the executioner's part was again all too evident in 1746 when lords Balmerino and Kilmarnock were beheaded for their part in the Jacobite Rebellion of 1745. The executioner on this occasion was John Thrift, a convicted murderer who was pardoned when he agreed to put his homicidal tendencies to work on behalf of the authorities by becoming an executioner. By no means master of his trade, Thrift clearly appeared to be exhibiting all the signs of great nervousness and as the crowd watched him ascending the scaffold to do his deadly business, he fainted and had to be revived with some wine. Given the circumstances, it was perhaps surprising that he was encouraged by none other than Lord Kilmarnock to pull himself together but this was only partially successful because, having grasped the axe, he then threw it down again after bursting into tears once more. He then fell on his knees and pleaded for Kilmarnock's forgiveness. More soothing words were said and eventually Thrift, presumably encouraged by Kilmarnock's kindness, took the axe and cut his lordship's head off with a single blow. Balmerino was less fortunate. Thrift needed five blows to remove his head. After the first attempt the nobleman managed to turn his face towards the executioner and further discompose him with a ghoulish and sinister leer. The crowds watching the proceedings voiced their derision and contempt in no uncertain terms and Thrift remained an object of ridicule for the rest of his life. His funeral a few years later was accompanied by a drunken, jeering mob, who bombarded both coffin and mourners with a variety of noxious missiles.

Simon Fraser, Lord Lovat, was no less than 80 years of age when he was executed for high treason. Lest one should feel sorry for a man of that age having to undergo this ordeal in public, it should be pointed out that he had obtained his title and estates by abducting the widow of the previous Lord Lovat and forcing her into marriage with threats of violence. It is said that he then forcibly consummated the marriage in front of a large gathering of members of the Fraser clan. An enormous crowd turned out to watch Lovat's execution and a specially erected grandstand collapsed killing a dozen, twenty or as many as eighty people, depending on which accounts you read. Lovat found this catastrophe highly amusing. He is purported to have said, 'The more mischief, the better the sport.' The block and axe used to dispatch him are today on view in the Bloody Tower. He was the last person to be judicially beheaded in Britain, on 9 April 1747. His head was sewn back on before he was placed in his coffin.

Lovat was one of those men who can only be described as a 'bad egg'. Upon being sentenced to death, he made the rather unusual request that the execution be carried out using the 'Scottish Maiden', a forerunner of the much better known guillotine. His wish was not granted and John Thrift again was the executioner. He must have been practising assiduously because this time he severed Lovat's head with one blow. Mystery surrounds the subsequent fate of Lovat's remains. Instructions were given for the body to be buried within the precincts of the Tower, and indeed a lead coffin with an appropriate nameplate nearby was buried in the Chapel of St Peter ad Vincula. But whether the coffin really contains the egregious Lovat's remains has never been established for certain and it is rumoured that his body was smuggled up to Kirkhill near Inverness in Scotland and buried there, with the severed head in a box close by.

In 1780 some of Tower Hill's less well-known victims included three people convicted of taking part in the Gordon Riots: a one-armed sailor and two prostitutes. All three were hanged. It can have been little compensation to them to know that they were in good company, and that they were meeting their fate at a place where many others of far more privileged birth had also drawn their last breaths.

A stone in the pavement at the west end of Trinity Gardens serves as a reminder of Tower Hill's notorious past as a place of execution.

FOUR

Smithfield

'What anarchy and din'

In the twelfth century William FitzStephen, clerk to Thomas Becket, described West Smithfield as a smooth field where every Friday there is a 'celebrated rendezvous of fine horses to be sold'. Smithfield was a grassy place just outside the city walls which soon established a reputation as a livestock market. From the seventeenth century the westward expansion of the city began to engulf the market and many complaints were made about drunken herdsmen and unruly cattle being allowed to wander among the houses and shops. In addition to the market Smithfield had a number of other great institutions, notably St Bartholomew's Church and St Bartholomew's Hospital, both of which were established in Smithfield by the late twelfth century, and the Charterhouse, which was set up as a Carthusian monastery in 1371. Despite the existence of these august institutions, Smithfield is perhaps better known for its history of raucous, turbulent, bizarre and grotesque spectacle. From the fourteenth century it had been home to tournaments and duels as well as the debauchery and rowdiness associated with the famous Bartholomew Fair. The fair was held in mid- to late August, around the time of St Bartholomew's Day (24 August – the same time at which the present-day Notting Hill Carnival takes place), between 1133 and 1855. Wordsworth described it vividly in his *Prelude* of 1799:

> I saw giants and dwarfs, Clowns, conjurors, harlequins, amid the uproar of the rabblement, perform their feats. What a shock for eyes and ears! What anarchy and din Barbarian . . . Monstrous in colour, motion, shape, sight, sound! . . . The hurdy-gurdy, at the fiddle weaves, Equestrians, tumblers, women, girls, and boys . . . All moveables of wonder, from all parts, Are here – Albinos, painted Indians, Dwarfs, The Horse of knowledge, and the learned Pig, The Stone-eater, the man that swallows fire, Giants, Ventriloquists, the Invisible Girl, . . . The Bust that speaks and moves its goggling eyes, The Wax-work, Clock-work, all the marvellous craft of modern Merlins, Wild Beasts, Puppet-shows, All out-of-the-way, far-fetched, perverted things, All freaks of nature, all Promethean thoughts of man, his dullness, madness, and their feats All jumbled up together, to compose A Parliament of Monsters, Tents and Booths.

From the fourteenth century Smithfield witnessed a history of bloody incidents. The leader of the Peasants' Revolt of 1381, Wat Tyler, was killed in a confrontation at Smithfield when he was was stabbed by the Lord Mayor, William Walworth. Tyler sought refuge in St Bartholomew's Hospital but was dragged out to be beheaded (it is uncertain whether he was already dead prior to beheading). In addition, Smithfield was for over 400 years one of London's main sites of execution, a fact Shakespeare noted in *Henry VI*: 'The witch in Smithfield shall be burned to ashes.' A long procession of individuals met a gruesome end at Smithfield, including William Wallace, various Lollards and numerous Protestant martyrs during the reign of Mary Tudor (1553–8). (Smithfield to the west of the city must not be confused with East Smithfield, which was adjacent to the Tower of London and another location for executions, albeit in much smaller numbers.)

In April 1956 about a hundred Scots gathered to commemorate the opening of a memorial on the wall of St Bartholomew's Hospital. Around £1,000 had been raised to pay for a memorial dedicated to William Wallace on the site of his execution. Wallace was tortured and brutally executed 700 years ago and the plaque records that, 'He fought dauntlessly in defence of his country's liberty and independence . . . eventually betrayed and brought to London and put to death near this spot on 23 August 1305 . . . His memory remains for all time a source of pride and honour and inspiration to his countrymen.'

Wallace's story has taken on a particular significance in both historical and mythical terms. In 1296 the English under Edward I (r. 1272–1307) had temporarily subdued Scotland, which led to deep resentment, aggravated by the imprisonment of many Scottish nobles who had been heavily taxed and were still expected to serve the king in his military campaigns against France. Revolt quickly took hold and spread across Scotland, and in May 1297 Wallace slew the English Sheriff of Lanark, William Heselrig. Wallace's rebellion gained momentum as he was joined by other Scots who saw themselves oppressed by English rule. They struck at Scone, Ancrum and Dundee. The young Andrew Murray led an even more successful rising by taking Inverness and Urquhart Castle. With most of Scotland liberated, Wallace and Murray now faced direct conflict with the English, and although the English nobility had a number of grievances with Edward they united behind him to take part in the Battle of Falkirk in 1298.

By this time Wallace had established a reputation for diplomacy as well as fighting and he was assigned a new role as an envoy for the Scots to the courts of Europe. But when the French looked for Edward's assistance in suppressing a revolt in Flanders, they abandoned their former allegiance to Scotland. This severely damaged Scottish hopes of a victory against the English and the Scottish leaders capitulated and acknowledged Edward as overlord in 1304.

Wallace, however, would not compromise and was not prepared to accept English rule. By so doing he not only signed his own death warrant but also became a nuisance to both the English and the Scottish nobles who were prepared to switch sides to suit their needs.

Wallace, now deemed an outlaw, continued his resistance but was captured on 3 August 1305 by Sir John Menteith near Glasgow. After a brief imprisonment in Dumbarton Castle, Wallace was taken to London to face a show trial in Westminster Hall. The journey took three weeks as he was exhibited in towns and villages in England en route. When he eventually arrived in London he was taken to a house in Fenchurch Street. The following day he was tried at a hastily arranged court in Westminster Hall, where he was charged with treason, murder, robbery and 'various other felonies'. The accusation went on to state that he had invaded the Kingdom of England [and] killed those who were loyal to the King of England including 'old and young, brides and widows, babes and their mothers . . .'.

Forbidden to have a jury, Wallace responded to the accusation of treason by denying the charge and saying that he had never been Edward's subject in the first place. The inevitable verdict of the court was that Wallace should be dragged from the Palace of Westminster to the Tower of London and from there through the city to Smithfield to his execution. The judgment of guilty was a formality and now Wallace faced the public humiliation of being paraded through London.

On 23 August – the day before the fair at Smithfield – Wallace was wrapped in an ox hide and dragged by horses 4 miles through London to Smithfield. There he was hanged as a murderer on a very high gallows made specially for the occasion. An expectant crowd looked on as he was cut down while still alive and then mutilated and disembowelled; having been convicted of treason, he was probably emasculated as well. As a punishment for the 'great wickedness which he had practised towards God and His holy church by burning churches', his heart, liver, lungs and other internal organs were thrown into the fire and burned. Finally, he was decapitated and his carcass cut up. His head was placed on a pole on London Bridge. The gruesome task of placing decapitated heads on the gateway at the Southwark end of London Bridge fell to the Keepers of the Heads, who were granted leases to live in the gateways – a tradition that had been in use from at least the early fourteenth century to the late seventeenth century. Parts of Wallace's body went to Newcastle, an area Wallace had destroyed in 1297–8, Berwick, Perth and Aberdeen, and perhaps Stirling, as a warning to the Scots. By such brutal and decisive action

Edward destroyed the man but in doing so ensured the birth of a legend.

Executions at Smithfield continued for over four centuries after the death of Wallace, although the records of many of them are vague. One reason for the vagueness lies in the name used for the place of executions, the Elms, as this was used for both Smithfield and Tyburn. However, over the two centuries after Wallace's death, building around Smithfield increased and the elm trees were felled, as the sixteenth-century writer John Stow recorded: 'Smithfield . . . then called the Elms, for there grew many elm-trees; and this had been the place for execution for offenders. Since which time the building there hath been so increased that now remaineth not one tree growing.'

By 1394 Smithfield had ninety-four inns and the meadows and gardens had given way to a labyrinth of alleys, lanes and courtyards. Cock Lane nearby was the only place in medieval London where licensed prostitutes could solicit for trade. The area had acquired a reputation for raffishness and decadence.

At the end of the fourteenth century the established Church came under criticism from John Wycliffe (1324–84), a Yorkshireman educated at Oxford. He was one of the first recognised critics of the Church and his supporters, known as Lollards, rejected the Roman Catholic Church, arguing that the Bible was the supreme authority, that the clergy should hold no property and that there was no basis for the doctrine of transubstantiation (the belief that bread and wine changes into the substance of the body and blood of Christ during the Eucharist). The name Lollard was derived from the medieval Dutch word meaning 'to mutter'. The Lollards were mainly itinerant preachers but they did have some support among a group of knights at the king's court. They included Sir William Neville, Sir John Montague and Sir William Beauchamp.

Wycliffe wanted reformation of the Church, arguing that it should give up all its worldly possessions. Predictably, such dangerous ideas led to persecution and not surprisingly Wycliffe was condemned as a heretic in 1380, and again in 1382. He spent the last years of his life translating the Bible into English before his death in 1384. Afraid that his grave would become a religious shrine, the Bishop of Lincoln gave orders that Wycliffe's body should be dug up and thrown into the river. Many of Wycliffe's supporters came from around the Thames Valley, in particular the Buckinghamshire Chilterns. Wycliffe himself was at least spared the brutal persecution that fell on and destroyed many of his supporters.

Richard II (r. 1377–99) had a strong faith but initially he tolerated the Lollard supporters in his own court. However, in the mid-1380s he began an active campaign against heresy in his kingdom and moved against the Lollards. During Henry IV's reign (1399–1413), the Crown and Church united against the Lollards and anti-heresy legislation was passed in 1382, 1401 and 1414, giving the authorities the legal right to burn heretics. The Act *De Haeretico Comburendo* of 1401 allowed the king to order sheriffs and justices of the peace to burn heretics. Anyone accused of heresy was given the opportunity to recant his beliefs, and those who chose to do so suffered a much less severe punishment. The most typical method of burning involved heaping faggots around a wooden stake to which the prisoner was attached with chains or iron hoops. With only a small fire, the condemned would burn for a few minutes in agony until death resulted from heat-stroke or loss of blood plasma. The executioner could maximise the pain by arranging the intended fire so the victim's skin would burn in sequence, from the calves up to the thighs, hands, body, upper chest and face. Victims might also die from suffocation. In later burnings the condemned were strangled at the stake before being burned.

William Sawtrey is cited as England's first Lollard and Protestant martyr. He was burned at the stake in March 1401, although there is some confusion as to the precise location of his execution with some accounts such as that by Foxe stating Smithfield and others suggesting St Paul's Cross. Others followed and were executed in various places in London. John Badby, a tailor from Evesham, was convicted of heresy in 1410 and refused to recant his beliefs. He was subsequently brought to Smithfield, where he was placed in an empty tub, tied in iron chains and fastened to a stake surrounded by dry wood. The Prince of Wales, later Henry V, gave Badby another chance to recant when he attempted to counsel him. Yet again Badby refused, at which the wood was lit and finally Badby cried 'mercy'. The flames were quickly doused and Badby was asked for the final time to reject his 'heresy'. Still he refused and this rejection consigned him to the flames. When Henry V succeeded to the throne in 1413 Smithfield continued to receive many of the Lollards, including London merchants Richard Turming and John Claydon in 1415 and the priest William Taylor in 1423.

John Claydon was accused of having seditious books in his house. According to the Mayor of London, the books were 'the worst and most perverse he ever did read or see'. When Claydon was committed to the fire at

Smithfield, 'he was there meekly', along with fellow martyr George Gurmyn, with whom he had often discussed matters of faith. William Taylor was accused of heresy but recanted and received absolution. Having gone through the ritual of forgiveness, Taylor pushed his luck and was caught yet again a year later in 1419. Deprived of his priesthood, Taylor spent a long time in prison before being brought to Smithfield on 1 March 1422 and burned at the stake. The steady flow of Lollards continued and nine years later Thomas Bagley, Vicar of Monenden near Malden, 'a valiant disciple and adherent of Wycliffe', was also condemned for heresy and burned.

Throughout the fifteenth and early sixteenth centuries both secular and ecclesiastical authorities made efforts to stamp out the Lollards, although the repression gradually became less intense. The only way the Lollards could survive was as an underground movement, passing on their beliefs within families and through trade contacts. During the reigns of Henry VII (1485–1509) and Henry VIII (1509–47) there were at least twelve Lollard trials, including that of Joan Broughton, the first woman to suffer martyrdom in medieval England. Joan, an old widow of 80 years or more, was burned at Smithfield on 28 April 1494, along with her daughter.

Lollards and heretics continued to be burned throughout the reign of Henry VIII. Among them were William Succling and John Bannister in October 1511 and John Stilincen in September 1518. Stilincen had previously recanted but was brought before Richard FitzJames, Bishop of London, and condemned as a heretic. Among a vast crowd of spectators he was chained to the stake and burned to death. James Brewster from Colchester followed him in 1519.

West Smithfield had many 'fair inns and other comely buildings' by the sixteenth century, according to the great London chronicler John Stow. In the maze of crowded lanes surrounding the area were large tenements, inns and brewhouses, as well as the livestock pens for the market. Ned Ward in *The London Spy* described the type of cookshops in Smithfield and what could be had there: 'measly Pork and Neck beef stood out in wooden Platters, adorn'd with Carrots and garnish'd with the leafs of Marygolds'.

During the period when Henry VIII was seeking his divorce from Catherine of Aragon and establishing the break with the Roman Catholic Church, Richard Byfield was thrown into prison and whipped for supporting Protestant doctrines. Byfield was flogged on a number of occasions and eventually taken to the Lollards Tower in Lambeth Palace where he was chained by the neck to the wall. In 1532 he was led to Smithfield to face the same fate as other heretics. In the same year a cook called Richard Rose was boiled to death for poisoning the gruel made for the household of the Bishop of Rochester. Two people died. Rose was placed in an iron cauldron over a fire and his death was slow and excruciating; it took him two hours to die. This method of execution was also meted out to John Forest, one of Catherine of Aragon's chaplains who had continued to support her throughout the divorce with Henry VIII. In April 1538 Forest was taken before Archbishop Cranmer but refused to acknowledge Henry as Supreme Head of the Church. For his temerity he was sentenced to death at Smithfield, where he was reportedly roasted alive for two hours in a cage over a log fire before he died.

In the religious turmoil of the 1530s Protestants were keen to obtain copies of William Tyndale's translation of the Bible but it had been banned and the penalty for reading it was severe, as John Tewkesbury discovered. According to Foxe, Tewkesbury was held in the porter's lodge at Thomas More's Chelsea house where he was pinioned 'hand, foot, and head in the stocks' for six days without release. He was then whipped and had his eyebrows twisted with small ropes until blood spurted from his eyes. Later he was sent to the Tower and racked until he was nearly crippled. Such was the torture inflicted on him that by the time he appeared at the stake at Smithfield he was almost dead. Similar agonies were inflicted on Andrew Hewit and John Frith in 1533. Frith had come to England and distributed copies of Tyndale's Bible but was caught when the books were found in his bag. Death by burning was extremely painful but in the case of these two the wind blew the flames away from them and it took more than two hours of agony before they died. Frith was said to have courageously 'embraced the fagots'.

An unusual incident of heresy in 1538 concerned the case of a madman called Collins who was 'burned to ashes, amidst a vast crowd of spectators' with his dog at Smithfield. Collins had objected to a priest who had elevated the host during a church service. For Collins this smacked of Catholicism and he was so enraged he lifted his dog above his own head in an attempt to mock the priest's action. The man, who was clearly insane, should have had a much lighter sentence. However, executions during Henry's reign were so numerous that Hugh Latimer, Bishop of Worcester, felt moved to comment on the high number of executions taking place in London in a sermon in May 1549.

Included in those executions were the rich and the powerful, such as Thomas Cromwell, the king's key adviser during the 1530s. He was executed at the Tower in 1540, condemned by the very Act of Treason he had been instrumental in introducing a few years earlier. During the same year three Catholics, Richard Fetherston (who had defended Catherine during the divorce), Thomas Abel and Edward Powell, were hanged, drawn and quartered as traitors along with three Protestants, Cuthbert Barnes, Thomas Garret and William Jerome, who were burned as heretics. All six were drawn through the streets to Smithfield upon three hurdles, with a Catholic and a heretic on each hurdle.

The fate of 25-year-old Anne Askew reflected the religious turmoil of the times. Anne, who had been disowned by her husband for being a Protestant, came to London, where she was arrested for distributing leaflets. She was subjected to such severe torture that she had to be carried to the stake at Smithfield, where she was burned in a chair with three other heretics. A stand was erected outside the gatehouse of St Bartholomew's Church where the Privy Council and the Lord Mayor sat to view Anne's death. Her friend Joan Bocher was also burned there three years later for arguing that Christ had not been born as a man to the Virgin Mary.

After Henry's death in 1547 his young and sickly son Edward succeeded him. During his short reign (1547–53) Protestant doctrine advanced slowly and the Acts for the burning of heretics were repealed. However, the religious changes imposed during the reigns of Henry VIII and Edward VI were to be wholly undone by Henry's daughter Mary, a devout Catholic, when she succeeded to the throne in 1553. Many Protestants had supported

Mary as the rightful heir to the throne but they clearly had little idea of the persecution that would follow. Within two months of her becoming queen, Protestants were being arrested on the flimsiest of charges and many others fled abroad. Shortly after the formal ceremony of reconciliation with Rome on 30 November 1554 the medieval heresy laws were revived, which led to the burning of 283 Protestant martyrs, 56 of them women, between February 1555 and November 1558.

Burning at the stake had become the usual punishment for religious dissenters since the beginning of the fifteenth century. However, during Mary's reign it took on a particular significance and defined the key period of Protestant martyrdom in England. Persecutions began in January 1555 when a number of eminent Protestants were subject to hostile examination by a commission of leading bishops. Many refused to recant and were condemned to burn. One man who became synonymous with the repressive measures taken against Protestants during Mary's reign was Edmund Bonner (1500–69), Bishop of London. Bonner, who had supported anti-Catholic measures under Henry VIII, was characterised by John Foxe as a monster:

This cannibal in three years space three hundred
                                                    martyrs slew
They were his food, he loved so blood, he spared none
                                                    he knew.

Public executions were guaranteed to draw large crowds and the burning of the first Protestants under Mary would be no exception. Fellow Protestants stood in the crowd as a mark of respect and support for the victims. On occasion they would attempt to persuade the executioner to hasten death by placing gunpowder around the martyrs.

The first Protestant to be publicly burned at Smithfield in Mary's reign was John Rogers, vicar of St Sepulchre's at Newgate. Rogers had met the celebrated martyr William Tyndale and was inspired to convert to the Protestant cause. Twenty years later he was languishing in Newgate prison. He was asked to revoke his doctrines but refused, thus assuring his place as a martyr. He asked to see his wife before his execution but this request was refused, and on 4 February 1555 he was led the short distance from his prison to Smithfield through the large crowd. Among the mass of people who came to watch him die were his eleven children and his wife, who was holding their baby at her breast. According to John Foxe, Rogers was 'burnt to ashes, washing his hands in the flame as he was burning'. It was said that as he burned, a flock of doves flew over Smithfield – which some interpreted as a sign from heaven. Other martyrs who had appeared before the commission were executed elsewhere, many in the places where they had preached.

Defiant martyrs refusing to renounce their beliefs were becoming all too common. Two Protestant bishops, John Cardmaker and John Warne, followed Rogers three months later. When they arrived at the stake at Smithfield Cardmaker was taken aside and addressed by the sheriff while Warne's execution was being prepared and the wood and reeds set alight around him. The hope was that Cardmaker would recant at the sight of Warne burning but, refusing to succumb, he too went to the flames.

It was not only well-known or eminent Protestant figures that were persecuted. The climate was dangerous;

no dissenter was safe and anyone who showed signs of heresy was vulnerable. The search for those holding heretical views extended into towns and villages and local vicars were required to inform on suspected parishioners. The martyrs who suffered under Mary came from diverse backgrounds, from the learned to the obscure. Alongside the bishops there were many tradesmen, including butchers, barbers, drapers and weavers. One such weaver was Thomas Tomkins from Shoreditch, who was burned at the stake at Smithfield in May 1555. During the summer of 1555 most of the burnings took place in Bonner's diocese in London and Essex, thus reinforcing his reputation as 'Bloody Bonner'. As the burnings continued unabated throughout the year Mary announced that she was pregnant, further damaging Protestant hopes that Elizabeth might not succeed to the throne. However, as it turned out they had no cause for alarm, as the physicians knew that Mary was incapable of giving birth.

The Revd John Bradford, one of the first Protestants to be arrested at the beginning of Mary's reign, had been in various prisons prior to his execution. In the compter prison in Broad Street he met a 19-year-old apprentice, John Leaf. At 9 a.m. on the morning of 12 July 1555 Bradford and Leaf were taken to Smithfield tied face-down on two hurdles. Typically a large crowd had gathered for the event. Bradford's brother-in-law Roger Beswicke was in the crowd and took Bradford's hand as he passed. Bradford began to address the crowd, telling them to refuse to bow to idolatry. At this point the sheriff struck Bradford on the head with his staff and cut his head open. Despite this blow, Bradford bravely attempted to comfort Leaf at the stake. The faggots were lit and both men died relatively quickly.

Another martyr imprisoned when Mary came to the throne was John Philpot, Archdeacon of Winchester. After eighteen months and a number of examinations from Bonner, Philpot was taken to Smithfield at 8 a.m. on 17 December 1555. When he arrived the ground was so muddy that two officers offered to carry him to the stake – an offer he declined. Philpot proceeded to say psalms and prayers and was then secured to the stake and burned. During the winter of 1555/6 more Protestants were arrested in London, including John Tudson, Thomas Whittle, John Went, Thomas Brown, Isabel Foster, Joan Lushford and Bartlet Green. In January 1556 all seven were burned together at Smithfield.

Three years into Mary's reign 88 heretics had been burned, 16 of them at Smithfield. Some folk in London protested at the burnings but to no avail. In January 1556 the Lord Mayor and Sheriffs of London were sent instructions from the Privy Council that any obdurate person should be punished for heresy. In April six men, including weaver John Cavel, shearman Richard Spurge and fullers Thomas Spurge and George Ambrose, were burned together. Three more followed the next month. The persecutions continued throughout 1557 with three men and two women executed in April at Smithfield.

By November 1557 secret Protestant congregations were beginning to form, but regularly changed their meeting places in order to avoid arrest. Two members of one such congregation were Cuthbert Simpson and John Rough, a Scottish Protestant. Rough had seen an execution at Smithfield and was emotionally moved after witnessing the burning of James and Margery Austoo. The authorities were aware of the secret congregation and used Roger Serjeant, a tailor from Buckinghamshire, to infiltrate the group. Serjeant did his work well and duly informed on the group, who were arrested at a meeting at the Saracen's Head in Islington. Simpson was racked while Rough had his cheek burned for half an hour. John Rough and Margaret Mearing were burned on the same fire on 22 December but Simpson had to wait a little longer. After spending some time in the stocks he was burned at Smithfield along with Hugh Foxe and John Devenish on 28 March 1558.

The burnings continued and the following month over forty men and women were arrested for attending a Protestant meeting in a field at Islington. Twenty were detained and sent to Newgate, where they were promised a pardon on condition that they attended Mass. Thirteen refused and seven of them were burned at Smithfield in June 1558. On the day of the executions a large and sympathetic crowd assembled to watch. As the condemned were about to be burned, the sheriff read out a proclamation from the queen threatening arrest and punishment for anyone showing sympathy with the seven. The crowd soon let their feelings be known and ignored the threat by shouting and protesting at the burning of the men. None the less, such executions were backed by those in power, such as bishops, high sheriffs and of course Bonner, who was known to flog heretics in the grounds of his house, at least partly for his own gratification.

By late 1558 Mary was 42 and ailing. She had failed to produce an heir to the throne, she had lost Calais and seen the departure of her husband King Philip, who had left England in July 1557 never to return. Elizabeth, Mary's half-sister, who lived at Hatfield, had to tread very carefully during Mary's reign for fear of losing her own life. By November 1558 Mary was dying at St James's

Palace in Westminster. She demanded to see Elizabeth in order to ask her to maintain the Catholic faith, but this was another lost cause. On 17 November 1558 Mary died and was succeeded by Elizabeth, much to the joy of her Protestant subjects. Of the 283 Protestants burned during Mary's reign, 78 had been in London and 56 at Smithfield. A few years later Tyburn would become the designated place for the execution of Catholics, who in their turn would be celebrated as martyrs. When John Foxe concluded his account of the Marian martyrs he wrote that after the execution of 'Roger Holland there was none suffered in Smithfield for the testimony of the Gospel, God be thanked'. There were, however, still more executions to follow at Smithfield, as Foxe lamented, when three foreign Anabaptists were burned there in 1575.

Both Protestants and Catholics had suffered for their religion and the persecution would continue in Elizabeth's reign (1558–1603). Missionary and Jesuit Catholics who sought to convert people back to the faith found themselves condemned for treason. Over 100 priests were executed at Tyburn, although Smithfield also witnessed some executions of Catholics, including Edward Arden from Warwickshire. His father William Arden was a second cousin of Mary Arden of Wilmcote, William Shakespeare's mother. In 1575 Edward was high sheriff of the county but eight years later he was indicted in Warwick for plotting against the queen, as were his wife, son-in-law John Somerville, and Father Hugh Hall. They were all taken to London and condemned on the evidence of Father Hall, who was released in return for the information he had offered. Arden died at Smithfield on 30 December 1583 still protesting his innocence.

Protecting heretics and traitors carried severe consequences. Nicholas Horner, who was arrested for harbouring Catholic priests, was kept in a damp cell for a long period, during which time he had one leg amputated after contracting blood poisoning. After his release he remained undeterred and continued to hide priests and refused to conform to public worship as required by law. He was arrested again but this time he lost more than his leg as he was hanged, drawn and quartered at Smithfield on 4 March 1590. On the same day Christopher Bales, a Catholic priest, was executed in Fleet Street opposite Fetter Lane. Prior to his execution Bales had been tortured by the queen's notorious agent Richard Topcliffe (1532–1604). Having established a reputation for persecuting Catholic recusants and Jesuits over a period of twenty-five years, Topcliffe effectively became the chief officer in charge of enforcing the anti-Catholic penal laws. He racked prisoners at his own house and proudly boasted that he had a machine at home that was even more brutal than the racks more commonly used.

As London's population grew during the seventeenth century so did the alleys, lanes and buildings around Smithfield. The fair there became increasingly bizarre. In 1614 Ben Jonson's play *Bartholomew Fair* promised to show all the phantasmagoria on display, such as the 'strutting Horse-courser, with a leere-Drunkard, . . . the Tooth-drawer . . . a consort of Roarers for musique . . . the Ginger-bread-woman . . . the Hobby-horse-man . . . the Pigge-woman . . . the Seller of Mouse-trappes, and so of the rest'. By the 1640s the fair had become so large that it involved no less than four parishes: Christ Church, Great and Little St Bartholomew's and St Sepulchre's.

The civil wars of the mid-seventeenth century embroiled Britain in a bitter and bloody turmoil and Smithfield played host to at least one victim of this conflict. Thomas Pits was charged with betraying a parliamentary garrison – Russell Hall in Staffordshire – to the enemy. In October 1644 a large crowd watched Pits on the scaffold confessing to being a 'dissembling hypocrite'. He blessed Charles I and desired that Parliament would remove all the king's evil counsellors. Pits tried to convince the crowd that the king was honest but misguided. He then proceeded to tell of his own downfall and how he was the victim of treachery. Such last speeches were intended to serve as warnings to others and the one offered by Pits was no exception. He told the assembled crowd to stay close to God and his cause. He then 'lifted up his hands towards heaven, and gave three strokes upon his breast' – and was then thrown from the ladder and from this world.

After the upheavals of the civil war and the period of the Commonwealth (1640–60), London emerged from the restraints of Puritan rule. Theatres, plays and alehouses were once more regularly frequented and sexual immorality became fashionable. Samuel Pepys kept detailed accounts of his own sexual activities. He recorded in September 1661 a visit he made to a 'pitiful alehouse' in Smithfield, where he 'had a dirty slut or two' approach him. However, he wrote 'my very heart went against them, so that I took no pleasure but a great deal of trouble in being there and getting from thence for fear of being seen'. Pepys also commented on his visit to Bartholomew Fair, where he met his 'Ladies Jemimah and Paulina' and saw the 'monkeys dance, which was much to see . . . but it troubled me to sit among such nasty company'. He seemed constantly surprised that women were capable of knocking back a quart of wine in one go and becoming as 'drunk as devils'.

The Great Fire of 1666 reached as far as the edge of Smithfield, its approach marked by the statue of a cherub, a symbol of gluttony, at the corner of Cock Lane and Giltspur Street. Crowds had flocked to Smithfield for centuries to find entertainment and sexual pleasures. They came to see an assortment of curiosities on show in the taverns and at the fair. A mixture of the grotesque and the bizarre were always on display. During the eighteenth century the crowds flocked to Bartholomew Fair to gape at the cow with two heads, the boy with one head on two bodies and the man covered in scales, as well as dwarfs such as Madame Teresa and a regular parade of giants. The execution of religious martyrs was now a sign of past times.

The heady days of executions at Smithfield became fewer as Tyburn and later Newgate became the main sites. In 1674 a woman was burned at Smithfield for the crime of clipping (removing precious metal from the edges of coins). Some executions had taken place at East Smithfield since the sixteenth century, although they were never on the scale of West Smithfield. One such case at East Smithfield at the beginning of the eighteenth century was that of the married couple Michael and Catherine Van Berghen. They originated from Holland and by 1700 kept a public house in East Smithfield, where Geraldius Dromelius acted as their servant. Oliver Norris decided to have a drink there one evening. At 11 p.m. Norris left the alehouse in an intoxicated state but still alert enough to realise he had been robbed of his purse. He returned and accused Van Berghen and his wife of the robbery, which they vehemently denied. The argument became heated. Van Berghen seized a poker and hit Norris with it, fracturing his skull, at which point the servant intervened and proceeded to stab Norris to death. The Van Berghens decided to take the dead man's clothes and wig and then dumped the body in a ditch. The next morning Norris's body was found and identified by people who had seen him drinking in the pub the night before. The Van Berghens and their servant were arrested and executed on 10 July 1700 near the Hartshorn brewhouse in East Smithfield, close to the place where the murder was committed. The bodies of the men were hung in chains between Bow and Mile End and the woman was buried.

There was a rather tragic consequence to this execution. The *London Post* recorded that the crowd of spectators was so huge 'that there was a great deal of mischief done, but the particulars we cannot learn, only that one scaffold fell'. The falling scaffold killed one boy and wounded several people. One of the sheriff's officers, who was on horseback, was so crushed with the crowd that his horse fell down under him, 'and he was carried off for dead; and there was nothing to be heard almost but shrieks and cries of murder'.

An unintended 'execution' at Smithfield in 1756 concerned one James Egan, a shoemaker of Drury Lane. Egan, along with Stephen M'Daniel, John Berry and James Salmon, had conspired in framing and accusing innocent people of murder in order to claim rewards. In many cases they had been successful in securing prosecutions which led to the death of the unfortunate victims. In one such case the gang asked a poor man to take a horse to an inn at Smithfield but he was then seized by Egan and taken to the alderman accused of stealing the horse. Eventually he was hanged. Many innocent people fell prey to the gang's activities and were sentenced to death simply as a result of the gang's greed. However, justice finally caught up with Egan and his fellow criminals. Berry and M'Daniel were sentenced to stand in the pillory at Hatton Garden in Holborn while Salmon and Egan were to stand in West Smithfield. This was to be followed by imprisonment for seven years. However, such was the popular hatred towards this odious gang that M'Daniel and Berry had to be removed from the stocks because their lives were in danger. The pillory at West Smithfield was thronged with people waiting to 'greet' Egan and Salmon, pelting them with stones, brickbats, potatoes, dead dogs, cats and a variety of other objects. The constables tried to intervene but were overpowered and Salmon and Egan were left to the mercy of an enraged mob. The blows they received occasioned their heads to swell to an enormous size and the crowd pulled the offenders' clothes so much they were nearly strangled. After about half an hour in the pillory a stone was thrown at Egan; it hit him on the head and he died instantly.

The execution of John Perrot at Smithfield in 1761 was more in keeping with the times. Perrot had arrived in London from his native Newport Pagnell at the age of 24 and began to trade in foreign white lace. He later opened a draper's shop and dealt in a variety of goods. He established a reputation as a merchant and had little problem in finding credit. But Perrot was in fact a wealthy rogue who reputedly embezzled £25,000 of goods received on credit. The goods of course had to be converted into ready money and to do this he employed an agent, Henry Thompson, to sell them for him. It was only a matter of time before Perrot's activities were investigated and so it was no surprise when a Commission of Bankruptcy sued against him on 19 April 1760. A full disclosure of his estate and effects was revealed and it showed not only that Perrot had debts of over £13,000 but that he had also been exceptionally extravagant in his spending.

Perrot did not cooperate and was kept in Newgate for six weeks. When finally he did disclose his accounts they included £2,700 for housekeeping, £700 for clothing, £920 on tavern and coffee-house expenses and £5,500 for attending 'with the fair sex'. This latter money had apparently been given to Sarah Powell, his mistress of six years. However, Sarah Powell may not even have existed but a Mary Anne Ferne, who visited him during his spell in Newgate, had purportedly received large sums of money and presents as well as a house. The creditors had no doubt that Perrot had been concealing money. This came to light when a woman by the name of Mary Harris was dismissed from the services of Mary Ferne, Perrot's mistress. Harris gave information to the commission, which responded by issuing a warrant to search Ferne's apartment. In addition to the very expensive furniture, bundles of bank notes cut in half were found at the bottom of a trunk; they matched those in Perrot's house. This evidence was sufficient to impose the death sentence on Perrot. He was placed in irons and pressed to disclose all his effects relating to his estate. He refused, but on the morning of his execution he finally confessed and asked that his body be buried in the church near his birthplace. He also asked to be allowed to spend more time in the chapel and less time at the place of execution. He stayed in the chapel for nearly two hours and then had his irons removed. At 10.15 on the morning of 11 November 1761 he said farewell to a fellow prisoner and was immediately put in the cart and led to Smithfield to be hanged.

The days of execution at Smithfield thus finally came to an end, although the fair continued until 1855 when the city authorities closed it down as it was widely considered to be a place of debauchery which encouraged public disorder. The market, which had been active since the twelfth century in the trading of horses, sheep, cattle and pigs, was established as a cattle market by the City of London Corporation in 1638. This continued until the sale of live cattle was transferred in 1855 to the Metropolitan Cattle Market in Islington and a new market at Smithfield was opened in 1868. Reminders of those who perished at the stake and on the scaffold can still be seen on plaques outside St Bartholomew's Hospital. Ghostly screams of martyrs put to death close by are said to be heard at the gatehouse of the Church of St Bartholomew the Great – on stormy, moonlit nights of course.

FIVE

Newgate and Old Bailey

> You owe me ten shillings,
> Say the bells of St Helen's.
> When will you pay me?
> Say the bells of Old Bailey.
>
> *Old nursery rhyme*

The first mention of a purpose-built prison in the vicinity of Newgate appears in 1189. From early times Newgate was the prison for London and Middlesex and it came under the joint jurisdiction of the sheriffs of those places who appointed its gaoler. Located in the north-west corner of the city, Newgate housed particularly serious offenders from outside London in addition to local miscreants. As early as the fourteenth century the prison gained an evil reputation not only for the barbaric conditions in which the inmates were kept but also for the cruelties of its keepers. A constant theme in the history of Newgate is the especial fear and loathing it generated. This led the populace to give vent to their collective hatred by attacking it whenever possible, the first occasion apparently being in 1381 when Wat Tyler's peasant followers inflicted considerable damage on the fabric of the building.

A major rebuilding took place in 1423 with money provided by the executors of Richard Whittington's will.

The new prison was ironically nicknamed 'Whittington's Palace' or simply 'The Whit'. It was already in a semi-ruinous state by the time of the Great Fire of London which caused damage so severe that it had to be rebuilt. A splendid new building was completed in 1672, but its fine exterior was in stark contrast to the appalling squalor inside. Newgate became notorious for its inadequate and filthy supplies of water, the almost non-existent ventilation and the appalling stench which emanated from it and permeated the surrounding neighbourhood in certain weather conditions. Outbreaks of gaol-fever, a particularly virulent form of typhoid, occurred regularly and killed many of its inmates.

In 1770 another rebuilding was commenced. The work was incomplete when the London crowds attacked and destroyed much of it by fire during the anti-Catholic Gordon Riots in 1780. The mob released many of the prisoners before going on to attack a number of lesser prisons. Newgate was regarded as one of the strongest and most important prisons in Britain at that time and the fact that it was largely destroyed by an incensed and drunken London mob was a considerable affront to the authorities. Interestingly one man who played a prominent role in this attack on Newgate was Edward Dennis, then the public hangman. He was apprehended and sentenced to death for his part. While he was in the condemned cell, with remarkable insouciance he petitioned for his son to succeed him in the hangman's role – which brings into being the extraordinary possibility that the son might have to hang his father. This did not happen, however, because Dennis was not only reprieved but also restored to his hangman's post. He then resumed his official duties and shortly afterwards hanged some of his fellow rioters!

A further Newgate prison was completed in 1783. Conditions inside continued to be appalling and attracted forthright criticism from well-known penal reformers such as John Howard and Elizabeth Fry. In 1814 a parliamentary enquiry was launched into conditions in Newgate but improvements were slow in coming because the issue of prison reform generated little political support. In 1815 a debtors' prison (or compter) opened in Whitecross Street and Newgate's substantial debtor population was transferred there. In 1850 a select committee identified Newgate as one of England's worst prisons, both for the way in which it was managed and for the standards of its accommodation. In 1852 Holloway Prison was opened and many prisoners were moved there, leaving Newgate to house prisoners awaiting trial at the Old Bailey or execution. In 1902 Newgate Prison was demolished, but the loss of this familiar landmark went largely unlamented. The Central Criminal Court, which became known as the Old Bailey, was built on the site and was completed in 1907. Faced with Portland stone, it is surmounted by a 12-foot-high gilded statue of Justice holding a sword in one hand and a set of scales in the other. The judicial functions associated with the Old Bailey can be traced back to a Sessions House for London and Middlesex which opened at Smithfield in 1334. This was replaced in 1539 by a new Sessions House close to Newgate. When this burned down in the Great Fire of 1666 an imposing stone building was erected on the same site. The Middlesex Sessions House was renamed the Central Criminal Court in 1834 after its jurisdiction was extended to include the counties of Surrey, Essex and Kent.

To stand outside the Old Bailey today is to be confronted by the weight of history. The building stands as mute witness to the turmoil of emotions engendered by its history of imprisonment, torture and executions, both private and public, and even the occasional reprieves that were granted. A City of London plaque now adorns the Newgate Street façade. Rather misleadingly it states, 'Site of Newgate, demolished 1777'. However, this date refers to the initial demolition of the agglomeration of ancient buildings in the 1770s.

In 1714 a notoriously brutal turnkey called Spurling was ushering a number of prisoners into the dock in the Sessions House when one of them pulled out a pistol and shot him dead. This action was applauded by a number of other prisoners, including some women. This incident had occurred in full sight of everyone in the court and those involved were peremptorily sentenced to death. On 19 September 1714 they were hanged outside in the yard. The body of Johnson, the man who had fired the fatal shot, was later taken to Holloway and displayed in chains alongside the decomposing corpses of a number of other executed felons.

In 1783 executions were transferred from Tyburn to a sizeable open space in the street known as Old Bailey which in those days ran alongside part of Newgate prison. On execution days a scaffold was erected close to the Debtors' Door in the prison wall. Through this door the condemned prisoners were brought for their public swansong. For some this offered a brief moment of glory – for once in their lives everybody was interested in them and they were the centre of attention. Later on the scaffold was mounted on wheels and was brought out of Newgate for each execution, drawn by two horses.

The first execution in Old Bailey took place on 9 December 1783 when executioner Edward Dennis ended the lives of ten felons. In 1785 the gallows were even busier as twenty men were hanged in just one morning. The new execution site lacked Tyburn's spacious surroundings, Old Bailey being funnel-shaped and increasingly narrow as it approached Ludgate. While this may perhaps have made the crowds easier to control, the constricted space was a potential source of danger in the event of panic or any emergency in the closely packed throng.

Prisoners varied widely in the manner in which they approached their execution. Those who excited most admiration from warders, visitors and the crowd around the scaffold were the few who steadfastly refused to be perturbed by the situation and ate and drank heartily and in some cases whistled, sang and joked as if they had not a care in the world. One or two ate so much in their last few days that they appeared to be making more than ample provision for the journey into the unknown! Their desires were often indulged by the authorities. A murderer named Jeffreys, for example, ordered and was served roasted duck when he was placed in the condemned cell.

Although executions now took place literally on the doorstep of Newgate, the strong carnival element surrounding such events was little diminished and the crowds continued to be as excitable as ever, while the pickpockets and prostitutes enjoyed rich pickings. Hucksters selling pies, fried fish and all manner of snacks and beverages elbowed their way through the seething crowds and did a roaring trade.

On the night before an execution, the peace of the small hours was invariably disturbed by the sounds of revelry from those who had arrived early in order to get the best view of the morning's proceedings. This noise was doubtless all too audible to the occupants of the condemned cells, as was the hammering of the carpenters building the gallows, at least in the days before the more permanent one came into use. From the condemned cells the prisoners were taken into an apartment called the Large Room, where they were met by a crowd of officials, newspaper reporters and friends. Their irons were struck off and then their arms tightly bound around their bodies with cord. The prison chaplain would be vociferously urging the miserable wretches to confess and pray for forgiveness, but all that most of them could do at this stage was sigh, sob, moan or stammer out desperate last-minute appeals for mercy. The procession of prisoners and officials then made its way slowly to the Debtors' Door on Old Bailey. As they appeared in the street a great roar would go up from the crowd, temporarily drowning out the solemn tolling of the bell of St Sepulchre's. A cry of 'Hats off, hats off' reverberated through the crowd as headwear was doffed and everyone jostled their neighbours in the confined space in order to get the best view possible.

A few people, derided as moaning Jeremiads, had expressed concern that a disaster could happen in such a densely packed horde – and their warnings proved to be well founded. In 1807 a large crowd, estimated at 40,000 by some and twice that figure by others, turned up to watch the execution of an unsavoury pair named Haggerty and Holloway, who had brutally murdered a lavender seller called Steele during a robbery on Hounslow Heath in 1802. A third member of the gang, Benjamin Hanfield, had been convicted for another crime and sentenced to transportation; becoming ill, he was convinced he was dying and duly confessed to his part in Steele's murder, implicating Haggerty and Holloway in the process. The pressure in the crowd was so intense that people began to panic. Several people, including a man selling pies, slipped and fell over. Such was the throng that anyone who fell was trampled on and few were able to get to their feet again. One young woman with a baby at her breast just managed to hand the infant to a man before slipping down and being crushed to death. Miraculously the baby survived, having been passed safely from hand to hand over the heads of the crowd and placed by some caring soul into a cart nearby. On that awful day twenty-eight members of the crowd died, crushed or suffocated. Nearly seventy more were severely injured. After this, barriers were erected in some of the streets abutting on to Old Bailey but it is surprising that further tragedies of this sort did not occur.

The keenest enthusiasts for a hanging often slept on the steps of the prison or in St Sepulchre's churchyard nearby in order to obtain a ringside view in the morning. There were sometimes enough of them to create an unruly mob and the night before the execution would be spent in revelry, with singing, dancing and, if the mood developed, brazenly overt individual and group sex sessions. At 8 a.m. precisely the procession emerged from the Debtors' Door of Newgate Prison. It included the sheriffs in their robes and full regalia and the Ordinary of Newgate dressed in his full canonicals. The rest of the group consisted of the warders, various jacks-in-office, the hangman with his assistants, the guards and the prisoner or prisoners. The prison bell tolled sonorously. The prisoner would be cheered or booed on to the scaffold depending on the crowd's opinion of him or her and the nature of the offence. The hangman, by virtue of his office, was nearly always subjected to catcalls and mockery except on those occasions when his victims had committed offences that disgusted the crowd. Then he was – briefly – a hero.

In March 1789 a woman named Murphy was executed outside Newgate for coining – making counterfeit coins. Coining was long regarded as extremely serious, probably because an unstable currency underpinned the effective rule of the monarch and the integrity of the state. To undermine it was therefore tantamount to treason. Murphy was the last person convicted of this crime to suffer such a fate. Her husband had also been convicted for the same offence and had been hanged earlier that day with seven others; when his wife's turn came, she was chained to a small gibbet. After spending some moments in prayer, she was placed on a stool which was then removed to leave her suspended. After she had been hanging for about half an hour and all signs of life had been extinguished, faggots were piled up to cover her body and then set on fire.

Extraordinary although it may seem to modern eyes, burning was employed for the execution of women convicted of crimes such as treason, the murder of their husbands and coining. It was seen as a more acceptable alternative to hanging for it prevented the exposure of their bodies to the crowd's prurient gaze. The intention was that the woman would be dead by strangulation or from suffocation through lack of oxygen before the flames touched her. Another to die in this way was Phoebe Harris in 1786.

The hangings that took place outside Newgate provided an opportunity for the Governor of the prison to lay on an exclusive social event to which he would invite his immediate family, the Ordinary and a small select group of people of distinction. Doubtless he hoped that some of the latter would be prepared to return the favour in some way in the future. An excellent view of the proceedings could be had from the prison and after the execution the party would withdraw to take breakfast. This was usually preceded by a glass or two of brandy, and involved a hearty meal, which, a trifle insensitively, always included grilled or devilled kidneys. Having eaten their fill, the party would then return to view the cutting down of the corpse. As ever in London, the element of theatre was an essential part of public hangings.

In 1802 one of Newgate's most celebrated executions took place when Governor Wall was hanged. He had been convicted of the murder of a soldier named Benjamin Armstrong who was under his command at Goree in Africa. Wall's high rank and the time that had elapsed since the crime had been committed elicited great interest in the case and his subsequent fate. Appointed Governor of Goree in 1779, Wall was heartily loathed by all under his command for his bullying and inflexible severity. Shortly before he was due to retire and return to England in 1782, a group of soldiers – who perhaps should have known better – petitioned him concerning what they thought were unfair stoppages to their pay. Wall's furious response was that this action was mutinous. Believing Armstrong to be the ringleader, he ordered him to be tied to a gun carriage and to receive 800 lashes. Slaves were ordered to carry out the punishment. They set to with great gusto for fear that if Wall thought they were slacking, they would be subjected to the same treatment. The unfortunate Armstrong suffered internal injuries from which he died a few days later.

Wall was arrested in 1784 but managed to escape to France where he changed his name. It is probable that he found life in Napoleonic France uncongenial or even dangerous because he returned to England and eventually gave himself up. His trial took place eighteen years after the offence. He stoutly defended himself on the grounds that his actions were taken during the suppression of a mutiny, and he contemptuously denied the allegation made by one witness that he had executed offenders by trying them across the mouth of a cannon which was then fired.

An eyewitness gave an account of Wall's last moments:
The prisoner entered. He was death's counterfeit, tall, shrivelled and pale; and his soul shot so piercingly through the port holes of his head, that the first glance of him nearly terrified me. I said in my heart, 'God forbid that I should disturb thy last moments!' His hands were clasped and he was truly penitent . . . He then, turning to the Ordinary, questioned him, 'Do tell me, sir: I am informed I shall go down with great force: is that so?' After the construction and action of the machine had been explained, the doctor questioned Wall as to what kind of men he had at Goree. 'Sir,' he answered, 'they sent me the very riff-raff.' The poor soul then joined the doctor in prayer and never did I witness more contrition at any condemned sermon than he then evinced.

Hangman Botting, hardened to the crowd's abuse, found himself their hero for once, such was the abhorrence with which Wall was regarded. The wretched man took over eleven minutes to expire. No sooner was he dispatched than the hangman was busy selling pieces of the actual rope used at a shilling an inch, while in nearby Newgate Street an emaciated old man was selling what he claimed were pieces of the genuine rope for sixpence an inch. Just round the corner a huckster was busy selling pieces of yet a third rope!

Spencer Perceval made his mark on history by becoming the only British prime minister to be assassinated in office. Like Abraham Lincoln, he had a premonition of his death the night before he died, dreaming that he was shot while passing through the lobby of the House of Commons. Clearly shaken by the dream, when he woke he poured out his feelings to his family, who anxiously urged him to stay away from the House that day. This he agreed to do – until an urgent message arrived asking for his presence in a crucial and controversial debate. Lurking in the lobby of the House was John Bellingham, nursing a sense of grievance and outrage because some time earlier he had been imprisoned in Russia for debt. He had appealed to the British authorities for redress but their response was that there was nothing they could do because the conviction had been entirely correct under Russian law. Incensed by this response, Bellingham had written to the Bow Street magistrates outlining his complaints and making it clear that if they would not assist him, he would take the law into his own hands. Foolishly he had also furnished them with his name and address.

Seething with pent-up hatred and frustration, Bellingham observed the comings and goings at the House of Commons for a few days. His original intention was to attack Lord Leveson Gower, a former ambassador to Russia, whom Bellingham believed had let him down. On

11 May 1812 Bellingham was standing in the lobby of the House when Spencer Perceval rushed in, keen to get to the debate. Bellingham shot him at close range, either mistaking him for Leveson Gower or perhaps recognising him as prime minister and thinking that he would do just as well. Spencer Perceval's last words were rather curious: 'Oh I am murdered!' Despite the likelihood that Bellingham was of unsound mind, his trial was rushed through with conspicuous speed and he was hanged outside Newgate on 18 May, only a week after firing the fatal shot. Had he committed the crime just thirty years later, the McNaghten Rules would almost certainly have saved him from execution on the grounds that he was not responsible for his actions. The execution was notable for the unusually large crowd and the fact that an ox ran amok and gored a few unfortunates but luckily without causing fatalities. Lord Byron (1788–1824) was among the celebrities in the crowd that day.

Two years later, in February 1814, John Ashton, a highwayman, was hanged in Old Bailey. He was one of five criminals scheduled to be hanged on that day. He quickly caught the attention of the crowd when he started capering about on the scaffold shouting, 'I'm Lord Wellington! I'm Lord Wellington!' But this extraordinary outburst was merely the prelude to an entertainment which provided full value for money. Soon afterwards the trap was pulled and Ashton fell out of sight, only to bounce straight back on to the platform, the noose still in place and he himself apparently unhurt. Despite the hood over his head, he laid about him with considerable spirit and many of those on the scaffold received blows they would remember for a very long time. Eventually he was overpowered and placed on the trap once more; this time he failed to reappear. The entertainment was over for the day but many in the crowd were to enjoy free drinks when they described it in pubs over the next few weeks.

In 1815, the year of Waterloo, Eliza or Elizabeth Fenning, the 'Dumpling Murderer' was executed. She was 21 years of age and worked as the cook in a household in Chancery Lane. Her master was an unpleasant and hectoring man but Elizabeth went on record as saying that she was well enough content with her position. One evening the family and the servants were tucking in to a dinner prepared by Elizabeth which included a generous number of dumplings. Everyone, including Elizabeth herself, became violently ill and investigations discovered what appeared to be arsenic in the dumplings. No one died but a wave of vengeful hysteria swept Elizabeth to trial where she was sentenced to death. Little evidence was produced to substantiate the claim that she was a deliberate poisoner and it is highly likely that the diners had been affected by acute food poisoning. There was widespread popular revulsion against this travesty of justice and large crowds turned out when Elizabeth was hanged, not to cheer but to commiserate. She died on the day she was to have been married.

Mary Green was hanged for uttering counterfeit currency on 22 March 1819. Left to hang for the usual length of time, her body was then cut down and taken away by friends – whereupon she showed signs of returning life. A doctor was called and within a short time Mary made a complete recovery. She went on to live to a considerable age.

The years after the Napoleonic Wars saw Britain in the economic doldrums, and large-scale distress and popular discontent were met with government repression. On 1 May 1820 five of the Cato Street conspirators were executed outside Newgate. They were members of a group of political dissidents who had concocted a hare-brained scheme to assassinate the entire cabinet while they were enjoying the hospitality of the Earl of Harrowby, Lord President of the Council, at his residence in Grosvenor Square. The plan was to carry out the assassinations and then go on to seize a number of strategic points in London and establish a provisional government. The ringleader was Arthur Thistlewood, who had served in the Marines. One of his closest associates was James Ings, a butcher by trade and a man of particularly bloodthirsty propensities, who revelled in informing his fellow conspirators about how he personally was going to decapitate lords Castlereagh and Sidmouth and keep their heads as souvenirs. He also revealed his intention of cutting off Castlereagh's right hand, preferably while he was still alive.

The conspirators' ranks had been penetrated by government spies and they were seized in a loft in Cato Street, ironically not far from Tyburn, but not before Thistlewood had killed one of those sent to apprehend them. As traitors they were sentenced to be hanged and then beheaded, and the promise of such a spectacle drew an exceptionally large crowd. Many members of the cabinet were widely hated and the authorities were anxious that a rescue attempt might be made so they deployed a large number of troops to control the crowds and even had artillery pieces at the ready! Astonishingly to modern eyes, the boys of Westminster School were awarded an extra day's holiday so that they could watch the spectacle.

The keenest spectators were there in good time and saw the five coffins being brought out and placed on the scaffold, which was generously sprinkled with sawdust. The block was then placed on the platform, ready for use. The solidly packed mass of spectators then waited in eager anticipation, latecomers having little chance of getting any kind of view of the proceedings. Eventually the prisoners appeared, ushered towards the scaffold behind the Ordinary, who was intoning the offices of the moment. Three of the condemned men contemptuously sucked oranges and all five got a cheer from the crowd as they ascended the scaffold. Thistlewood, Ings and two of the others went to their deaths bravely and defiantly. The fifth died quaking with terror. Ings loudly declaimed that he hoped God would be more merciful to him than men had been. He also bellowed snatches from various rebellious songs and gave three cheers for the crowd. Two of the conspirators died slowly and agonisingly, and the hangman's assistant was required to pull on their legs to finish them off.

The entertainment was by no means over. The corpses were left hanging for an hour before being decapitated by a masked figure, who used a surgeon's knife rather than the more traditional axe which had been placed near the block for the purpose. Doubtless the crowd had been looking forward to watching the axe fall and were disappointed; decapitation with a knife was much less dramatic, even though he was such a virtuoso with the knife that many took him for a surgeon. But perhaps they were propitiated when the assistant hangman held up each head in turn in full view of the crowd and bellowed out, 'This is the head of Arthur Thistlewood, a traitor', and similarly for the others, after which the head was unceremoniously dumped on the pile of waiting sawdust. Thistlewood and company were the last prisoners to be both hanged and beheaded in Britain.

Henry Fauntleroy was an intelligent and resourceful man of great charm. He enjoyed an extravagant and vibrant lifestyle, which included a succession of highly attractive mistresses, all of whom demanded that the price of their companionship was to be pampered and showered with expensive gifts. One of these ladies earned the nickname 'Mrs Bang'. Driven by his libido to acts of increasingly reckless generosity, Fauntleroy soon found himself threatened by insolvency and so he drifted into crime. As a banker, he enjoyed privileged knowledge about his clients' financial affairs. Over several years he embezzled very large amounts from carefully selected accounts by forging powers of attorney. Nemesis was inevitable but such was Fauntleroy's egotism that he even tried to bribe the officers who came to arrest him. In court, many highly respected witnesses attested to his good character and to the end Fauntleroy denied any wrongdoing. It was all in vain. So-called 'white-collar crime' has always excited interest and Fauntleroy's execution for forgery outside Newgate in 1824 attracted the largest crowd since the Cato Street conspirators had played a starring role there. Fauntleroy went to his death calmly and with great courage. Curiously, an Italian man called Edmund Angelini offered to be executed in Fauntleroy's place on the grounds that he himself was a much less useful member of society, not being a married man and father like Fauntleroy.

The year 1828 saw the execution for forgery of Joseph Hunton, a Quaker. Of humble origins, he had married a wealthy woman and used the money thus acquired for extremely unsuccessful speculation on the stock exchange. He lost heavily and in an attempt to discharge his debts, started signing forged bills and cheques. Aware that the authorities had rumbled him, he fled to Plymouth and boarded a packet ship for New York. He made a brave attempt to disguise himself and be inconspicuous but his efforts were all in vain. He was apprehended wearing a light-green frock coat, a pair of light-grey pantaloons, a black stock and a foraging cap – and must have stuck out like the proverbial sore thumb! Tried at the Old Bailey, he was found guilty and sentenced to death. Fellow Quakers rallied to him and he went to his death bravely. The case focused attention on the excessive severity of the death penalty for the offence of forgery. The last execution for forgery took place in 1829.

Bishop and Williams were body-snatchers, who, when corpses proved to be in short supply, created their own. In one case they drugged and drowned a little Italian boy in Bethnal Green and then tried to sell his body to the anatomists. This sort of crime excited extreme revulsion and large crowds turned out in Old Bailey in 1831 determined to vent their loathing on these men, regarded as among the lowest forms of criminal life. Barriers were broken down as members of the crowd poured forwards, trying to seize the men. Had they succeeded, they would probably have torn them apart. As it was, three members of the crowd were trampled to death in the mêlée.

The Greenacre case of 1837 aroused enormous interest. A headless female torso was found in some buildings in Edgware Road and an inquest returned a verdict of wilful murder. Shortly afterwards a woman's head was discovered trapped in a lock on the Regent's Canal, and this matched the body. Two legs were found about a month later but it was some time before a positive identification of the body parts could be made. They were those of a widow, Hannah Brown. Suspicion fell on James Greenacre, who was engaged to marry Hannah, almost certainly for her money. The couple intended to emigrate when they were married. Apparently they had quarrelled about the use to which her money should be put. It is likely that Greenacre knocked her down senseless; thinking he had killed her, he proceeded to dismember her (while still alive, albeit unconscious). As ever, disposal of the victim was the murderer's first priority. Bizarrely, he wrapped the woman's head in a silk handkerchief and, placing it under his coat, carried it through the city streets and even on a horse bus before disposing of it in the Regent's Canal. This awful crime inevitably captured the public imagination and Greenacre was hanged outside Newgate in front of a large and enthusiastic crowd. The scene was described by Gordon Honeycombe in *More Murders of the Black Museum*:

They began gathering outside the prison well before midnight, when a sort of fair was held: piemen sold penny sandwiches and Greenacre tarts; ballad-mongers touted their wares; some hawkers sold pictures and life stories about Greenacre . . . as well as fake confessions. Others distributed religious tracts; and pickpockets plied their trade. Coffee-shops and pubs were open; first-floor rooms opposite the scaffold could be hired for as much as £12; windows were thronged. Every new activity was greeted with excited cheers and whistles, hisses and boos, even when women fainted and boys were trampled underfoot . . .

François Benjamin Courvoisier, a young Swiss valet, was found guilty of murdering his master, the high-born and elderly Lord William Russell, in his bed. This murder took place in Mayfair, the kind of fashionable neighbourhood not readily associated with violent crime. A frenzied attack had taken place, during which Russell's head had been almost severed from his neck. There were signs of a break-in and many valuables were missing. Police enquiries gradually focused on Courvoisier but the evidence against him was weak and circumstantial. However, while the case was actually being heard, a witness came forward who was able to identify Courvoisier as the man who had deposited a brown-paper parcel with him; when the police opened the parcel, it was found to contain the late victim's stolen possessions. It seems that Russell strongly suspected Courvoisier of having systematically robbed him over a period and so the latter decided to silence him before he could present his evidence to the authorities. He decided to purloin some more of his master's property while he was at it.

Hundreds of spectators arrived during the evening preceding the execution on 6 July 1840 and spent the night in the street in order to obtain a ringside view of the scaffold. Nearby houses which offered a good view were packed to the rafters and there were even people perched on the roofs overlooking Old Bailey. Those who wanted to watch in greater comfort paid £2 for a window with a view, but the additional amenities on offer in Lamb's Coffee House pushed the price for their windows up to £5. Many well-to-do voyeurs parted with good money that day and one extremely modish lady managed to fall out of the window on to the crowd below, such was her anxiety not to miss the action. The novelist William

Makepeace Thackeray (1811–63) was not a habitué of hangings but he did see Courvoisier's death, describing it graphically in his essay, 'Going to see a Man Hanged'. The event left him with feelings of shame, revulsion and fear. Charles Dickens witnessed the same hanging and was surprised to pick out Thackeray in the milling crowd (although at 6ft 3in tall he must have been quite conspicuous!). Dickens found the scene absolutely sickening and concluded that although executions were necessary, they should be carried out in private behind the prison walls.

Daniel Good was an Irish coachman who, one evening in 1842, rather stupidly stole a pair of trousers in Wandsworth High Street. A young shop assistant saw him and reported the offence to a passing constable, PC Gardiner. The latter recognised the thief's description and set off for the mansion near Roehampton where he knew Good worked. On searching the coach-house he unearthed a rather flaccid object which he took at first to be a dead, plucked goose – but to his horror he soon realised it was a naked female torso. Good chose this moment to lock the constable in and dash away from the scene. PC Gardiner must have been appalled by the fact that he had let a possible murderer escape in such a fashion. Soon police reinforcements arrived. Further searches revealed some partially burned female body parts, the remains of clothing and various sinister-looking implements such as knives and an axe, all of which looked as if they had been involved in particularly gruesome murder. The remains were identified as those of a young woman called Jane Jones, otherwise known as Jane Good, Daniel's estranged wife. She was almost certainly pregnant and had apparently been killed for the few pounds' worth of clothes and other articles which constituted her worldly goods. Good eluded the police for about a fortnight but found himself in the dock at the Central Criminal Court in May 1842 charged with murder. The case elicited enormous interest, not only because of the brutality involved but also because of Good's elaborate attempt to create an alibi and to shift the blame on to a young serving-girl to whom he had previously declared his love. Enormous crowds assembled outside Newgate on the morning of 23 May 1842 and gave Good, who was still protesting his innocence to anyone who would listen, an extremely hostile reception. Calcraft was the executioner and he did the job quickly and efficiently. The case was of major importance in the history of crime in Britain. It was largely as a result of this particularly shocking murder that it was decided to establish a plain-clothes detective force of officers who would specialise in the investigation of certain types of serious crime.

In 1860 an elderly and comfortably off widow was found battered to death in a house in Whitechapel. Although the motive seemed to be robbery, nothing of any real value appeared to have been taken. The police were puzzled by the presence of many rolls of wallpaper in the house and wondered whether the lady had invited a salesperson into the house in order to choose materials for redecorating. Enquiries following up this idea led nowhere. There was no evidence of forced entry. The police were baffled. Eventually a man named Mullins came forward, claiming that the killer was an agent working on behalf of the murdered woman, who had rented out many properties in the area. The information Mullins provided only served to focus attention on him as the possible murderer and the police soon built up a case which led to his conviction for murder. Few people convicted of murder have ever protested their innocence as vehemently as Mullins did, but his efforts were in vain and he was hanged in Old Bailey in front of a particularly large crowd.

In February 1864 five felons were hanged together. They were mutineers who had murdered their captain and seized the merchant vessel *Flowery Land*. Multiple hangings always attracted a large number of spectators and many upper-class 'swells' had been wining, dining and revelling for several hours overnight in anticipation of the morning's entertainment. Most had rented rooms at an exorbitant price to guarantee a first-class view of proceedings. As St Sepulchre's bell struck eight the crowd became somewhat hushed but eagerly expectant, craning forward as the procession appeared from the Debtors' Door. All but one of the prisoners were *in extremis*. They had been given brandy to fortify them but still had to be assisted on to the scaffold. Only Lopez, the last to die, managed to wave to the crowd. This raised a cheer. The bodies were cut down after an hour and later the same day were interred within the precincts of Newgate.

The authorities had anticipated an especially large and probably troublesome crowd for this event and so had built a heavy timber barricade across the entire front of Newgate. The result was that pickpockets and robbers were able to plunder the crowd with almost total immunity, because the police were on the other side of the barrier! The vast crowd (one estimate was an unlikely 200,000) was described by an observer as consisting largely of 'the lowest scum of London'; he went on to say, 'It was difficult to believe one was in the centre of a civilised capital that vaunted its religion and yet meted out justice in such a form.' He described the executions:

Not till four o' clock in the morning did the ministers of justice begin to appear. There was a rumbling of cart wheels – the dull thud of hammers and carpenters' mallets; and, through the rainy murk that hung over the heads of the mob, a gang of labourers, working by lantern-light, were seen putting the finishing touches to the structure of the scaffold. Then, unobtrusively, the Debtors' Door was opened; and, from this exit, peeped out an ancient and decrepit man, who sidled forth, cautiously tested the drop and (followed by roars of execration) quickly slipped back into the prison. At half-past seven St Sepulchre's bell started its tolling. The solemn strokes of the bell, added to the ominous knocking of the workmen and the distant hubbub of a savage and excited crowd, must have combined to give a peculiarly tragic intensity to the atmosphere. A few last preparations – sand scattered near the drop, lest the minister of religion attending the prisoners should lose his footing on the greasy boards – and the stage was ready. Below the scaffold stretched a vast ocean of upturned human faces, pale, strained, eager; anxious spectators clung to roof-ridges, parapets, railings and the tops of stationary vans; while a pathetic procession emerged . . . functionaries, jailers and official witnesses, all surrounding the knot of condemned men, cadaverous, pinioned and 'literally as white as marble'. Calcraft – for that was the name of the executioner – now proceeded to do his work with a ghastly nimbleness all the more surprising when one considered his advanced age. Heads were shrouded, ankles were strapped, and finally, a hempen noose was slung around the neck and attached to a hook that dangled from a cross-beam. The silence was now awful . . . suddenly a muted crash that reverberated through the street announced that justice had been done; and Calcraft, fastening himself in turn on the victims' feet, proceeded to pull his hardest till he was satisfied their struggles were over.

Possibly the largest crowd that ever assembled to view an execution outside Newgate was that which turned up in 1864 to watch the death agonies of Franz Muller, a young German living in London, who committed what is believed to be the first murder on a railway train. Thomas Briggs, a prosperous banker, was attacked and robbed late one evening on the North London Railway between Bow and Hackney Wick. He was sporting a fine gold watch and chain that perhaps provoked the greed of his assailant. Fatally injured, Briggs was thrown out of the compartment and was later found dying by the side of the tracks. There were few clues in the railway carriage compartment, except for a black beaver hat with a low crown which definitely did not belong to Briggs. Police enquiries made little progress until a cab-driver came forward to say that the hat belonged to a young German man who had at one time been engaged to his daughter. Muller meanwhile had left for the United States on a sailing ship but two detectives were dispatched on a fast steamship and were waiting for Muller when his vessel docked at New York. Muller had made no attempt to be inconspicuous on the voyage. He was described by fellow passengers as 'overbearing' and had even got into an argument with one of them, in the course of which he received a black eye. Muller was apparently short of money and for a wager offered to eat 5lb of German sausage at one sitting. Perhaps unsurprisingly, this enterprising attempt at fund-raising was unsuccessful. Whether this was because he could not stomach all the sausages or because he failed to attract the necessary sponsorship is not known.

Muller was extradited and stood trial at the Old Bailey. He staunchly denied the crime but is reputed to have confessed with his dying breath. The case attracted enormous interest and was accompanied by a wave of virulent anti-German hysteria. The crowd watched Muller go to his death with quiet courage. Some sense of the ravening nature of the crowd is provided by William Field, an usher at the Old Bailey, who said, 'It was a terrible crowd, shouting, yelling, shrieking, uttering ribaldry and obscenity; men drinking from bottles and women smoking . . .'

The Muller case is of considerable historical significance. The appalling scenes at his execution undoubtedly contributed to the case for the abolition of public hangings. The potential danger of violent attack within the confines of a passenger compartment was starkly highlighted. The outcome was the legal requirement that all railway carriages should be fitted with a means of enabling a passenger in distress to communicate with the driver while the train was in motion. This of course was what became known as the communication cord. Additionally some railway companies fitted their carriages with apertures which made it possible to look from one compartment into another. This was nicknamed the 'Muller Hole' or 'Muller Light'. Muller's hat, with its characteristic low crown, rather perversely became fashionable and was known as the 'Muller Hat'. It went on to become indelibly associated with Sir Winston Churchill during his years in high office. Despite the volume of circumstantial evidence submitted in court, there are some who even today believe that Muller was the victim of a miscarriage of justice.

The last execution in Old Bailey – and indeed the very last public execution in Britain – took place on 26 May 1868 when hangman Calcraft ended the life of a young Irish republican, Michael Barrett, who had tried to blow up the Middlesex House of Detention in Clerkenwell in an attempt to release some of his fellow patriots who were imprisoned there. A spectacular explosion brought down some of the prison wall but it also demolished a terrace of houses opposite, killing six people immediately, fatally injuring another six and seriously injuring at least forty others. This act excited a wave of hatred towards the Irish, and despite the extra security measures large crowds turned out to execrate Barrett and speed him to his death. Legislation had already been passed ending public executions, and subsequent executions at Newgate took place inside the prison and away from the eyes of the voyeuristic public. Many of those who witnessed Barrett's death were aware that this was the last public execution they would ever see. This in itself was enough to guarantee a large crowd. Calcraft had received threats on his life and there were probably many in the swarming mass who hoped that this might provide additional entertainment that day. In the event no such attempt occurred.

After Barrett was hanged, the scaffold was re-erected inside the prison in one of the exercise yards. This yard was overlooked by a gloomy garret in which the hangman spent the night before an execution; many of them whiled away the time by carving their initials in the woodwork. The first execution to take place in the new location was that of a singularly repulsive individual called Alexander Mackay, who had beaten his mistress into a pulp with a rolling pin and a furnace rake. Now executions took place in almost complete silence except for the clangour of Newgate's great bell. These so-called 'private' executions were not popular with the officials concerned because the presence of large, noisy crowds baying for blood had offered an element of vicariousness into the proceedings, sharing the blame, which was lacking in the much more confined and exclusive atmosphere inside the walls.

The burial ground at Newgate was known as Birdcage Walk. Along this dismal passage, also known as 'Dead Man's Walk', the felons passed on their way from the condemned cell to the execution shed, aware that they were walking over the mortal remains of previous inmates. Their corpses were stripped naked and thrown into shallow graves full of quicklime. Carved on the walls were the initials of some of those buried under the pavement. One such inscription – 'B L D L W' – referred to the sailors described as the '*Flowery Land* Pirates', who were hanged in 1864. Close by were the initials of the Cato Street Conspirators, 'T B I D T'.

While some felons were overwhelmed by fear as the time of their execution drew close, others were determined to go down with all guns blazing. Henry Wainwright was one such. Hanged at Newgate on 21 December 1875, he exhibited no signs of nerves; with his head held high, he rounded on the select gathering of those who had come to watch his execution and snarled, 'Come to see a man die, have you, you curs?' Wainwright was the first man to be hanged in London for seven years. Street children in London started playing a new game called 'Wainwright' which re-enacted his trial and execution. On one occasion a boy playing the role of Wainwright on the scaffold nearly died with a noose around his neck.

Mary Piercey, also known as Mary Wheeler, was tried for murder at the Old Bailey in 1890. A peculiar-looking woman, with a horse face, receding chin and extremely long neck, she was the aggrieved party in a 'love triangle'. Her jealousy and frustration led her to kill Phoebe Hogg, the 'other woman'. It was an exceptionally violent murder because Phoebe's head was almost severed from her body. Piercey also murdered Phoebe's baby. The press dubbed her the 'long-necked murderess' and those who viewed the court's proceedings were puzzled by her curiously abstracted manner, her seeming indifference to the unfolding drama that would decide her fate. Although she seemed to be enduring some inner torment, she refused to cooperate with her defence counsel who wanted her to agree to face a reduced charge of manslaughter. Some alleged that she had a male accomplice but this was never confirmed and Mary took the rap alone. She was hanged in Newgate on 23 December 1890.

London, and in particular the East End, was convulsed by the appalling murders supposedly carried out by 'Jack the Ripper' in 1888. They attracted unprecedented publicity, not only because of their appalling brutality but because of the sinister way in which they were perpetrated – and because they remained unsolved. The furore had only just abated when Neil Cream was executed in Newgate on 15 November 1892. A Glaswegian born in 1850, Cream was a singularly unprepossessing man with thin hair, a thick moustache, a squint and many nervous mannerisms. Despite his appearance, he sported modish clothes and was given to boasting about his sexual conquests, relating the details with a lurid relish to anyone who would listen. He showed his male friends the pornographic postcards he always carried with him and told them about the heightened sexual prowess he obtained from pills which he claimed contained substances such as strychnine. He qualified as a doctor of medicine in Canada, making a particular study of poisons, and rumours said that he used these poisons to assist with illegal abortions. He had a predilection for 'ladies of the night' and would try to press on them tablets which he described as tonics but which actually contained lethal poisons. He seems to have obtained his perverted sexual pleasures by persuading the women to take some of his pills whereupon he first had sex with them and then returned home to enjoy a bout of masturbation while imagining them writhing with pain and terror in their death throes. He killed several women, mostly in the Lambeth area of London, and the story is told that his dying words were, 'I am Jack the . . .'.

Amelia Dyer, the 'Reading Baby-farmer', was executed at Newgate on 10 June 1896. A former Salvation Army officer and still a regular worshipper, she was ostensibly respectable and apparently destined for permanent anonymity. However, she shot to notoriety when it was revealed that she made a living by charging considerable sums to provide long-term foster care for babies, usually those born to unmarried women who could not bear the social stigma attached to their position. Amelia was a model prisoner while awaiting execution, except for her habit of singing hymns in her cell in an appallingly tuneless fashion, which disturbed other inmates. However, she had a threatening way of scrutinising the warders which made them feel distinctly uncomfortable. The story goes that on her way to the scaffold she passed the Chief Warder of Newgate and quietly imparted the unsolicited and unwelcome information that she would meet him again in the future. Later on the man was on duty one evening just before Newgate closed for good and was enjoying a tot of whisky with some colleagues when he looked up and saw Amelia's face with its unmistakably malevolent smile looking at him through a grille in the door. Badly shaken, the warder opened the door – and saw nothing but a woman's handkerchief fluttering to the floor. The holding of women convicts in Newgate had finished some years earlier. Was it a ghost? Few prisons were more likely to have had a collection of ghouls and spectres than Newgate.

Hangings came to an end at Newgate in May 1902 when George Woolfe was executed. He had brutally murdered his girlfriend, Charlotte Cheeseman, and dumped her body on some marshland. She was very much in love with him and fully expected that he would marry her, but he suddenly and brutally ended their relationship by telling her that he had met someone else he preferred. It is likely that she was pregnant and was putting pressure on him to do the right thing. He therefore decided she stood between him and a life of bliss with his new love and so she had to go.

The scaffold at Newgate was taken down but with an admirable eye to economy it was to be reused at Pentonville Prison. The human remains buried in Birdcage Walk were removed and reburied at Ilford cemetery. Some of the fabric of the prison was reused in the building of the Old Bailey. In the ante-room of the keeper's office in Newgate were displayed three rows of plaster busts of murderers who had been hanged just outside its precincts. These busts had been made almost immediately after death and on all of them the marks of the rope where it had cut into the victim's neck were faithfully reproduced.

The Ordinary of Newgate played an important role in the execution of felons in Newgate. This office dated from the early sixteenth century and involved one of the four chaplains of St Bartholomew's Hospital who was appointed to visit Newgate and attend to the spiritual needs of the inmates, particularly those who had been condemned to death. He was answerable to the Court of Aldermen of the City of London. Part of the function of the Ordinary was to ride in the cart with the condemned prisoners to the place of execution and to try to provide spiritual succour for them in their ordeal. If they had not already done so, the Ordinary would also attempt to get them to make a full confession of their crimes (and to implicate their accomplices whenever possible). At the place of execution the Ordinary led the prayers and hymn-singing.

Henry Goodcole, the first full-time chaplain of Newgate, ministered to the prisoners between 1620 and 1641. With an eye to maximising the financial rewards attached to the post, he began to produce for sale printed broadsheets which piously described the enormity and heinousness of each criminal's offences and the condign fate that God was reserving for him. They also provided exactly those titillating and scurrilous details, either true or suitably embellished, which found a ready market among a public avid for sensationalism. Goodcole's endeavours started a new tradition. The selling of these sheets, known as 'Dying Confessions' or 'Accounts', brought in a sizeable income and meant that the post of Ordinary was eagerly sought after in spite of the fact that the office and the duties that went with it frequently incurred ridicule and hostility both from prison inmates and the crowds at the hangings. The presence of the Ordinary fussing about his duties became an established part of the theatre of hanging days at Tyburn and Old Bailey.

One of the most successful of these self-seeking Ordinaries was the Revd Paul Lorrain, who took the post in 1700 and went on to issue over 200 broadsheets during his tenure of office. Understandably, he was most aggrieved when Parliament began to levy a tax on printed publications because this seriously affected his profits. He petitioned the House of Commons for exemption from the tax on the grounds that his works contained material intended to deter readers from pursuing criminal ways.

Over the years the 'Confessions' evolved from broadsheets into pamphlets containing basic facts about the trial, a synopsis of the sermons preached to the condemned, a description of his or her life and crimes, personal material such as letters purportedly written to or by the condemned and having a bearing on the case, and a description of the execution itself. It was widely believed that Ordinaries were only too happy to embroider confessions where the real details were insufficiently sensational or to include blood-curdling but entirely imaginary information submitted to them by felons intent on shameless leg-pulling even at this late time in their criminal careers. It helped the Ordinary if he could develop a positive working relationship with the prisoner. Some prisoners refused to cooperate at all, although others used the opportunity to denounce those whom they had a grudge against in the hope of obtaining a commuting of their sentence.

A delay of four to six weeks between sentence and execution was common and in that period there was always the possibility of a reprieve. Clearly it was a time of immense stress for all but the most hardened or phlegmatic of prisoners. Many visibly aged during this period and the Ordinary often found that those who had contemptuously rejected his early ministrations were eager to pour their hearts out with confessions and confidences as the awful prospect of death drew closer and closer. The behaviour of even the most hardened recidivists was often dramatically modified under these circumstances. In 1744, while a felon called John Lancaster was having his irons struck off before being taken for execution, he is reputed to have turned to those about him and said, 'Glory be to God for the first moment of my entrance to this place! For before I came hither my heart was as hard as my cell wall and my soul was as black as hell. But oh, I am now washed, clearly washed, from all my sins and by one o'clock shall be with Jesus in Paradise!' He went on to exhort those around him to shrive themselves of their sins and said, 'Come to the Throne of God immediately, and without fear, for you will find him a gracious and merciful God who will forgive you as he has forgiven me.' A few hours later he was hanged at Tyburn.

A similar story was told of Harris, the 'Flying Highwayman', whose previous demeanour had been brazen and defiant, but as the cart passed Hatton Garden on its way from Newgate to Tyburn he suddenly burst into tears, clapped his hands and declared loudly, 'Now I know that the Lord Jesus has forgiven my sins and I have nothing to do but die.' He seemed deliriously happy and went to his death with a beatific smile on his face, while repeatedly stating that he and his horse had never ever jumped a turnpike gate. Stories like those of Lancaster and Harris have more than a hint of the apocryphal about them.

For much of the time the pastoral work of the Ordinary of Newgate fell on largely unreceptive ears. Few prisoners attended normal services in the chapel, even as a distraction from the everyday boredom of prison routine. However, the chapel was usually full to bursting with prisoners, visitors and officials on the Sunday before a hanging, when the 'Condemned Sermon' was preached in the prison chapel. The turnkeys charged admission to members of the public who came solely to scrutinise the manner in which the condemned prisoner was bearing up to the ordeal of waiting for execution. All eyes were therefore on the prisoners as they sat close to a black-painted coffin resting on a black cloth-covered table. Some prisoners excited the admiration of the crowd for their swaggering insouciance, others appeared to have undergone a religious conversion and made a display of new-found piety, but most were in a state of shock and merely gazed around vacantly, having more or less lost their reason.

Prisoners condemned to death were money-spinners for the Newgate turnkeys because they became in effect temporary exhibits and the public were allowed in, at a price, to view them. The number of visitors and the prices charged depended on the popularity or notoriety of the prisoner concerned. In 1724 Jack Sheppard, a minor robber but a resourceful and talented escapologist, proved a great asset as visitors thronged to see him during his last few days. He even had his portrait painted in the condemned cell by the prestigious artist Sir James Thornhill (1675–1734), taking time off from the decorative artwork for which he was better known. The highwayman 'Sixteen-String Jack' Rann was another whose extrovert nature was brought out by the hordes of friends and well-wishers who crowded into his cell shortly before he was executed in 1774. But for each person who found the inner resources to display composure of this sort, there were many more whose last days were spent quaking with fear or dementedly appealing for mercy.

Until 1809 Surgeons' Hall stood conveniently nearby in Old Bailey. The bodies of executed felons were obtained for dissection there under legislation passed in 1752. A curious experiment was performed on the body of a man named Foster, who had been hanged as a murderer. His corpse was subjected to a 'galvanic' experiment described in the *Annual Register* for 1803:

On the first application of the process to the face, the jaw of the deceased criminal began to quiver, and the adjoining muscles were horribly contorted, and one eye actually opened. In a later phase of the experiment, the right hand was raised and clenched, the legs and thighs were set in motion and it seemed for all the world as if the wretched man was on the point of being restored to life! The object of these experiments was to show the excitability of the human frame when animal electricity is duly applied: and the possibility of its being efficaciously used in cases of drowning, suffocation, or apoplexy, by reviving the action of the lungs and thereby rekindling the expiring spark of vitality.

Possibly even more curious is the story that during these experiments one of the observers was struck by Foster's arm as it jerked upwards convulsively and unexpectedly. The trauma of being struck by a cadaver was apparently sufficient to cause the man to die later on the same day!

Few condemned felons successfully escaped from Newgate in its later years. One who did was Henry Williams in 1836. Those awaiting execution were allowed to exercise in an open yard surrounded by a 50-foot-high wall of smooth granite topped with vicious revolving iron spikes. His gaolers did not know that Williams had once been a sweep's boy and had learned all manner of tricks for climbing apparently unassailable surfaces. Despite being seriously lacerated by the spikes, Williams made his hair-raising ascent, got on to the roof and by a series of death-defying leaps reached other roofs and eventually freedom and safety. Enjoying his new-found liberty, he made his way to a pub in Southwark for a well-earned pint of beer. Another who got away was a sailor named Krapps. Using knotted sheets as improvised ropes, he descended from the roof of the prison into Newgate Street, to the accompaniment of cheers and congratulations from passers-by. Most attempts to escape ended much more ignominiously, however.

At 18 Old Bailey stands the 'Magpie and Stump' public house, the origins of which date back several centuries although the present building dates from the twentieth century. During the years 1783 to 1868 when public executions took place in Old Bailey successive landlords cashed in to offer a hospitality package to rich patrons who were devotees of a good hanging. For a substantial fee they could stay overnight, gorge themselves on an 'execution breakfast' and then obtain a privileged view of the gory proceedings in the street below from their bedroom window. Mystery surrounds the pub's curious name. It may be that the sign was intended to depict the arms of the Boleyn family, which included a white falcon perched on the root of a tree. Possibly the local Londoners, quick as ever to see a joke, substituted a more prosaic bird for the falcon and a stump for the tree root. Another explanation is that the 'Stump' element was added to the original 'Magpie' as a joke, this stump referring to the truncated necks of those executed nearby. The Magpie and Stump was often featured in the popular television series *Rumpole of the Bailey*.

At the junction of Old Bailey with Giltspur Street, Newgate Street and Holborn Viaduct stands the Church of the Holy Sepulchre without Newgate, commonly known as St Sepulchre's. Its position means that it has many associations with the world of crime and executions. It is mentioned in the ancient nursery rhyme 'Oranges and Lemons' with the words, 'When will you pay me? Say the bells of Old Bailey'. The Revd John Rogers, a rector of St Sepulchre's, was among England's Protestant martyrs and had the distinction of being the first Protestant to die for his beliefs during the reign of Mary Tudor (1553–8). No shrinking violet, he had used his pulpit to launch a forthright attack on what he saw as the idolatry and superstition of Catholicism, for which he was arrested, tried, condemned and burned at Smithfield.

In 1585 one Awfield was executed at Tyburn as a traitor who had distributed 'lewd and seditious books'. The parishioners of St Sepulchre's where he worshipped displayed their opinion of him by refusing to have him interred within the church's precincts. His body, which had been brought from Tyburn for interment, then had to be unceremoniously dumped back in the cart and returned to Tyburn for burial there.

At midnight before the day of an execution, when one or more condemned prisoners would be taken from Newgate to Tyburn, 'going west' to their deaths, the sexton of St Sepulchre's would pass through an underground passage, part of the door to which can still be seen in the south wall of the church, to Newgate. There he would ring his handbell (now displayed in a glass case inside the church) and intone a number of admonitory verses at the door of the condemned cell. Later he would stand outside the church, still ringing his bell, and address the passing procession with the following words: 'You that are condemned to die, repent with lamentable tears: ask mercy of the Lord, for the salvation of your own souls, through the merits, death and passion of Jesus Christ, who now sits on the right hand of God, to make intercession for as many of you as penitently return unto him . . .'. There was more in the same vein.

Between about 1750 and 1830 the macabre activities of the 'Resurrection Men' were at their height. The burial ground of St Sepulchre's provided them with 'specimens' which they sold to the lecturers teaching anatomy at nearby St Bartholomew's Hospital. After the bodies had been exhumed, they were placed on a handcart and wheeled across the road to an inn where they were collected by the anatomists' men. A small watch-house erected in 1791 to guard against their activities can still be seen.

Old Bailey has other historical associations. In 1830 James Bossy was the last person to be punished in the pillory that had stood there for many years. He was unlucky because he had been convicted of perjury, which by this time was the only offence for which this punishment had not already been abolished. The misery of a spell in the pillory should not be underestimated because it offered an effective combination of public humiliation and torturous discomfort. Those placed in the pillory looked ridiculous but this was the least of their worries; they often experienced agonising cramps, were frozen, soaked to the skin or severely sunburned depending on the weather, and were frequently assailed by all manner of stinking noxious matter, stones, brickbats and verbal derision, depending on the extent to which their offences had provoked the anger of the crowd. Fatalities in the pillory were not unknown, especially when offenders were effectively stoned to death by crowds who had taken particular exception to their crimes. On occasions the hangman had to run for his life as soon as he had placed the offender in the pillory as the angry crowds vented their spleen on the hapless occupant by showering him with hard and sometimes lethal missiles. One prisoner who died in the pillory was 'Mother Needham', who was hated by the crowd because she preyed on innocent country girls arriving in London looking for work and lodgings. Under the guise of befriending them she won their confidence, but then in effect sold them as sex slaves to older men of lecherous proclivities. She was pilloried in 1731 at the junction of Park Place and St James's Street, near the house she used as a base for her heinous activities. Stoned by an enraged crowd, she received injuries from which she died a couple of days later.

The crowd extended very different treatment to offenders whose crimes they applauded. One such was

Japhet Crook, a forger. He was placed in the pillory at Charing Cross but not a single missile was thrown at him; instead he exchanged quips and pleasantries with a friendly and supportive crowd. This may not have been a severe ordeal for Crook, but what followed most certainly was. His ears were sliced off with a scalpel and his nostrils slit with scissors. His fortitude was such that he uttered not a single cry but when the hangman approached bearing a red-hot branding iron, his courage gave way and as the iron was applied he screamed. The hangman dared not complete the branding for fear that the crowd might seize and murder him and a dazed, traumatised and bloodied Crook was then carried away for a term of incarceration in the King's Bench Prison in Southwark.

The Old Bailey was one of many sites in London which had contained pillories for several hundred years. They all consisted of an upright post, usually on a raised platform, topped by a hinged pair of planks with holes pierced in them for the hands and the neck. Traditionally the pillory had been used to punish dishonest traders such as bakers who baked underweight loaves, butchers who sold more than usually tainted meat and brewers who watered down their beer. Thus used, the pillories allowed the public as the affronted parties to participate in the punishment – everyone hated dishonest traders. Later on a wider range of offenders found themselves occupying the pillory. Punishment in the pillory ended in 1837.

No. 30 Old Bailey now stands approximately on the site where Jonathan Wild's 'Office for the Recovery of Lost and Stolen Property' was located. Ostensibly a businessman who for a fair price would locate and return items stolen in London's crime-ridden streets, in fact he was arguably the capital's first 'Napoleon of Crime', who masterminded a vast criminal network and was in his time the most dangerous man in London. He was housed in Newgate before riding in the cart to be hanged at Tyburn in 1725. His skeleton is in the possession of the Royal College of Surgeons in Lincoln's Inn Fields.

One notable Londoner born in Old Bailey was the antiquary and historian William Camden (1551–1623), while Oliver Goldsmith (1730–74) spent several years in Green Arbour Court off Old Bailey. According to the American writer Washington Irving, who went to visit Goldsmith there, Green Arbour Court may have had an attractive name but it was no Shangri-la. The buildings were mouldering and festooned with washing and the place was noisy and threatening, most definitely not the place for a writer of Goldsmith's tender susceptibilities. Fortunately for Goldsmith, the success of works like *The Vicar of Wakefield*, *The Good-Natur'd Man* and *She Stoops to Conquer* enabled him to put Green Arbour Court behind him and move on to more salubrious surroundings.

As a prison Newgate played a pivotal role in the popular culture of London for hundreds of years. It was referred to as 'The Whit' after Sir Richard Whittington or 'The Stone Tavern' or 'The Nark'. We have seen how Old Bailey, close by, attracted huge and unseemly crowds which unashamedly, even gleefully, revelled in the agonising deaths of a panoply of condemned criminals. Some were well known and notorious but most of the scaffold's victims were ordinary folk who committed squalid and stupid crimes out of foolishness or desperation. Even when executions ceased to take place in the prison and the Central Criminal Court was built on the site, drama was never far away. The Old Bailey, to give the court its popular name, has been the setting for some of the most famous trials ever to take place in Britain, including those of Hawley Harvey Crippen for the poisoning of his wife, the traitor William Joyce, also known as 'Lord Haw-Haw', and the Kray twins, who modelled themselves on Al Capone and made the East End their fiefdom in the 1950s and 1960s.

SIX

Tyburn

Tyburn doth deserve before them all
The title and addition capital,
Of Arch or great Grand Gallows of our Land,
Whilst all the rest like ragged Lackeys stand.
John Taylor, the 'Water Poet' (1580–1653)

John Taylor's tribute to Tyburn reinforced its significance as the most notorious site of execution not only in London but in the whole of Britain. From its origins in the late twelfth century to its removal in 1783, many tens of thousands of people met their end at the 'Fatal Tree'. For centuries Tyburn was as familiar to Londoners as any other of the city's outstanding landmarks such as the Tower, St Paul's and London Bridge. The area around Marble Arch, where Tyburn was located, is now an exceptionally busy part of central London but throughout its history as a place of execution it was an area of countryside 3 miles to the west of the city. In the twelfth century it was a watery, low-lying area which 'offered a small gravel plateau first occupied by an obscure monastery'. None the less for centuries a regular flow, sometimes almost a flood, of people made their way to Tyburn and gathered around the gallows on foot, on horseback, in coaches or on the viewing stands to watch the executions there. Although the name no longer properly exists, it was derived from one of the rivers located to the west of the city. The River Tyburn runs from Hampstead through Swiss Cottage down to Regents Park, where it flows south, under Oxford Street and eventually into the River Thames in the Westminster area.

By the eighteenth century the crowds would spill over into the nearby roads around the junction of Tyburn Road (now Oxford Street) and Edgware Road. They would sit or stand on the walls around Hyde Park in order to get a good view, and some even resorted to climbing ladders. Tyburn loomed large in the public imagination of those who made London their home.

In 1184, about twenty years before Tyburn's beginnings as a place of execution, William FitzStephen, secretary to the Archbishop of Canterbury Thomas Becket, wrote the first general account of London. He described houses in the suburbs as having beautiful gardens and commented on the great forest with woodland pastures and coverts of wild animals. The only pests of London, he declared, were the 'immoderate drinking of fools and the frequency of fires'.

The gallows were situated on the old Roman road to Oxford, a muddy track where the grisly remains of the victims would have greeted traffic coming in to London from the west. As late as the early eighteenth century, when the suburbs were expanding westwards, Oxford Street (previously Tyburn Road) was described as 'a deep hollow road, full of sloughs; with here and there a ragged house, the living place of cut-throats, insomuch that I never was taken that way by night, in my hackney coach, to worthy uncle's who gave me lodgings at his house in George Street, but I went in dread the whole way'.

It is difficult to trace executions at Tyburn before 1196. This problem is exacerbated by the fact that both Tyburn and Smithfield were referred to as the 'Elms', and hence when the condemned were recorded as being 'executed at the Elms' it is not always clear which site was meant. The first execution at Tyburn is thought to have been that of William FitzOsbert, also known as 'Longbeard', in 1196. He was accused of sedition after leading a revolt of merchants and artisans against the payment of taxes levied for the ransom for Richard I. The Dean of St Paul's, Ralph of Diceto, recorded that William, 'his hands bound behind him, his feet tied with long cords, [was] drawn by means of a horse through the midst of the city to the gals near Tyburn [where] he was hanged'.

Over forty years later in 1242 William de Marisco suffered hanging, drawing and quartering, a punishment that was to be a regular feature of Tyburn's history. Marsh was accused of murdering Henry Clement, a messenger sent by the Irish peers to the king, and also of attempting to assassinate King Henry III. Marsh was 'hangyd at Tyburne', after which he was cut down while still alive and disembowelled and his body divided into four parts.

Although evidence is thin for the period from the mid-fourteenth to the sixteenth century some notable people met their end at Tyburn. Roger Mortimer, Queen Isabella's lover, conspired with her to depose Edward II from the throne, thus opening the way for the succession of the young Edward III in 1327. Captured two years later at Nottingham Castle, Mortimer was brought to London and committed to the Tower. According to the *Grey Friars Chronicle*, he was subsequently 'hangyd and drawne at Tyburn for tresoun'. His body was left to hang for two days and two nights before being buried in Greyfriars Church.

By the end of the fourteenth century there was famine in England and feelings were running high against Richard II's extravagant lifestyle. Not surprisingly, several attempts were made on the king's life. The Duke of Gloucester was one of a group of nobles imprisoned for opposing the king. However, suspicions were aroused when the duke was found dead within a few weeks of his arrest. Rumours began to spread that Richard had ordered four knights to kill Gloucester. These knights were eventually brought to account and executed at Cheapside. The first to suffer was John Hall, who was charged with having kept the door of Gloucester's room open, allowing the knights to enter and smother him to death. On 17 October 1399 Hall was drawn from the Tower to Tyburn where he was hanged, quartered and then had his bowels burned.

Richard's successor Henry IV (r. 1399–1413) was also the subject of plots intended to overthrow him. In 1402 a number of men were executed at Tyburn for writing seditious material against him. Although other notable executions followed, such as that of Sir John Mortimer in the 1420s, evidence of the execution of ordinary people is absent largely because they were considered insufficiently important to record. There are, however, a few fragments of information. We know that Benedict Wolman, the head of Marshalsea Prison, was hanged at Tyburn in 1416 for conspiring to kill the king. The thief Will Wawe was hanged in 1427, William Goodgroom, a horse dealer, in 1437 and John David, an apprentice, in 1446. John Scott, John Heath and John Kenington were likewise executed at Tyburn in 1495 for slandering the king and some of his council. Many others remain anonymous, including the locksmith executed in 1467 for robbery and four yeomen of the Crown hanged in 1483. There was an unusual incident in 1447 when five men were being prepared for their execution. As the men were being stripped of their clothes in order that the hangman could claim their garments, a last-minute reprieve arrived. The hangman refused to give back the clothes, obliging the five prisoners to walk back to London naked. Given the circumstances, the ribald comments and guffaws of onlookers must have seemed a small price to pay for their lives.

One remarkable case, which was echoed in Shakespeare's *Henry VI*, occurred at Tyburn in the 1440s and involved the astrologer and magician Roger Bolingbroke, along with Canon Thomas Southwell of St Stephen's Chapel, Westminster. Both men were charged with treason for attempting to kill Henry VI (r. 1422–61) by sorcery with the intention of replacing him on the throne with the Duke of Gloucester. Bolingbroke was taken from the Tower to Tyburn where he was hanged, drawn and quartered.

The first Tudor monarch, Henry VII (r. 1485–1509), faced a dangerous revolt in 1497 when men from Cornwall refused to pay taxes to finance an invasion of Scotland. The revolt escalated when some 15,000 men marched up from the south-west and became involved in a pitched battle at Blackheath near London in June; more than 1,000 were killed. Two of the leaders, the lawyer Thomas Flamank and the blacksmith Michael Joseph, were hanged, drawn and quartered at Tyburn and had their heads set upon poles on London Bridge. It was not the only challenge Henry VII would face. His claim to the throne was contested by a number of people. One such pretender was Perkin Warbeck, who adopted the identity of Richard of York, the younger of the two 'Princes in the Tower'. Born in 1474, Warbeck was brought up at Antwerp and served a succession of employers as a boy servant. In 1491 he was in Cork as the servant of a Breton silk merchant. While he was there he heard of the intrigue against Henry VII and became the tool of those who plotted against the king, such as the earls of Desmond and Kildare. Perkin believed that when people saw him dressed in the silks of his master they would take him for a person of distinction, and he insisted that he must be either the son of George, Duke of Clarence, or a bastard son of Richard III. The following year he was summoned to Flanders by Margaret, the widowed Duchess of Burgundy and sister of the late Edward IV. She saw in Warbeck a means of injuring the king who had brought down her family. As Richard, Duke of York, Perkin Warbeck was entertained grandly in France and in Vienna he was treated as the lawful King of England. His story gained sufficient plausibility that he was accepted as Richard by Charles VIII of France and the Scots even invaded England on his behalf. Exploiting the situation in the south-west, Warbeck proclaimed himself Richard IV. However, his moment of fame soon passed and after the execution of many of his followers Warbeck was drawn on a hurdle from the Tower and executed on 23 November 1499.

By the sixteenth century London had expanded its boundaries way beyond the original walled city and the road from Newgate to Tyburn saw an increase in traffic, particularly in cattle going to and from market. The increase in London's population – especially in the number of poorer people – became a matter of concern for successive governments. The state responded by instituting the poor laws and imposing harsher punishments for criminal offences. Tyburn continued to receive the poor and the persecuted in large numbers, and never more so than in the reign of Henry VIII. His reign witnessed momentous changes, particularly in religion, and these had severe consequences for the many who were caught out and found themselves at one or other of the places of execution in London. Until the 1530s the English people in general shared an allegiance to the Catholic faith but Henry VIII's divorce from Catherine of Aragon was the catalyst for the Protestant Reformation which witnessed, under successive monarchs, unprecedented confiscation of land and treasure. The break with the Roman Catholic Church during the 1530s saw savage attacks against persistent Catholics, who were accused of treason, while large numbers of Protestant dissenters were accused of heresy.

Anyone speaking out against Henry's marriage to Anne Boleyn was deemed to be a traitor. One notable victim of this legislation was Elizabeth Barton, the 'Holy Maid of Kent', who was a maidservant from Aldington in Kent. Barton was credited with having a 'divine gift', although she actually suffered from a form of epilepsy, and she entered the Benedictine Nunnery of St Sepulchre at Canterbury in 1527. When Henry formally divorced Catherine in 1533, Barton was so outraged she prophesied that Henry would die within a month of his marriage to Anne Boleyn. This prediction was considered dangerous and Elizabeth was arrested on grounds of treason. After suffering torture at the Tower she was executed at Tyburn in April 1534, along with Edward

Bocking, John Dering and two monks from Canterbury, Richard Risby and Henry Gold. It is reputed that her head was the only female one ever to be spiked and exhibited on the Drawbridge Gate of London Bridge.

Some other early victims of the break with Rome were three Carthusian monks of London, Robert Lawrence, Augustine Webster and Father John Houghton, who were all executed at Tyburn. They were fastened to a hurdle and dragged by horses to the site of execution, where many thousands had gathered. Being drawn through the streets on the bumpy stones was torture in itself and it was common for the condemned to be in a semi-conscious state by the time they reached the gallows. The executioner bowed before them and asked forgiveness, and then proceeded to hang them and 'dragged out [their] bowels . . . heart, and all else, and threw them into a fire'. William Exmew, another Carthusian monk, followed on 19 June 1535, along with Humphrey Middlemore, for being 'obstinately determined to suffer all extremities rather than to alter their opinion' with regard to the primacy of the Pope.

The largest rebellion in response to Henry's religious changes and the dissolution of the monasteries was the Pilgrimage of Grace. This spread across the north of England in 1536 and was supported by many thousands. Inevitably the rising was crushed and the leaders captured. Two months later, in May 1537, twelve Catholics, the abbots of Fountains, Jervaulx, and Sawley abbeys, Lord Darcy, Sir Henry Percy and several others associated with the rebellion were executed at Tyburn.

In 1540, after his failed marriage with Anne of Cleves, Henry married Catherine Howard but within two years she was executed at Tower Hill for adultery with Thomas

Culpepper. That Culpepper ever expected to carry on a secret affair with the queen defies belief and predictably rumours began to circulate. Culpepper paid a heavy price for his indiscretion and was executed at Tyburn on 10 December 1541, along with Francis Dereham. As a Gentleman of the King's Privy Chamber, Culpepper was spared hanging and disembowelling and was instead allowed the privilege of the axe.

Such was the scale of executions during Henry's reign that Hugh Latimer, Bishop of Worcester, commented in a sermon in May 1549 that 'there were three weekes sessions at Newgate and fourthnyghte sessions at the Marshialshy, and so forth'. In 1516 Thomas More recorded that twenty were sometimes hanged at one gallows.

The last martyr to be executed at Tyburn under Henry was Germaine Gardiner in March 1544, who had denied the king's supremacy. However, religious martyrs were not the dominant victims of the scaffold in this period. Instead the mass of anonymous felons who were victims of economic and social distress continued to remain the regular fare for Tyburn. During the reign of Henry's son Edward VI the diarist Henry Machyn recorded that in May 1552 six felons were executed at Tyburn; two months later James Ellis, described as the great cutpurse and thief, was hanged. In December two 'tall' men and a 'lackey' were executed for robbery. In January 1553 two men were killed for the murder of a gentleman and one was hanged and quartered for counterfeiting the royal signet.

At the age of 37 Mary Tudor ascended the throne in 1553 and immediately restored the Catholic faith. Her marriage to Philip, heir to the King of Spain, sparked off a rebellion in Kent, led by supporters of the former Protectors Somerset and Northumberland. This culminated in the death of 40 rebels and 90 others who were executed around London. However, only one, William Thomas, Clerk to the Council, was taken to Tyburn.

Mary, too, faced the threat of rival claimants to the throne. A rather spurious claim was made by 18-year-old William Constable, a miller's son, who stated that he was the surviving Edward VI. He was sentenced to be whipped along the route from Westminster Hall to Smithfield. He clearly failed to learn his lesson for nine months later he was again accused of the same offence. This time he was hanged and quartered in March 1556, the same month that 'ten thieves were hanged for robbery' at Tyburn.

London witnessed significant social, legal and political changes in the period from Henry VIII's reign to the Restoration of 1660. The population grew from around 50,000 to almost 500,000. There was also an expansion in trade and this increase in commercial activity brought consequences in terms of the number of people finding themselves at Tyburn on charges of coining (especially counterfeiting and clipping). By the end of the sixteenth century there were also developments in scaffold ritual. The procession from prison to gallows now stopped for a drink along the route and prayers were said with the chaplain before arriving at Tyburn. The last dying speech of the condemned on the scaffold varied. Some asked for forgiveness, others proclaimed their innocence, while religious devotees often exploited the opportunity to make pious pronouncements to the large crowd. In many cases the felon's valedictory speech involved a condemnation of the authorities. Some prisoners remained in silence while others were so drunk that all they could do was ramble on incoherently.

After execution the corpses from Tyburn were often thrown into a pit near the gallows – as happened to Oliver Cromwell's body. During the 1820s, when the area around Tyburn was being redeveloped, quantities of human skeletons were discovered. John Stow's *Survey of London* (1598) mentions Ralph Stratford, Bishop of London, who in the year of the Black Death in 1348 bought a piece of ground called Pardon Churchyard, also known as 'No Man's Land', which he dedicated to the burial of the dead. Twenty-three years later in 1371 a monastery was built nearby and the monks set aside 3 acres of land for the purpose of burying executed felons.

On a visit to England from Basel in 1599 Thomas Platter wrote in his diary a description of the process of execution and burial, and commented on the many prisoners who were taken 'out of the town to the gallows, called Tyburn, almost an hour away from the city'. After the execution he noted that the condemned were buried in a neighbouring cemetery, 'where stands a house haunted by such monsters that no one can live in it, and I myself saw it. Rarely does a law day in London in all the four sessions pass without some twenty to thirty persons – both men and women – being gibbeted.'

If Smithfield had been a prominent site of execution for Protestant martyrs during the reign of Mary, then Tyburn would provide the place of execution for Catholics during Elizabeth's reign. Elizabeth succeeded to the throne in November 1558 but many Catholics regarded Mary, Queen of Scots (1542–87) as the rightful claimant to the throne and she became a focal point for Catholic sympathies (as well as for anti-Catholic hostility). Plots which attempted to replace Elizabeth with Mary were uncovered and some of the conspirators found themselves at Tyburn. They included Thomas Norton and his nephew Christopher Norton, who were condemned for high treason and sentenced to be 'hanged, headed and quartered' for their part in the 1569 uprising. Another plotter, Francis Throckmorton, was executed for the conspiracy named after him in July 1584. Under torture he confessed that he was engaged in a grand 'Enterprise' to assassinate Elizabeth. In the same year the plotters George Haydock, John Nutter, Thomas Hemerford, James Fenn and John Munden were drawn on hurdles with five other priests to Tyburn. James Fenn was stripped of all his clothing except his shirt, but when the cart was driven away his shirt was pulled off his back, so that he hung stark naked, 'whereat the people muttered greatly'. Many of the plots against Elizabeth had centred around Catholics who refused to swear the oath of allegiance recognising the queen as Supreme Governor of the Church, and subsequently they were condemned as traitors.

A significant development in Tyburn's history was the erection in 1571 of the famous triangular gallows, the 'Triple Tree'. The gallows were strong and imposing, and capable of hanging twenty-four people at a time, eight on each beam. Estimates have put the height of the triangular tree at between 15 and 18 feet. It was recorded that on 1 June 1571 'the saide [John] Story was drawn upon an herdell from the Tower of London unto Tiborn, where was prepared for him a newe payre of gallows made in triangular maner'.

Doctor John Story, the first Regius Professor of Civil Law at Oxford, was imprisoned in 1563 for his persecution of Protestants under Mary. Although he escaped he was eventually recaptured and charged with high treason. The gallows crowd was hostile towards

1. The execution of Charles I at Whitehall on 30 January 1649. Arrogant, inept and devious in public matters, he went to his death with great dignity and courage. Philip Henry, an eye-witness, related that as the King's head fell, 'There was such a groan by the thousands then present as I have never heard before and desire I may never hear again.'

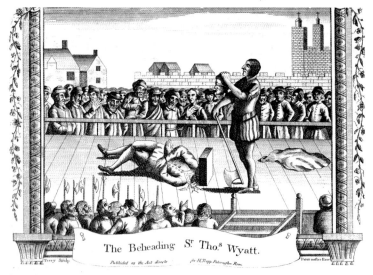

The Beheading S.ʳ Tho.ˢ Wyatt.

2. The execution of Sir Thomas Wyatt. He led an abortive Protestant rebellion against Queen Mary in 1554 but was captured and beheaded at Tower Hill. He was quartered and his bodily parts were put on display at various sites around London.

The IDLE PRENTICE Executed at Tyburn.

3. The *Idle 'Prentice* is hanged at Tyburn, 1747. Here William Hogarth provides possibly the best visual representation of the scene at Tyburn as the crowds prepare for a hanging amid scenes of robust, bawdy revelry.

4. William Kidd, the famous pirate, was hanged at Execution Dock in May 1701. His remains were then placed in a cage hanging from a gibbet in a prominent position further down the Thames where they could be seen by passing ships and act as a warning against piracy.

5. Female huckster walking the streets of London selling broadsheets purporting to be the *Last Dying Confession of the Condemned Prisoner*. These were often on sale days before the execution. Sometimes rivals would be peddling equally spurious alternative versions of the *Last Confession*. They sold like hot cakes.

6. Sarah Malcolm. She robbed and strangled her employer and was hanged in Fleet Street in 1732. She was drawn by Hogarth two days before her death.

7. The Sessions House, precursor of the Old Bailey or Central Criminal Court, where offenders from London and Middlesex were tried. Here thousands of men and women were tried and condemned to death. Later they made their final journey through the London streets to die at Tyburn, close to the present-day Marble Arch.

8. Aristocrats were normally accorded the privilege of being beheaded rather than hanged. However the crimes and personality of Earl Ferrers provoked so much disgust that he was hanged in May 1760. Vast crowds turned out along the route and at Tyburn. Ferrers died bravely, having ridden to the execution in his own landau dressed in an immaculate white suit.

9. A view of the Old Bailey and Newgate Prison. Newgate was probably the most hated and feared of London's prisons and it was destroyed by the mob on a number of occasions. When executions ceased at Tyburn in 1783, they took place outside the prison door in Old Bailey.

10. *Above, left:* A pirate about to be hanged at Execution Dock. This was at Wapping, downstream of the Tower of London. The chaplain or Ordinary can be seen trying to extract a last-minute confession while on the extreme left a marshal holds up the silver oar, symbol of the authority of the Admiralty. 11. *Right:* Execution of the Cato Street Conspirators outside Newgate Prison in May 1820. They had plotted to assassinate the Prime Minister and other leading politicians. After hanging for an hour, they had their heads expertly cut off by a mysterious masked man. These were Britain's last legal beheadings.

THE EXECUTION OF HENRY WAINWRIGHT.

13. The execution of Henry Wainwright in 1875. The expense of keeping a mistress led to financial troubles so he shot her and then cut her throat, before dismembering her and putting her bodily parts in brown paper parcels with the intention of burying them.

12. *Opposite, below:* Henry Fauntleroy was a philanderer, forger and crooked banker. Forgery was a capital offence and he was hanged outside Newgate in November 1824. Here he is having his irons removed in Newgate shortly before his execution.

14. John George Haigh, the infamous 'Acid Bath Murderer'. In an attempt at mitigation, he claimed that he was a vampire who had murdered others in order to get sustenance from their blood. He was hanged by Albert Pierrepoint at Wandsworth Prison on 10 August 1949.

Story, who certainly left his mark. When the executioner was in the process of disembowelling him, Story, it was said, summoned sufficient strength to raise himself and strike a blow at the executioner – although he paid for his insolence in pain, screaming with agony at his butchery. Many Catholics attempted to affirm their status as martyrs through their last dying speeches on the gallows, with actions that were intended to impress spectators. The martyrs regarded themselves as like the early Christians who had attempted to frustrate mob entertainment by accepting their fate passively.

In December 1581 a number of Catholic priests were executed at Tyburn. The most notable among them was the Jesuit Edmund Campion. They were dragged through the muddy streets to Tyburn where a large crowd was waiting. The mood of the crowd was far from friendly, against the background of a threat of invasion from Spain and the arrival of Catholic missionary priests who were viewed as dangerous foreign agents. Campion sang all the way to his execution and even when he was cut down from the rope he stood upright and shouted 'Lord, Lord, Lord' while struggling with the executioners. In the crowd was Henry Walpole, who was so inspired by the martyrs that he joined the Jesuits and some years later became a martyr himself when he was executed at York. Between 1581 and 1603, 180 Catholics were executed for treason, most of them at Tyburn.

The scaffold had now become a regular platform for martyrs wishing to preach their beliefs, a point that was not lost on the authorities. In an attempt to undermine the display of martyrdom, it was arranged that Catholics should be executed alongside criminals. However, Catholic priests then appropriated this to their advantage by drawing a parallel between their own situations and the crucifixion of Christ with common thieves, and they feverishly tried to convert felons to Catholicism during their imprisonment or even on the way to execution. The priest William Patenson converted six of the seven felons who occupied the condemned cell with him in Newgate.

Political tensions and conspiracies continued until the end of Elizabeth's reign, exacerbated by the war with Spain after 1585. The queen's physician Roderigo Lopez, who had settled in England, became embroiled in a plot against the queen. His fall from favour began when a group of Philip's supporters in Spain tried to use him in a plot to poison her. Lopez was arrested when correspondence was seized by the English espionage service and along with some fellow conspirators he was arrested and charged with treason. Under torture, the conspirators confirmed his guilt. He was carried in the customary fashion on hurdles from Westminster to Tyburn. On the scaffold Lopez affirmed that he loved the queen as he loved Jesus Christ, 'which from a man of the Jewish profession was heard not without laughter'. Lopez and the two others convicted with him were then 'hanged, cut downe alive, holden down by strength of men, dismembered, bowelled, headed, and quartered, their quarters set on the gates of the citie'.

The following year, 1595, the poet Robert Southwell, whose writings had been popular, was hanged at Tyburn for preaching to Catholics at Uxenden Hall near Harrow-on-the-Hill. Unfortunately for Southwell he came up against the notorious torturer and queen's agent Richard Topcliffe, who subjected him to the most brutal torture. On the gallows the hangman slowly strangled Southwell, but when an officer began to cut the rope off the still breathing priest, Lord Mountjoy and other witnesses interrupted and ordered him to let Southwell alone to die. He was said to have inspired sympathy on the gallows when some of the crowd appealed to the executioner to let him hang until he was dead.

The sixteenth century also saw important developments in the persecution of people accused of witchcraft. Trials and executions increased after the Witchcraft Act of 1563 and continued throughout Elizabeth's reign. Unlike many large-scale persecutions in Europe, English witch trials involved prosecutions against individuals on a much smaller scale. Following the Witchcraft Act Tyburn saw the executions of Margaret Harkett in 1585 and Anne Kerke in 1599. Further revisions to the Act were made in 1604, and some years later Elizabeth Sawyer and Joan Peterson were executed in 1621 and 1652 respectively. The 60-year-old widow Margaret Harkett from Stanmore, who was accused of bewitching her neighbours, was described as 'this ungodly woman . . . this witch'. Similarly Anne Kerke was accused of directing her magic against others. At her trial the judge, in order to disprove the belief that a witch's hair could not be cut, took ten or twelve hairs from her head. However, the sergeant attempting to cut the hairs said the scissors turned around in his hand. Elizabeth Sawyer was the subject of *The Witch of Edmonton*, a play first performed in 1621 at the Cockpit Theatre in Drury Lane. Elizabeth was brought to Newgate for causing the death of a neighbour by witchcraft. Three women were ordered to make a search of Elizabeth's body, after which they reported that they found a teat the length of half of a finger – which was sufficient evidence to condemn her. Joan Peterson, the 'Wapping Witch', who lived on Spruce Island near

Wapping, was charged with using witchcraft to kill Lady Powell, despite a lack of evidence. At her trial Joan was searched and predictably was found to have a 'teat of flesh in her secret parts'. Joan protested her innocence but on 12 April 1652 she was hanged.

By the reign of Charles I (1625–49) London was expanding rapidly, a point made by a contemporary who wrote that the capital 'is grown too fast for the Kingdom'. At the end of the seventeenth century Celia Fiennes commented that London now 'makes up but one vast building with all its suburbs'. New fashionable squares and streets were spreading westwards towards Tyburn, particularly in the neighbourhoods of Marylebone and Mayfair.

In 1605 a minor change in the ritual of execution took place when a bell began to be rung outside Newgate Prison for those awaiting their fate. As the condemned prepared themselves for their journey to Tyburn, the bellman would toll for them at St Sepulchre's and address them thus: 'Gentlemen, consider now you are going out of this world into another, where you will live in happiness or woe for evermore.' The first prisoners to hear the cries of the bellman were Jonathan Woodward and James Philpot, two notorious housebreakers. The following year the bell tolled for Catholic Robert Drury, who died a martyr at Tyburn on 26 February 1607. It was declared that he and other prisoners were to be:

> Laid upon a hurdle and so drawne to the place of execution . . . then to have their secrets cut off and with their entrails thrown into the fire before their faces, their heads to be severed from their bodies, which severally should be divided into four quarters.

Drury wore a new black cassock and new shoes for his execution. On the scaffold he claimed that he had never told a lie, and then after a thoughtful pause added 'not willingly'. Many others followed, including Thomas Garnet and John Roberts, a Benedictine priest. Roberts was hanged and quartered in December 1610 with sixteen other persons condemned for various offences. He used the gallows to preach a valedictory sermon and the sheriff even rebuked hecklers in the crowd who tried to stop him.

The last dying speech more often reflected the words of the prison Ordinary or chaplain than those of the condemned felon, although religious martyrs needed little help with their message. The authorities always hoped for a confession, to reinforce the purpose of execution and to serve as a warning for onlookers. Francis Newland, who was executed for murder in 1695, said from the gallows, 'I am at peace with all the world . . . I suffer a most just reward, for my past sinful life and conversion.' However, there were many who did not repent and continued to protest their innocence. One such was Edward Altham, who was executed for rape in 1688. He declared his innocence on the gallows so powerfully that he won the crowd's sympathy. Similarly George Goffe, executed in 1700 for burglary, confessed to his earlier sinfulness but added that his fate was the result of a malicious prosecution by man rather than a just judgment from God. Supporters of the condemned would offer some comfort by trying to claim the body from the anatomists, while in the case of the priest Thomas Maxfield in 1616 fellow Catholics adorned the gallows with garlands and flowers and strewed the ground with bay leaves and sweet herbs.

Religious martyrs are better documented than the procession of countless felons who went to Tyburn for crimes such as larceny or coining. In 1538 Edmund Coningsby was executed for counterfeiting and in 1540 four felons were hanged and quartered for clipping gold. Two men were executed in September 1554 for 'the coining of naughty money' and three more in July 1555. In August 1562 Philip Furey, a goldsmith, was hanged for coining, followed by Henry Rolfe in 1572, Thomas Green, another goldsmith, in 1576 and Henry Elks in 1586. Francis Salisbury and Thomas Houghton were executed at Tyburn in November 1697 for forging a counterfeit sixpenny stamp to emboss vellum, paper and parchment. At the end of the seventeenth century 'nests' of coiners were discovered and many were arrested, convicted and executed.

In 1626 Henrietta Maria, Charles I's Catholic queen, visited Tyburn, kneeling beneath the gallows to offer prayers and devotion to the Catholic martyrs executed there during Elizabeth's reign. Her action caused a diplomatic furore and her courtiers were sent back to France for their part in the incident. However, given the queen's devotion to her faith it was unlikely that she had needed much prompting to make the short journey to Tyburn.

Two years later Charles's leading adviser George Villiers, the Duke of Buckingham, who was described by the great nineteenth-century historian S.R. Gardiner as among the most incapable ministers of this or any other century, was assassinated. Buckingham's rapid accumulation of power and wealth had made him a deeply unpopular figure. When he visited Portsmouth in August 1628 a naval officer called John Felton emerged from the crowd and stabbed him to death. Few mourned Buckingham but Felton, who was subsequently executed at Tyburn, became a national hero and gained great sympathy, and the political furore surrounding Felton created a republican *cause célèbre* in certain quarters.

Crime in high society, especially that involving sexual scandal, has always guaranteed widespread salacious interest and this was certainly so with Mervin Touchet, Earl of Castlehaven. He was indicted on three counts – assisting other men to rape his own wife and buggery with two of his manservants – and was duly executed at the Tower, but his servants were hanged at Tyburn in July 1631, their confessions and last speeches from the scaffold having been eagerly gobbled up by the huge and prurient crowds.

The period between the outbreak of civil war in 1642 and the restoration of the monarchy in 1660 saw little change in the nature or scale of executions at Tyburn. Huge crowds continued to attend. For example, Philip Powell and Peter Wright, who were executed along with thirteen other felons on Whit Monday 1651, drew a crowd of over 20,000. Shortly after the establishment of the newly formed republic in June 1649, Tyburn witnessed the execution of twenty-four people at the same time in front of a crowd of many thousands.

In 1660 the monarchy was restored and Charles II was welcomed home with great pomp and ceremony, amid the pealing of bells and the cheering of thousands of people. However, there were scores to be settled. Of the 59 men who had signed Charles I's death warrant, 41 were still alive, 15 of whom had fled the country. In all, 10 of the regicides were brutally executed and another 19 gave themselves up. Three escaped to New England while others went to Europe. Colonel Daniel Axtell and Francis Hacker were brought to the gallows in October 1660, while John Okey, Miles Corbet and John Barkstead were executed at Tyburn in April 1662. Okey displayed much penitence on the scaffold and his severed quarters were given to his friends and allowed a decent burial. Corbet's head was displayed over the city's gates, Barkstead's above Traitor's Gate at the Tower.

The most famous of the regicides was the Lord Protector, Oliver Cromwell, who had died in September 1658, nearly two years before the Restoration of the monarchy. Almost twelve years after Charles's execution the exhumed bodies of the regicides Oliver Cromwell, Henry Ireton (Cromwell's son-in-law) and John Bradshaw (the judge at Charles's trial) were brought to the Red Lion Inn at Holborn to rest overnight on their way to Tyburn. Some writers, including Howard McMains, support the view that Cromwell's remains were in such an awful condition that they were secretly interred in Red Lion Square. Although there is little evidence to support this, McMains believes that the corpse identified as Cromwell's at the Tyburn scaffold was in fact that of an ordinary dead soldier. If this is so then it throws doubt on the identity of the head buried in 1960 in Sidney Sussex College, Cambridge, which is believed to be that of Cromwell.

On 30 January 1661 at approximately 10 a.m. the three bodies were publicly hanged on the 'Triple Tree' and then cut down, decapitated and thrown into a pit at Tyburn. Despite the many claims as to what really happened to Cromwell's body, it is most likely that his eventual resting place by January 1661 was a pit near the gallows, along with thousands of others executed at

Tyburn. Mr A.J. Beresford, who lived at the south-west corner of Edgware Road, wrote to *The Times* on 9 May 1860 to comment on the excavations in the area which had uncovered many human bones. He added that these were 'obviously the relics of unhappy persons who were buried under the gallows'.

Although the Restoration saw a relaxing of the restraints imposed by the Puritans on pleasures, anti-Catholicism continued to be a force. In 1678 another outbreak of anti-Catholic hysteria occurred following rumours of a 'Popish plot'. At the centre of the rumour was Titus Oates (1649–1705), an Anglican priest who claimed there was a Jesuit-led plan to assassinate Charles II in order to hasten the succession of his Catholic brother James. Oates's story was a complete fabrication but it was sufficient to create a scare as well as sending a number of innocent men, such as Robert Green, Lawrence Hill, William Staley and Henry Berry, to their deaths at Tyburn. These events sparked a wave of anti-Catholic persecution in which thirty-five innocent people were executed and hundreds of others suffered greatly.

Other Catholic victims followed. Oliver Plunkett, the Catholic primate of Ireland, was sentenced to death for plotting to aid a French invasion of Ireland in 1678. He was drawn through the city of London to Tyburn and hanged, drawn and quartered. His bowels were taken out and burned in front of him before his head was cut off and his body divided into four quarters and disposed of. His head was rescued by his friends and now remains preserved in the Catholic Church of St Peter's in Drogheda in the Irish Republic.

The procession of the nameless to the gallows continued. For example, 'twelve men and three women' were executed in March 1680. Poverty forced many into crime. Mary 'Moll' Jones had married an apprentice who was so extravagant that Mary resorted to picking pockets just to survive. She was eventually condemned for stealing a piece of satin from a mercer's shop on Ludgate Hill and was hanged at the age of 25 on 18 December 1691. Many young women found work in London as domestic servants but this left them vulnerable to sexual advances by their master and other males in the house. Peter Linebaugh has shown that between 1703 and 1772, 12 per cent of the women hanged at Tyburn were executed for infanticide, and most of them were domestic servants. As Linebaugh states, the common themes for the women involved were poverty and loss of employment.

A last-minute reprieve from execution was the desperate hope of many who took the route to the gallows. After visiting an execution in 1664, Pepys recorded that the condemned man delayed the inevitable by long discourses and prayers in the hopes of reprieve. There were cases of a reprieve arriving literally at the last minute. Jonathan Simpson, who was convicted of highway robbery, was saved in this way at the last minute by his rich relations, but he failed to learn his lesson and after a number of other robberies returned to Tyburn on 8 September 1686, aged 32. In 1703 Thomas Cook set off from Newgate on what was usually a once-in-a-lifetime journey to Tyburn. He had reason to believe that a reprieve would arrive on the day before the execution, but when it failed to appear he put a brave face on it and had travelled as far as the gallows when, to his great joy, the reprieve finally arrived. He was taken back to Newgate while the authorities decided what to do with him next. But to his great mortification he received notice that the reprieve had been rescinded. He then had to wait several weeks before the next 'Tyburn Fair', when he set off from Newgate once more. Hours later he was dead.

Over the centuries the crimes of the condemned remained largely consistent but there were changes in their definition and scale. Those convicted of larceny, burglary, housebreaking, pickpocketing and highway robbery remained Tyburn's staple diet of offences throughout its history as a place of execution. Murder, arson, rape, bigamy and treason also continued to provide offenders, although on a lesser scale. Crimes such as witchcraft and infanticide were placed on the statute book in the sixteenth and seventeenth centuries, while between the fifteenth and the seventeenth centuries many were executed for their religion, accused of either heresy or treason, although the number of martyrs declined from the seventeenth century.

The eighteenth century offers more detailed accounts of those executed at Tyburn as well as the changes in the area generally, particularly the demise of the 'Triple Tree', which was replaced by a movable scaffold in 1759, and the eventual end of executions at Tyburn in 1783. Hangings usually took place on the first Monday of each month. In 1730 what is now the bustling Oxford Street was the rural Tyburn Road, and Tyburn itself was still some distance away from the more heavily populated areas of London. However, it was common for Londoners to walk or ride out into the suburbs and rural areas to take the air, eat, drink and play games in the fields. Rural settings were more suited to public executions since there were few if any residents to disturb and there was plenty of space for large crowds, both to watch the procession and around the gallows. Hogarth's illustration of the *Idle*

'*Prentice* on his way to Tyburn depicts a huge throng of people awaiting the execution. The 'Triple Tree' is visible in the background, with the executioner sitting atop one of the beams.

One desperate final hope for relatives and friends was that the hanged person might be resuscitated. In 1709 John Smith was hanged at Tyburn and left for some time before being cut down. He was then taken to a nearby house where he was given treatment from which he made a complete recovery. For the rest of his life he rejoiced in the nickname 'Half-Hanged Smith'. In 1736 Thomas Reynolds was hanged but when he was cut down and placed in his coffin he pushed back the lid and made an effort to climb out. The hangmen then descended on poor Thomas with the intention of stringing him up once more but onlookers intervened and carried him off. Although they made vigorous attempts to save his life, he died shortly afterwards. Occasionally victims were found to be still breathing when they were placed on the anatomists' table for dissection.

Execution day guaranteed crowds of thousands. All the roads and lanes to Tyburn were busy and, as Henry Fielding (1707–54) noted, Tyburn appeared like 'a wake or festival, where idleness, wantonness, and drunkenness and every other species of debauchery are gratified'. People would jockey for a good view and tensions inevitably built up in the crowd. Finally a great cry of 'Hats off! Hats off!' would go up as the procession made its way to the foot of the gallows platform. This was not intended as a mark of respect for the condemned prisoner but a demand that those near the front should take their hats off so that those at the back could see better! Further roars came from the eager crowd as the hangman stepped forward and the condemned prisoners ascended to the gallows. The hangman would then place a noose around each prisoner's neck and it became the practice for a hood or bag to be placed over the head. Often there were large numbers of people milling about on the gallows at this point as friends and relatives said their farewells, the Ordinary fussed about trying to extract eleventh-hour confessions and the condemned prisoners made speeches. A homing pigeon was released when the entourage reached Tyburn to let those at Newgate know of its safe arrival.

Two of the largest crowds assembled to witness an execution at Tyburn were those for Jack Sheppard and Jonathan Wild, but for very different reasons. Sheppard (1702–24), a thief and escapologist, won himself an immortal place in London's folklore when he was executed in November 1724. Much has been written about Sheppard. He became a popular hero and starred in innumerable broadsheets and ballads, although much of this material was inevitably exaggerated and distorted. Despite his previous escapes from Newgate, Jack was finally caught and held. He travelled in the customary cart from Newgate to the gallows, enjoying a triumphal progress. Tens of thousands turned out to cheer him and he revelled in the attention. A plan to rescue his body after the execution degenerated into a mêlée when his supporters came to blows with the men they thought were the surgeon's agents. Following the execution a mob went on the rampage in an orgy of looting and destruction. The Riot Act was read and order finally restored, although not without some difficulty. Jack's mortal remains were interred in the churchyard of St-Martins-in-the-Fields. He was just 22 years of age.

Six months later the execution of the notorious thief-taker Jonathan Wild prompted many thousands of people to turn out. In contrast with Sheppard, in Wild's case the crowd came to express their absolute contempt and loathing. Wild, who had built up a corrupt business on shameless exploitation of others' vulnerabilities, had long paraded his wealth and success for all to see. The night before his execution he unsuccessfully tried to commit suicide with an overdose of laudanum. The following morning, in a greatly weakened state, he faced a crowd who gave him a terrible time. He was booed and abused and pelted with a wide variety of missiles, including excrement and the rotting corpses of long-dead cats and dogs. The crowd rejoiced to see the once-powerful Wild brought down, humiliated and destroyed. Wild was hanged at the same time as the highwaymen William Sperry and Robert Handford (or Stanford), but it was Wild's death the crowd had come to see; the others were merely the supporting cast. Wild's skeleton can be seen in the Hunterian Museum at the Royal College of Surgeons in Lincoln's Inn Fields.

A varied collection of murderers took their last journey to Tyburn in the eighteenth century. Some had distinguished themselves in the armed forces, such as John Peter Dramatti, who was born in France but served in the English army with great courage. He was executed in July 1703 for the murder of his wife, who was said to be connected to the French royal family. John Morgridge from Canterbury was the kettle-drummer with the 1st Troop of Horse-Guards. Embroiled in a drunken brawl with a fellow officer, he drew his sword and killed Captain Cope. A reduced charge of manslaughter was rejected and Morgridge was subsequently executed in April 1708.

Ferdinando, Marquis de Paleotti, was the head of a noble family in Italy and a colonel in the imperial army. During a visit to England to see his sister he ran up large debts as a result of his heavy gambling. His sister tried to help him with his financial problems but he was not satisfied with this alone and ordered his servant to borrow some money from another source. The servant refused, at which the marquis drew his sword and killed him. At his trial he protested that it was disgraceful to put a nobleman to death, like a common malefactor, for killing his servant. His arrogance remained undimmed and he instructed the sheriffs to ensure that the Englishmen doomed to suffer with him did not defile his body. Despite his protests he was executed at Tyburn in March 1718.

Edward Bird had attended Westminster and Eton and then attained a position as lieutenant in a cavalry regiment. In a fit of rage he stabbed a waiter, Samuel Loxton, to death with a sword because his bath had not been prepared as soon as he ordered it. The night before his execution Bird attempted to commit suicide by taking poison and by stabbing himself several times. Despite this he was taken to the gallows in a mourning coach, attended by his mother and the Ordinary of Newgate. He begged a pinch of snuff, which he took, and was then hanged on 23 February 1719, at the age of 27.

Another murder resulting from swordplay culminated in the execution of John Stanley, an army officer. As a young man Stanley's father took him to Spain to witness several military engagements, and it was said that the young man delighted in trampling on the bodies of the deceased after the fighting had ended. Insufferably vain, Stanley went on to become involved in drunken brawls and gambling. His violent streak was never far away and eventually he murdered his mistress, for which crime he was executed in December 1723.

Thomas Wilford did not have the same advantages in life as John Stanley. Born of poor parents in Fulham, Wilford had only one arm and was taken into the workhouse where he ran errands for paupers. Here he met Sarah Williams. They married and took lodgings in St Giles's. Within a week of the marriage Wilford found out that Sarah had been seeing an old flame. This sent him into such a rage that he attacked Sarah, cutting her throat. He immediately confessed his guilt, saying he had killed the woman that he loved beyond 'all the world', and was willing to die for the crime he had committed. At his trial he was sentenced to death and hanged at Tyburn on 22 June 1752, exhibiting to the end the most genuine signs of contrition for his crime.

While murderers such as Stanley and de Paleotti killed servants with little compunction, a servant who killed his or her master was regarded with horror. Some were even accused of treason. Robert Greenstreet, who was apprenticed to Mr Souch, a fishhook-maker in London, repeatedly asked for an increase in his wages. His insistence eventually resulted in an argument in which Greenstreet stabbed his master to death. At his trial at the Old Bailey Greenstreet pleaded guilty and was duly executed on 14 December 1761. His body was given to the surgeons for dissection.

Norwich-born Deborah Churchill came to live in London and took up with a young man called Hunt. One night as she, Hunt and a friend were returning from the theatre, an argument broke out and both men drew their swords. Deborah tried to intervene but her actions distracted the other man, as a result of which he received a fatal wound. Hunt escaped but Deborah was arrested and indicted as an accomplice to murder. She denied her guilt to the last moment of her life and perished on the gallows in December 1708.

It has been estimated that during the first half of the eighteenth century sailors accounted for 25 per cent of the executions at Tyburn. William Corbett had made many sea voyages but was so addicted to drinking and theft that he found himself in trouble on a number of occasions. He took lodgings at the house of Mr Knight, a publican at Rotherhithe, and then proceeded to murder both Knight and his wife Anne. Then he searched the house for money and even put on some of Knight's linen and other clothes. Corbett was executed at Tyburn on 4 April 1764 and his body hung in chains on the road between Rotherhithe and Deptford.

Sarah Metyard and Sarah Morgan Metyard, mother and daughter, were milliners who grossly exploited the women sent to them from the workhouse to work. They kept the girls locked up and fed them on meagre portions of bread and water. So brutal were the mother and daughter that they beat a number of the apprentices to death and then tried to cover up their crimes by cutting the bodies into small pieces and dispersing the remains. Four years elapsed before the discovery of these horrid murders but at the ensuing Old Bailey sessions they were both sentenced to be executed on 19 July 1768. On the following Monday the bodies were conveyed in a hearse to Surgeons' Hall, where they were first exposed to the curious gaze of the public and then dissected.

On 5 May 1760 another huge crowd turned out to watch the execution of Lord Ferrers, whose rich and

aristocratic family could trace its lineage back to the royal
Plantagenet dynasty. When drunk, which he was for much
of the time, Ferrers became extremely violent. He married
for the second time in 1752 and subjected his new wife to
six years of systematic violence and cruelty. The household then passed into the stewardship of an old and
faithful family retainer called John Johnson, whom
Ferrers accused of cheating with the accounts. Johnson
protested his innocence but Ferrers shot him, wounding
him fatally. In his arrogant way, he assumed he would be
acquitted but his reputation had gone before him. He
showed no remorse and was condemned to death. Large
crowds gathered to boo him as he made his way to
Tyburn in a black coach and wearing a white satin
wedding suit. He was the first nobleman to be executed
on the common gallows.

Catherine Hayes, Mary Young (also known as Jenny
Diver) and Elizabeth Brownrigg all grace the pantheon of
English criminals, on an equal footing with any of their
male counterparts. Catherine Hayes was executed in 1726
for killing her husband, an act of petty treason. The
punishment for this crime was burning and Catherine
suffered this fate in May 1728. The usual procedure was
for the executioner to strangle the victim with a rope
around the neck so that she did not have to endure the
unspeakable agony of the flames. On this occasion,
however, the executioner bungled things and let go of the
rope too soon. Catherine therefore was still alive when
she was engulfed in the flames. She screamed in agony as
the crowd watched, both appalled and fascinated by the
sight and sound of Catherine's death throes. Mary Young
was one of London's most notorious pickpockets. At the
age of 15 she had left Ireland and moved to London,

where she took up a life of stealing. Despite being transported to the Virginian colonies, she returned to England to continue her trade but she was eventually caught and hanged at Tyburn on 18 March 1740, having greatly irritated the crowd by the lengthy time she spent on the scaffold engaged in prayer.

The case of Elizabeth Brownrigg has gone down in criminal history as one of the worst examples of cruelty and physical abuse of children. Indeed, Elizabeth was probably one of the most hated women ever to be hanged at Tyburn. The midwife at St Dunstan's workhouse, she used her position to win the confidence of the young vulnerable female inmates. She brought them back as apprentices to her unsavoury home in Fleur-de-Lys Court, where they were kept virtually as slaves, being systematically starved, whipped, tortured and otherwise abused. The appalling nature of her crimes incurred widespread anger and Brownrigg had to run the gauntlet of verbal abuse and a hail of dangerous missiles from a huge crowd as she travelled to Tyburn on 14 September 1767. Her body was taken to Surgeons' Hall, dissected and anatomised.

Condemned prisoners often worried about what would happen to their bodies after execution. John Casey rode with his brother in the cart to the gallows in 1721 and managed to defy the claims of the surgeons by seizing the body after the execution and giving it a respectable burial. On occasions relations made a special journey to London in order to protect the body. The wife of William Seston, for example, travelled all the way from Lancashire in 1721. Matthew Lee's brother and sister came from Lincoln, while Oliver White's father made the long journey from Carlisle to protect his son's body by keeping watch over his grave at night. In 1731 the father of Samuel Curlis walked 30 miles to London to see his son hanged and then took possession of the body beneath the gallows.

A significant number of highwaymen appeared at Tyburn but few lived up to the romantic ideal portrayed in fiction. However, some did come from respectable backgrounds and these reinforced the myth of the 'gentlemen of the road'. James Maclaine was perhaps the archetypal 'gentleman highwayman'. When he was just 18 his father died, leaving him a sizeable inheritance which he got through with great speed, and then had to take a job as a butler. Maclaine had charm and style, which he used to work his way through a large number of women, but he could not escape the death sentence for his crimes (although he did receive many female visitors while languishing in Newgate). Large crowds turned out to watch him on his way to his execution in 1750.

William Udall's father was an eminent distiller in Clerkenwell, London. Young William had a good education but, like many others before him, he squandered his early opportunities and instead resorted to highway robbery. After a number of violent robberies he was hanged on 14 March 1738. Nicholas Horner, who was executed in April 1719, followed a similar pattern. His father was a minister who had supported his son through many excesses. Robert Ramsey, executed in June 1742, was educated at Westminster School before plunging into gambling and then highway robbery in order to support his extravagant lifestyle. On the gallows he spoke to the surrounding multitude about the dangers of gambling and how it would lead to destruction. William Parsons was the eldest son of a baronet and a lieutenant in the army but he became a swindler and highway robber and was executed for returning prematurely from transportation in February 1751. Henry Powell went to the Merchant Taylor's School and then became a military surgeon. He twice deserted from the regiment in which he served and subsequently embarked on a life of crime. He was eventually arrested for stealing two shillings and sixpence from a woman on the highway. In his last speech he described his death as a 'just judgment for my sins against the Divine Majesty and my neighbour' and expressed the hope that 'those who survive me will take warning by my fatal end'.

Jack Addison had committed fifty-six robberies before his execution in March 1711; in contrast John Smith's career as a highwayman lasted only a week. Ironically, his very short life of crime began at Tyburn. Resting on a stile near the gallows, he and a companion waited for a suitable victim, eventually stealing a grey mare from William Birch. The following day Smith set out alone upon the mare and robbed three stage-coaches near Epping Forest, and a further four coaches over the next few days. Within a week he was arrested. He was executed in December 1704 at the very place where he had taken his first steps towards a life of crime. Tom Gray, imprisoned for highway robbery in Gloucester, escaped from the prison by setting it on fire, smothering three of his fellow prisoners to death in the process. He continued robbing until he was arrested and brought to Newgate, which proved more difficult to escape from. Before his execution in March 1713 Gray threatened the prison Ordinary, saying he would kill him if he dared venture to pray with him in the cart at Tyburn. In 1739 John Morris was hanged for highway robbery. In the course of perpetrating an earlier crime Morris's jawbone had been shot off. He had carefully saved all the pieces he could find and while he was awaiting execution he distributed them as good-luck charms to his fellow inmates of Newgate.

The permanent gallows at Tyburn was removed in the mid-eighteenth century and on 4 October 1759 the first executions took place on a new movable gallows that was erected and dismantled for every hanging day. However, there was growing pressure for public hangings to be moved from Tyburn to a more remote spot, with Camden Town being mooted as a possibility among a number of other locations.

Executions at Tyburn during the eighteenth century provide much information about the criminals and their crimes, trials and executions. Hundreds of those who died there lived in a vicious cycle of poverty, starvation, desperation and crime and this is reflected in the narratives of their cases. Many were in the last transports of terror. They went to their deaths for crimes that would be now considered trivial. Other prisoners displayed courage, some arrogance and others even a sense of the comic and the bizarre. Tom Gerrard was executed in August 1711. He had stolen horses and silver, burgled and set fire to houses, and even, rather ingeniously, trained his dog to pick pockets. Will Maw was a compulsive criminal who had been involved in coining, for which he had already been punished. He continued to rob but was so afraid of being caught that he arranged for his wife to buy a coffin and declare him dead. A funeral procession took place with some forty to fifty people attending. Some five years later he was recognised and told how he had faked his death to avoid prosecution. But he was still carrying on his old criminal ways and was eventually arrested and executed on 11 October 1711.

There is some confusion over the identity of the last person to die on the scaffold at Tyburn. Some sources cite William Ryland, the forger, who was hanged on 29 August 1783, but others claim it was John Austin, who was hanged on the same day. The old 'Triple Tree' was sold and legend says that some pieces were bought by a local innkeeper for use as stands for barrels, the hostelry concerned according to some accounts being the Carpenters Arms. The Tyburn Convent close by in Hyde Park Place keeps what it claims are other fragments of the 'Triple Tree' as a reminder of the Catholics who suffered for their beliefs at Tyburn.

Tyburn received a long line of forgers, murderers, bankrupts, bigamists, housebreakers, arsonists, rapists, rebels, traitors, heretics, smugglers, poachers, thieves and robbers. The ending of punishment at Tyburn came about not because of a more humane or enlightened attitude towards penal policy but because the disorder such events engendered disrupted trade and commerce in the city, particularly along the route from Newgate. The wealthy citizens then taking up residence in the highly fashionable streets and squares did not want the presence of unruly and irreverent crowds on hanging days. The decision to end executions at Tyburn did not meet with universal approval. In particular Dr Johnson fulminated that the 'old method drew together a number of spectators. If they do not draw spectators, they do not answer their purpose. The old method was most satisfactory for all parties: the public was gratified by a procession; the criminal was supported by it. Why has all this to be swept away?'

SEVEN

Charing Cross, Westminster and Whitehall

As I was going by Charing Cross,
I saw a black man upon a black horse;
They told me it was King Charles the First –
Oh dear, my heart was ready to burst!

Old nursery rhyme

A series of notable executions took place between Charing Cross and Westminster during the reign of the first three Stuart monarchs (1603–85) and all were landmarks in British history. Before the end of the twelfth century royal justice was administered, as were all other aspects of government, from where the king resided. However, John's signing of the Magna Carta at Runnymede in June 1215 put into effect a series of reforms, one of which decreed that common pleas should be heard in a fixed place. That place became Westminster Hall. By the late fifteenth century the main courts of law all functioned in the Great Hall at Westminster and its environs, remaining there until the late nineteenth century. State trials were held at Westminster Hall for centuries and many dramatic events of national importance took place there, including the trials of William Wallace in 1305, the Gunpowder Plot conspirators in 1606 and

Charles I in 1649, and the impeachment of Lord Melville in 1806.

During the fourteenth century the privy and public parts of the Palace of Westminster developed. Edward III (1327–77) built a high clock tower in the courtyard (near the site of the modern-day clock tower housing the great bell, Big Ben). During the reign of Richard II (1377–99) the Great Hall was the centre of English secular and ceremonial life. Richard had the Great Hall extensively remodelled to project the grandeur, power and authority of the English monarchy.

A track between Westminster and Charing Cross had existed in medieval times. By the Tudor period it had become a residential street in which a number of eminent people lived. Halfway between Charing Cross and Westminster is Whitehall, which was the main London residence of the royal court. Henry VIII died here in 1547. Whitehall had seen an extensive rebuilding programme during the 1530s, and during James I's reign (1603–25) a whole new palace was planned although only the Banqueting House was completed. None the less, the palace contained some 2,000 rooms and was adorned by the large art collection built up by Charles I (r. 1625–49).

Charles I, in a rather tragic way, connects the three points of Westminster, Whitehall and Charing Cross. In 1649, after the upheavals of the civil wars (1642–8), Charles was put on trial in Westminster Hall; a few days later he was executed at Whitehall. Eleven years later, when his son Charles II (r. 1660–85) became king, the regicides were hunted down and some were executed at Charing Cross. A statue of Charles I on horseback, sculpted in 1633, was placed in Charing Cross in 1674, with Charles looking down Whitehall towards his palace, the place of his trial and the site of his execution.

There had been other notable executions here before Charles since Charing Cross had long been a place of execution. In 1544 William John Tooley, a poulterer, robbed a Spaniard in St James's. He was taken to Charing Cross in a cart in front of a large crowd to be hanged. In his dying speech he asked to be delivered from the tyranny of the Pope, which, as far as John Foxe was concerned, ensured his right to be considered a martyr to the Protestant cause. After his execution the Privy Council ordered that Tooley should be further punished by ecclesiastical law for his 'heretical' prayer. Bishop Bonner duly published a writ excommunicating Tooley, and he was posthumously tried and his remains exhumed and burned. John Foxe, the sixteenth-century martyrologist, considered Tooley's execution excessively harsh, particularly in view of the extensive numbers of thieves who did not receive the death penalty. Foxe believed Tooley was victimised because he robbed a Catholic.

In the sixteenth century the Pope had been replaced as head of the English Church by Henry VIII. During the reign of Elizabeth I (1558–1603) those who were not prepared to accept Elizabeth as the Supreme Governor of the Church of England could expect severe punishment, and as a consequence more than a hundred Catholic priests were executed at Tyburn for treason. There was sensitivity verging on paranoia regarding the potential threat of Catholic plots and this mood lingered on into the eighteenth century. Various conspiracies against Elizabeth – Ridolfi's (1571), Throckmorton's (1583), Babington's (1586) and Lopez's (1594) were exposed and the perpetrators punished. But it was at the beginning of James I's reign that the most famous plot in British history took place.

The origins of the Gunpowder Plot, the conspiracy to blow up the Houses of Parliament on 5 November 1605, remain unclear. The generally accepted view is that it was an attempt to re-establish the Catholic religion, although some historians suggest it was the work of a group of agents provocateurs, anxious to discredit the Jesuits and reinforce the ascendancy of the Protestant religion. The plot centred around five conspirators, Robert Catesby, Thomas Winter, Thomas Percy, John Wright and Guy (or Guido) Fawkes, later joined by Robert Keyes. To modern eyes Fawkes emerges as the principal conspirator although he was in fact a minor player. Born in 1570 at York and brought up as a Protestant, he enlisted as a mercenary in the Spanish army in the Netherlands in 1593 and became a Catholic.

If the plot had succeeded it would have had devastating consequences. It was discovered after an anonymous letter was sent to Lord Monteagle, a Catholic, warning him not to attend the state opening of Parliament. Monteagle passed this letter on to the authorities, who ordered a search of Parliament – whereupon Fawkes was found guarding a cache of gunpowder in the cellars at midnight. All the conspirators except Robert Winter were killed by troops at Holbeche House, Staffordshire, or arrested by 12 November, and the survivors taken to the Tower of London to be tortured.

The eight conspirators were brought out from the Tower on a cold Monday in January; they passed through Traitor's Gate and boarded a barge to go upriver to Westminster Hall. The date was 27 January 1606 and the court was in no doubt what the intentions of the conspirators had been. They were the agents of Jesuits who had traitorously conspired with the purpose of 'Advancing . . . the pretended and usurped Authority and Jurisdiction of the Bishop of Rome, and for the restoring of the superstitious Romish Religion within this Realm of England'. Sir Edward Coke, the Attorney-General, reinforced this point: 'The Principal offenders are the seducing Jesuits, men that use the reverence of religion, yea even the most sacred and blessed name of Jesus, as a mantle to cover their impiety, blasphemy, treason and rebellion . . .'

This treasonable offence was to be achieved, the trial recorded, by digging 'a certain Mine under the said House of Parliament, and there secretly, under the said House, to bestow and place a great Quantity of Gunpowder'. Their guilt was never in question, as they had already been condemned several days before, and subsequently there was no defence and no verbal examination. The prisoners faced a hostile jury consisting of Robert Cecil, Sir John Popham, Charles Howard, Thomas Howard, Henry Somerset, Charles Blount, Henry Howard, Sir Thomas Fleming, Sir Thomas Walmesley and Sir Peter Warburton. The Counsel for the Crown were Sir Edward Philips and Sir Edward Coke. All except Digby pleaded not guilty, but the court laid down precisely the punishment for treason. The traitor

shall . . . be drawn to the place of Execution from his Prison, as being not worthy any more to tread upon the Face of the Earth whereof he was made [and] drawn backward at a Horse-Tail. And whereas God hath made the Head of Man the highest and most supreme Part . . .

he must be drawn with his Head declining downward, and lying so near the Ground as may be, being thought unfit to take benefit of the common Air.

Once on the scaffold he would be

strangled, being hanged up by the Neck between Heaven and Earth . . . Then to be cut down alive, and to have his Privy Parts cut off and burnt before his Face, as being unworthily begotten, and unfit to leave any Generation after him. His Bowels and inlay'd Parts taken out and burnt, who inwardly had conceived and harboured in his heart such horrible Treason. After, to have his Head cut off, which had imagined the Mischief. And lastly, his Body to be quartered, and the Quarters set up in some high and eminent Place, to the View and Detestation of Men, and to become a Prey for the Fowls of the Air.

This brutal punishment was deemed to be 'a Reward due to Traitors, whose Hearts be hardened: For that it is Physic of State and Government, to let out corrupt Blood from the Heart'. The eight conspirators were asked if they had anything to say before sentence was passed but 'there was not one of these [except Rookwood] who would make any continued Speech, either in Defence or Extenuation of the Fact'. Thomas Winter requested that he might be hanged both for his brother and himself. Bates and Winter pleaded for mercy while Grant, after a silence, declared that he was guilty only of a conspiracy intended but never effected. Rookwood acknowledged his offence to be so heinous that he justly deserved the punishment of the court. Fawkes spoke of the innocence of the priests and then acknowledged his own guilt, stating that he was ready to die for it.

The Lord Chief Justice, Sir John Popham, then pronounced judgment. After a pause Digby bowed to the Lords and said, 'If I may but hear any of your Lordships say you forgive me I shall go more cheerfully to the gallows.' The verdict was that on Thursday 30 January, Sir Everard Digby, Robert Winter, John Grant and Thomas Bates were to be executed at the west end of St Paul's Church. On the following day Thomas Winter, Ambrose Rookwood, Robert Keyes and Guy Fawkes were to be executed 'within the old Palace-Yard at Westminster, not far from the Parliament-House'. The prisoners were then taken back to the Tower by boat to await their fate. The only visitor they received was Father Strange.

Between the trial and the execution extensive preparations were made for the construction of a scaffold and the butchering blocks, and plans made for crowd control. Orders were given by the Lord Mayor that every door of every dwelling house along the route of the execution procession was to be guarded by an able-bodied person armed with a halberd. Complaints were made that the gate of St Paul's churchyard was an inappropriate place for executions. None the less, Digby, Robert Winter, John Grant and Thomas Bates were executed there. Their quarters were dipped in tar to preserve them while on show and their heads were displayed on London Bridge.

Next day, Friday 31 January, thousands of people lined the 3-mile route between the Tower and Old Palace Yard in Westminster to see Thomas Winter, Ambrose Rookwood, Robert Keyes and Guy Fawkes. As Rookwood was drawn past his house he saw his wife standing in a window. Despite being tied with ropes, Rookwood raised himself up and cried out, 'Pray for me, pray for me.' His wife responded, 'I will, and be of good courage. Offer thyself wholly to God. I, for my part, do as freely restore thee to God as he gave thee unto me.'

The first to mount the scaffold was 'a very pale' Thomas Winter. Asked to say some final words he replied that he had already told all to the Council and that he had come to die. He added only that the priests were not to blame. Winter was cut down after only a 'swing or two' and then suffered the agonies of the executioner. He was followed by Rookwood, who made a long speech asking forgiveness from king and state, and prayed to God to make James a Catholic. Rookwood probably redeemed himself with some of his words and was hanged for longer than Winter. By the time he was cut down he was already on his last breath. Next was Keyes, who climbed the ladder and tried to jump to hasten his death but the rope broke and he was quickly taken to the block and butchered.

The last of the conspirators to die was Guy Fawkes. Already suffering from the appalling torture he had undergone, Fawkes slowly mounted the scaffold but his foot slipped on the bloodstained boards. The crowd waited with eager anticipation as Fawkes asked for the king's forgiveness and added that he hoped his death would wash out his offence. He then knelt and prayed, after which the executioner's assistant removed his cloak and doublet and placed them with those of the other conspirators. Fawkes had difficulty climbing the ladder to reach the noose, but with some assistance he forced himself up it. As the hangman adjusted the rope, Fawkes stretched out his arms and jumped from the ladder, breaking his neck and thus denying the executioner a last opportunity to display his skills. The *Weekly News* for 31 January reported that:

> Last of all came the great devil of all, Guy Fawkes, alias Johnson, who should have put fire to the powder. His body being weak with the torture and sickness, he was scarce able to go up the ladder, yet with much ado, by the help of the hangman, went high enough to break his neck by the fall. He made no speech, but with his crosses and idle ceremonies made his end upon the gallows and the block, to the great joy of all the beholders that the land was ended of so wicked a villainy.

Under James I a more tolerant policy towards Catholics had been adopted but within the Catholic community a small and well-trained group of extremists remained committed to creating mayhem and destruction in the heart of London. This small cell was determined to re-establish the doctrine of the Church of Rome, although the majority of Catholics disowned them. Fawkes and a number of others had been trained abroad. Through a mixture of incompetence, the work of the security services and information received, the anticipated explosion never occurred.

While much was made of the Gunpowder plotters and Jesuits in general in the harsh criticism of the trial record, a surprising leniency was shown by the Jacobean government towards English Catholics. This was evident in the lack of subsequent persecution; James I wanted stability above all else and was not keen to punish peaceful Catholics solely for their religious opinions. A few days after the plot he spoke to Parliament saying that 'it did not follow that all professing that Romish religion were guiltie of the same [treason]'. None the less, the legacy of the date – 5 November – consolidated itself in the popular consciousness as the executions of the conspirators, particularly Fawkes, secured their place in history.

Six years after the execution of the gunpowder conspirators a notable thief was hanged at Charing Cross. John Selman was known variously as a 'foyster', 'nypper', 'pick-purse', 'cut-purse' or more commonly, a pickpocket. On Christmas Day 1611, King James, Queen Anne, the Duke of York and several members of the nobility were receiving the sacrament in the Chapel Royal at Whitehall when a stranger was noticed acting suspiciously. He was dressed in a black cloak, lined and faced with velvet. It was, of course, Selman. It is hard to believe he had gone into the chapel with the intention of robbing the king, but he had stolen 40 shillings from one of the assembled group. Immediately, two men set off in pursuit and arrested Selman, who admitted entering the royal chapel with evil intent. Six days later he was tried and found guilty. Faced with the death sentence, Selman fell to his knees and pleaded for the king's mercy, begging that his body be given a Christian burial. Seven days after being sentenced, on 7 January 1612 Selman was taken to the place of execution where a large, boisterous crowd had gathered. In his last dying speech he claimed: 'I am come patiently to offer up the sweet and dear sacrifice of my life, a life which I have gracelessly abused. I have . . . wasted my good name in the purchase of goods unlawfully gotten, and now [am] ending my days in too late repentance.'

Twelve years after the Gunpowder Plot, Westminster witnessed the execution of Sir Walter Raleigh (1552–1618), the great adventurer, courtier to Elizabeth I, navigator, author and poet. Born in Devon, Raleigh fought in France and later went to Ireland where he suppressed a rebel uprising in Munster. After his return to England he became a favourite of Queen Elizabeth I, who bestowed on him a knighthood and appointed him Captain of the Queen's Guard (1587). However, Raleigh managed to upset some people in high places and this was to contribute to his downfall years later. He even provoked the wrath of the queen herself when he married one of her maids of honour, Elizabeth 'Bessy' Throckmorton. In a jealous rage Elizabeth sent Raleigh to the Tower.

After his release he continued his explorations, pursuing his search for the famous city of El Dorado in 1595. In 1603 he was arrested again under suspicion of opposition to King James's succession, and finding himself back in the Tower he wrote his important, if incomplete, *History of the World*. After thirteen years in the Tower he was released in 1616 and set off yet again on another expedition (1616–18) in search of gold in the Orinoco region. This was a failure and also involved the destruction by fire of the settlement of San Tomas. Raleigh had violated the terms of his mission by destroying this Spanish town and on his return to England the Spanish ambassador urged the king to reinstate Raleigh's death sentence.

King James, keen to avoid a show trial, decided that a small group of commissioners should convict Raleigh, and on 22 October the Attorney-General charged him with promoting a war between England and Spain. Raleigh defended himself stoutly but six days later he was a broken man. The Lord Chief Justice explained that his treason could not be pardoned, adding that although Raleigh had been a valiant and a good Christian, execution was the only possible sentence. James I, succumbing to the demands of the Spanish, thus consented to the execution of a national hero.

The night before his execution Raleigh stayed in the Abbey Gatehouse, Westminster. He received several visitors, including his wife Bess who left him after midnight. He wrote a last letter to her, saying, 'You shall now receive my last words in these last lines . . . I send you all the thankes which my heart can conceive, or my words can rehearse for your many travailes, and care taken for me . . . Thy mourning cannot availe me, I am but dust.' He went on to discuss financial arrangements to make sure she would be supported after his death. He then advised her to be cautious of other men. 'When I am gone, no doubt you shall be sought for by many, for the world thinkes that I was very rich. But take heed of the pretences of men, and their affections, for they last not but in honest and worthy men, and no greater misery can befall you in this life, than to become a prey, and afterwards to be despised.' This was not a warning against remarriage, however, and he even suggested that this would be the best course of action for her and their son. 'I spoke not this to dissuade you from marriage, for it will be best for you, both in respect of the world and of God. Remember your poor childe for his father's sake.' With his last words of love he wrote, 'My deare wife farewell. Blesse my poore boy. Pray for me, and let my good God hold you both in his arms.' The next morning he took Communion, ate breakfast, smoked some tobacco and prepared for his last journey. Dressing for the occasion, he wore a satin doublet, black embroidered waistcoat, taffeta black breeches and coloured silk stockings, hat, embroidered night-cap and a black velvet cloak.

The execution took place in the Old Palace Yard, Westminster, on the same day as the Lord Mayor's Show. The large crowd assembled to watch included two men who would play a part in the historical events that led to civil war twenty years later, John Hampden and John Pym. Dean Tomson and two sheriffs led Raleigh up to the scaffold where he made his last speech. He thanked God for bringing him into the light to die, instead of in the prison of the Tower. He denied that he had been unfaithful to his king and forgave those who had conspired to bring him to his death. He concluded with the following words:

> And now I entreat you all to join with me in prayer, that the great God of Heaven, whom I have grievously offended, being a man full of all vanity, and having lived a sinful life, in all sinful callings, having been a soldier, a captain, a sea captain, and a courtier, which are all places of wickedness and vice; that God, I say, would forgive me, cast away my sins from me, and receive me into everlasting life. So I take my leave of you all, making my peace with God.

However, these were not quite his last words. As he took off his gown and doublet he asked the headsman to show him the axe. He was then reputed to have said, 'This is sharp medicine . . . that will cure all my diseases.' Courageously, he then placed his head on the block, having refused a blindfold, and gave the signal to strike. The executioner paused and then brought down the axe. It took two strokes to sever his head, which was displayed to the crowd before being placed in a red leather bag. His wife Bess took the embalmed head home in the bag that evening and kept it with her for the next twenty-nine years until she died at the age of 80. Raleigh's body was buried in St Margaret's, Westminster, to the south of the altar, and years later it was reunited with the head. For the scaffold crowd another execution was over and they would get on with their lives until the next one. As a measure of the transience of the moment Dean Tomson wrote, 'This was the news a week since but it is now blown over, and he is almost forgotten.'

Seven years after Raleigh's death, King James I died and was succeeded by his son Charles I (r. 1625–49), who soon found himself at loggerheads with Parliament. He dissolved Parliament in 1629 and did not recall it for a further eleven years. Many Puritans were worried by what they saw as 'Popish plots' and the absence of a Parliament during the 1630s only exacerbated the tensions. Events came to a head when it was decided to introduce a modified version of the English Prayer Book into Scotland, in the hope that the Scots would conform to this style of worship. However, Scotland, particularly the Lowlands, had long embraced Presbyterianism, a more rigid form of Protestantism, and the Scots were not prepared to accept what they saw as a Catholic tendency. Charles's attempt to subdue Scottish resistance failed and he found himself recalling Parliament in 1640. The conflict between Charles and Parliament escalated over the next fourteen months and civil war was declared in August 1642. Seven years later, following much bloodshed and upheaval, the king was called to account in January 1649 and put on trial on the charge of treason.

A special court was appointed to judge the king. He was accused of 'traitorously and maliciously' plotting to enslave the English nation in a 'wicked design' to 'subvert the ancient and fundamental laws and liberties of this nation and in their place to introduce an arbitrary and tyrannical government'. In this revolutionary situation the House of Commons resolved to take sole responsibility for the king's trial. The first problem was to obtain a sufficient number of judges to preside over this irregular court. Eventually 135 men sat as 'commissioners', acting as both judge and jury. The Lord President John Bradshaw, a former judge of the Sheriff's Court in London, resorted to wearing a specially reinforced hat to provide protection against outraged royalists. The most vigorous of the four prosecutors was the Solicitor-General John Cooke, a barrister of Gray's Inn. Finally it was decided that the king should be tried at the south end of Westminster Hall.

The king appeared at his trial wearing full royal regalia. Cooke read out the charges of treason and Charles asked the court by what powers he had been brought there, adding, 'Remember I am your king, your lawful king, and what sins you bring upon your heads, and the judgement of God upon this land; think well upon it, I say.' After some deliberation, Bradshaw said he was 'fully satisfied' with the authority of the court. Over the next few days evidence was brought against the king before sentence was passed.

On Saturday 27 January 1649, to signify the solemnity of the occasion, Bradshaw was dressed in scarlet robes for the first time. When Charles was brought into the court to hear the verdict there were shouts of 'justice' and some of 'execution' from the soldiers and the people assembled in the court. The king requested that he be granted a hearing before any sentence was passed but Bradshaw stated that the king had already delayed justice for several days by refusing to plead. Eventually Bradshaw announced the finding of the court: the king had been found guilty of all the said charges. Despite his appeals to speak, Charles was led from the court. He was permitted to see two of his children – Princess Elizabeth (aged 13) and the Duke of Gloucester (aged 8) – before he was taken back to Whitehall to await execution.

Tuesday 30 January 1649 was a bitterly cold day and Charles went to his death wearing two heavy shirts so that he might not shiver in the cold and appear to be afraid of the fate that awaited him. With colours flying and drums beating he was brought from St James's at 10 a.m.; he walked through the park with a regiment of Foot for his guard and accompanied by Doctor Juxon, the former Bishop of London. Charles entered the Banqueting House, where he drank a glass of claret and ate a piece of bread. However, as if to add to the drama, the execution was delayed for a matter of hours. Rumours circulated that an executioner could not be found. In fact, Parliament had not yet contemplated the question of the succession and hastily passed an Act making it an offence to proclaim a new king, thereby abolishing the office of monarch. The brief emergency Bill was hurriedly passed by midday and the king was kept waiting until nearly 2 p.m. He then walked through the Banqueting Hall, ironically beneath the Rubens ceiling glorifying the Divine Right of Kings.

From there Charles proceeded to the scaffold, which had been erected outside one of the windows of the palace. It was 'hung round with black and the floor covered with black, and the Ax and the blocke laid in the middle of the scaffold'. The whole was heavily guarded by companies of soldiers and there was a seething multitude of people who had come to witness the historic event.

The block was about a foot high. When the king saw it he asked 'if there were [any that were] higher'. Then he turned to face the assembled crowd and delivered his last speech. He affirmed his innocence, called himself a martyr to the people and forgave those who had brought him there. He then addressed the executioner (probably Richard Brandon, the official executioner for the city of London), saying, 'I shall say but very short prayers and then thrust out my hands', which was the sign to bring down the axe. Charles arranged his hair under his cap and then spoke to Juxon, who told him that he had but one short stage to go. Charles replied, 'I go from a corruptible to an incorruptible crown, where no disturbances can be.' Taking off his cloak and his George (the jewelled pendant of the Order of the Garter, bearing the figure of St George) he stooped down, laid his neck upon the block and after a short pause stretched out his hands. With one blow the executioner severed Charles's head from his body and then held it up to the crowd shouting 'behold the head of a traitor'. The crowd was quickly dispersed and the scaffold and everything associated with it cleared as soon as possible. The king's body was immediately embalmed and then placed in a coffin covered with black velvet; later it was taken to Windsor to be interred.

At Windsor, Charles's coffin was laid in a vault in the chapel beside two other coffins, believed to be those of Henry VIII and his queen Jane Seymour. Charles was interred on 19 February, three weeks after the execution, with no ceremony and only a few mourners. The words 'King Charles, 1648,' (1648 because this was the old calendar) were inscribed on the outside of the outer wooden coffin to mark the last resting place of the executed monarch.

The execution of Charles I was a defining moment in British history. Parliament felt that the proceedings against Charles had been necessary to secure the constitutional gains of the Civil War – the supremacy of Parliament, the independence of judges and the freedoms guaranteed by Magna Carta and the common law. He had been charged and condemned as 'a tyrant, traitor, murderer and . . . enemy to the Commonwealth of England'. But was he guilty as charged? Historians have debated this for years but rarely speak well of the trial, believing Charles was a victim of Puritan injustice. In fact the court displayed an unusual amount of patience with Charles. At the time of his trial a third civil war seemed possible and Charles could have been court-martialled and shot as the enemy commander.

Charles's coffin lay undisturbed until 1813 when the vault was opened for the funeral of the Duchess of Brunswick. On 1 April the Prince Regent, the Duke of Cumberland, the Dean of Windsor, Sir Harry Halford and two other gentlemen assembled at the vault while a search was made for the remains of King Charles. The leaden coffin was found and partially opened to reveal the body of the decapitated king in good condition, thanks to the gums and resins used to preserve it. One of the most distinguishing features, his beard, was perfect. The shape of the face was long and oval and many of the teeth remained. The head was found to be loose, and without any difficulty was held up to view.

A tract published at the time of the execution, entitled *The Confession of the Hangman*, stated that Brandon had acknowledged payment of £30; in addition he was given an orange stuck full of cloves and a handkerchief from the king's pocket. Brandon died a few months later, possibly from the stress brought on by the execution, and was buried in Whitechapel churchyard. Another publication printed in February 1649, the *Eikon Basilike* ('The Royal Image'), represented the dead king as a victim of tyranny. Charles, despite his miserable and troubled reign, died well and the *Eikon Basilike* helped to establish him as a Christian martyr. Parliament could not wipe away the support for the monarchy in the whole country and the Restoration of the monarchy in 1660 was greeted with much fervent rejoicing. It also brought closer the day of reckoning for those responsible for Charles I's death.

Puritanism faded after the Restoration. Theatres were reopened and the new king, Charles II, declared himself keen to support metropolitan improvements. Of the 59 men who signed Charles I's death warrant, 41 were still alive, although 15 had gone abroad. Ten were condemned to death at Charing Cross or Tyburn in October 1660. Of those ten Thomas Harrison, John Jones, Adrian Scroope, John Carew, Thomas Scot and Gregory Clement had signed the death warrant. Hugh Peters, Francis Hacker and Daniel Axtell had commanded the guards at the king's trial and execution, and John Cooke had acted as chief prosecutor. Three more regicides – John Okey, Miles Corbet and John Barkstead – were arrested and executed at Tyburn in 1662. A further nineteen were imprisoned for life; only a few escaped, three to New England and others to Europe. In August 1660 the passing of the Act of Indemnity and Oblivion served as a gesture of reconciliation to reunite the kingdom, and a free pardon was granted to everyone who had supported the Commonwealth and Protectorate, except for those who had directly participated in the trial and execution of Charles I. A special court was appointed in October 1660 and the surviving regicides were offered as human sacrifices in a rigged show trial.

At the time of Charles I, Charing Cross was described as having only a few dwellings, mainly to the east and north-east. There had been executions there before. Henry Machyn records that in 1555 three men were carried from Marshalsea in a cart to Charing Cross and 'there hanged . . . for robbing certain Spaniards of gold'. A Spaniard was also hanged there for killing a servant. However, the punishment of the regicides in 1660 would become by far the most famous of all the Charing Cross executions.

On Saturday 13 October 1660, between 9 and 10 a.m., Major-General Thomas Harrison was drawn upon a hurdle from Newgate to Charing Cross where a scaffold had been erected. Harrison was resolved to die bravely for his cause, although he had been critical of Cromwell's government as well as supporting the death of the king. At his trial he said that Charles's execution had not been done in a corner and added, 'I do not come to be denying anything . . . I did what I did out of conscience to the Lord.' As a Fifth Monarchist (a religious group who believed in the second coming of Christ), Harrison might have been a zealous believer but there is no doubting his sincerity, nor the brave and dignified way in which he confronted his death. He was the first of the regicides to face the brutal punishment. A woman who cleaned his prison room said that she 'knew not what he had done to deserve to be there and that he was a man full of God'. Indeed his godly character remained consistent throughout his ordeal. He told his wife he had nothing to leave but his Bible. As he was drawn to the scaffold it was said that he had a 'sweet smiling countenance', which never changed. On the scaffold he forgave his executioner and gave him 'all the money he had'. The crowd jeered, 'Where is your Good Old Cause now?', to which Harrison replied, 'Here in my bosom and I shall seal it with my blood.' He then gave his last speech, in which he said, 'Gentleman, by reason of some scoffing, that I do hear, I judge that some do think I am afraid to die . . . I tell you no, but it is by reason of much blood I have lost in the wars, and many wounds I have received in my body which caused this shaking and weakness in my nerves.' Harrison was a man of principle and the courage he displayed on the scaffold impressed many of the onlookers.

He was hanged with his face looking towards the Banqueting House at Whitehall. Half-dead, he was cut down by the executioner and then 'his Privy Members [were] cut off before his eyes, his Bowels burned, his Head severed from his Body, and his Body divided into Quarters, which were returned back to Newgate upon the same Hurdle that carried [him]'. In traditional manner his head was set upon a pole on the top of the south-east end of Westminster Hall and his quarters were displayed on the city gates.

Samuel Pepys attended Harrison's execution: 'I went out to Charing Cross, to see Major-General Harrison, hanged, drawn, and quartered . . . he looked as cheerful as any man could do in that condition. He was presently cut down, and his head and heart shown to the people, at which there were great shouts of joy.'

Two days later John Carew was carried in similar manner to the same place. Again, Pepys recorded the event: 'This morning Mr Carew was hanged and quartered at Charing Cross; but his quarters, by a great favour, are not to be hanged up.' Another contemporary comment was that 'His Majesty was pleased to give, upon intercession made by his Friends, his Body to be buried'.

On 16 October John Cooke, the chief prosecutor at the trial, and Hugh Peters were similarly executed at Charing Cross. In Newgate Cooke told the other prisoners that he 'would choose this death rather than from fever', and to his visitors he declared, 'We [the regicides] are going to heaven, and we are leaving you to the storm.' As he left the prison he bade farewell to his wife Mary and asked her not to go to the scaffold. Struck with grief, he said, 'Let us not part in a shower . . . in heaven all tears shall be wiped from our eyes.' He also wrote a solemn letter to her, full of moral guidance. In it he noted that: 'We are not traitors, nor murderers, not fanatics, but true Christians and good Commonwealth men . . . we sought the public good and would have enfranchised the people . . . if the nation had not more delighted in servitude than in freedom.'

Cooke spoke for a number of the regicides who saw themselves as defenders of reason and the law, and in this sense their principal contribution was in defending the constitutional safeguards for civil and religious liberties. He declared on the scaffold that he was the first man to be hanged for demanding justice. Interestingly, Cooke was the first lawyer to assert the right of the accused to stay silent. Additionally he advocated legal aid and a system that was tantamount to a national health service, and contributed to the forging of many democratic ideals.

The day was cold and wet as Cooke and Peters were taken from Newgate. Cooke chose to go to the scaffold first. Recognising Peters's state of terror, Cooke spoke compassionately of his friend: 'Here is a poor brother coming. I am afraid that he is not fit to die at this time. I could wish that His Majesty might show some mercy.' After his last words he was hanged, then quickly released from the rope and stripped of his clothes ready to face the gruesome ordeal that was to follow. His genitals were cut off and held before his eyes, and then the lining of his inner bowel was twisted out. Still conscious, Cooke looked on as his entrails were burned, but he was dead before his heart was displayed to the crowd. The stench created by the burning of his intestines brought complaints from the residents of Charing Cross and the executions of the regicides Axtell and Hacker were consequently moved to Tyburn.

Hugh Peters (1598–1660) was born in Cornwall and educated at Cambridge. A devout Puritan, he served as a chaplain in the parliamentary army. Although he played no direct part in the trial and execution of the king, his enthusiastic support for the regicides resulted in his arrest after the Restoration. A popular fable claimed he had been Charles's executioner, a charge he strongly denied. Peters was a zealous man whose appearance was not to his advantage, hence his nickname 'Jack Pudding Peters'. At his trial his courage deserted him and he had neither the honesty nor the capacity to suffer as the rest had done. He was observed to be drinking cordials to keep him from fainting. There was much popular indignation against the regicides and Peters had to run the gauntlet of an angry crowd as he was carried to the scaffold. He waited as Cooke endured the agonies of execution, until Colonel Turner called to the sheriff's men to bring him nearer 'that he might see it'. The executioner, already covered in blood, approached Peters 'and rubbing his bloody hands together asked, "How do you like this Mr Peters, how do you like my work?" Peters responded, "I am not terrified of it, you may do your work."' On the scaffold Peters at last summoned up some courage as he gave his speech. In an almost inaudible voice he said, 'This is a good day. He is come that I have long looked for; and I shall be with him in glory.'

On Wednesday 17 October other regicides followed. John Evelyn recorded that, 'about the hour of nine in the morning, Mr Thomas Scot, and Mr Gregory Clement, were brought in several Hurdles; and about one hour after Master Adrian Scroop and Mr John Jones together in one Hurdle were carried to the same place, and suffered the same death, and were returned and disposed of in the like manner.'

Gregory Clement had been a successful merchant and MP for Fowey in Cornwall but his fellow Puritans turned against him in the early 1650s when he was caught in bed with his maidservant. For some reason his name was scratched from Charles I's death warrant. Veronica Wedgwood suggested this was because of his adultery but it seems unlikely. In 1660 he went into hiding but was recognised because of his 'very extraordinary voice' and arrested. He tried to use the scratched-out name to his advantage, saying it was not his. Sadly for him the signature was still legible. He managed to retrieve some courage and faced his death regretting that he had been so weak as to deny the cause for which he was proud to die for.

Colonel John Jones, Cromwell's brother-in-law, said to a friend, 'I could wish thee in the same condition with myself, that thou mightest share with me in my joys.'

Charles II was present at these executions and later decided what to do with the remains of the regicides after their body parts had been paraded through the city. The heads of Harrison and Cooke were spiked on poles and fixed above the north end of Westminster Hall. On 20–21 October Samuel Pepys wrote:

> This afternoon, going through London . . . I saw the limbs of some of our new traytors set upon Aldersgate, which was a sad sight to see; and a bloody week this and the last have been, there being ten hanged, drawn and quartered . . . George Vines carried me up to the top of his turret, where there is Cooke's head set up for a traytor, and Harrison's set up the other side of Westminster Hall.

It was no coincidence that the regicides were executed near the spot where Charles I had met his end. The royalist John Evelyn wrote in his diary on 17 October 1660:

> This day were executed those murderous Traytors at Charing-Crosse, in sight of the place where they put to death their natural Prince, & in the Presence of the King his sonn, whom they also sought to kill . . . The Traytors executed were Scot, Scroope, Cooke, Jones. I saw not their execution, but met their quarters mangld

& cutt & reaking as they were brought from the Gallows in baskets on the hurdle.

London was still expanding and by the late seventeenth century Charing Cross was so busy it was said that anyone who wanted to know what was going on in London had only to go there to pick up the gossip. In the eighteenth century Samuel Johnson said, 'I think the Full tide of human existence is at Charing Cross.' The area would never again see such butchery as was inflicted on the regicides but gruesome executions continued at Tyburn. Charing Cross became a place where proclamations were read and offenders pilloried. The most famous person to stand in the pillory here was Daniel Defoe in January 1703 for his pamphleteering and political activities. His publication *Hymn to the Pillory* caused his audience to throw flowers instead of the customary harmful and noxious objects, and to drink his health. He was the darling of the crowd.

EIGHT

Executions North of the Thames

London life, with its noise and colour and
animation, is like a story by Dostoyevsky.
Alec Waugh (1898–1981)

Fleet Street in medieval times was a major road
joining the city and Westminster. A murder took
place in Fleet Street in 1607, the killers being hit-men
hired by Lord Sanquhar, a Scottish nobleman.
Retribution soon followed. Sanquhar himself was
executed in Westminster, the other two in Fleet Street
close to where the murder had taken place. One of the
murderers was a young Scottish nobleman, who, in
accordance with Scottish practice and perceptions of
class at the time, was hanged from a gallows several feet
higher than that on which his lower-born accomplice
died. Some accounts give the date of the murder and
subsequent executions as 1612.

You can still walk down Old Mitre Court, which leads
off Fleet Street towards the Temple. Here in 1732
Sarah Malcolm was hanged for a triple murder at the age
of 22. She had been brought up in a prosperous and
respectable family which became increasingly needy
because her father was a feckless spendthrift. Sarah was
forced to take employment as a laundress and among her
customers was a Mrs Duncomb. Sarah frequently went to

Mrs Duncomb's home to collect or drop off washing but one day she attacked and strangled not only the old lady but also a serving woman and a young girl before robbing the premises. Her bloodstained clothes were soon found and the articles she had stolen were recovered. On being apprehended, Sarah tried to implicate some of her relations but they all produced convincing alibis. When Sarah was searched the very large sum of £53 was found hidden in her hair. Sarah was a woman of striking appearance and two days before her execution she sat to be sketched by none other than William Hogarth. She was dressed splendidly in scarlet, bought specially for the occasion. Such was the interest her case generated that her corpse was put on display and large numbers of people paid good money to view it.

Theodore Gardelle was of Swiss extraction and a more than competent painter of miniatures who settled in London in the middle of the eighteenth century. In 1761 he murdered his landlady although he very nearly botched the job. The motive appears to have been robbery, although it has been suggested that he had persistently tried to seduce her and that after one final rebuff his patience had run out and he attempted to rape as well as rob her. It was a foolish thing to do because she proved to be considerably stronger than he was. Not only did she easily parry his blows but she also proceeded to beat him up. Finding himself in dire straits, he picked up a poker and used it to inflict a number of injuries; as she weakened, he stabbed her to death. He partially dismembered her body and then tried to burn what was left. As a crime, it lacked finesse and Gardelle was quickly apprehended and hanged at the junction of the Haymarket and Panton Street.

In the 1840s the Corporation of the City of London was urgently looking for a site for a house of correction to accommodate those serving short sentences. After some difficulty (created largely by the fact that those with influence had no wish to live close to a prison), a site was eventually found at Holloway in north London. It was in a somewhat dismal area that was already beginning to be covered with street after street of mean housing. The initial building on the site outwardly resembled nothing so much as a mock castle. Holloway was absorbed into the state system of prisons in 1877. In its early days Holloway housed numbers of male prisoners but since 1902 it has been almost exclusively a female prison.

The first execution at Holloway took place on 9 January 1923. Edith Thompson and her lover Frederick Bywaters had been found guilty of murdering her husband Percy. Edith was a romantic, sensual woman, avid for new and exciting experiences to relieve her humdrum existence in suburban Ilford with Percy, who bored her to tears. Bywaters, who was eight years younger, helped to put some colour back in her cheeks. One night Edith and Percy were walking home after a visit to the theatre when Bywaters sprang out from an alley and attacked Percy, stabbing him fatally. Witnesses said that they heard Edith telling him to stop. However, the contents of a number of love-letters she wrote to Bywaters were produced as evidence, and fairly damning it was too. The letters revealed that she was obsessed with the idea of murdering Percy, and in one letter she even boasted that she had ground up some pieces of glass and put them in his porridge. Although there was some public sympathy for Edith, her appeal was dismissed. She was hanged at Holloway at the same time as Bywaters met his end at Pentonville, less than a mile away. Edith found it extremely difficult to cope with the pressure and had to be carried, heavily sedated, to the scaffold. Ellis, the hangman, declared that it was the most harrowing execution he had ever carried out. He numbered such celebrities as Dr Crippen and Sir Roger Casement among his victims, but his work only seemed to bring him misery and in 1932 he committed suicide.

In 1954 Mrs Styllou Christofi, a Cypriot, was hanged at Holloway. In a fit of jealousy she had killed her German-born daughter-in-law, brutally battering her with a lump of iron before strangling her and then trying to burn the body. During the trial the jury was informed that some years earlier Christofi had been acquitted, through lack of evidence, of murdering her own mother-in-law back home in Cyprus. It is likely that this unsavoury woman was at least partly insane, and probably should have been treated as such instead of being executed. She never exhibited the slightest sign of remorse.

Ruth Ellis was a physically attractive but emotionally unstable young woman who murdered her lover in 1955 in a case which became one of the most celebrated in British legal history. Her murder of the vapid young wastrel David Blakely at the Magdala Tavern close to Hampstead Heath brought to a shocking end their extremely turbulent relationship. Ellis had met Blakeley in 1953. Like her, he was outwardly sophisticated and worldly, but a habitué of the same slightly seedy, down-at-heel bars and clubs which proliferated on the fringes of London's West End. She was employed as a 'hostess' but she also seemed to have some responsibility for the accounts in the various dives in which she worked. Ruth had had a short, acrimonious marriage and her two children were now looked after by her parents. She drank hard and was promiscuous (but no more so than Blakely), and her brief periods of cohabitation with him always ended in mutually jealous quarrels and tantrums. Eventually Blakely decided to break off their relationship once and for all but told friends that Ruth was in such an emotional state that he was afraid of what she might do by way of retaliation. He was right to be worried. Ruth obtained a gun – exactly how has never been satisfactorily ascertained – and tracked down her ex-lover, shooting him several times in the pub's car park.

Ruth seemed curiously numbed and indifferent after the frenzy of emotion that had led her to kill Blakeley. She exhibited no apparent remorse and made it clear that she had gone to the Magdala with the specific intention of killing him. That being so, the law said she had to die and she seemed entirely resigned to her fate. While the killing itself was cold-blooded and calculated, Ruth was clearly under intense emotional strain at the time and the case was used to strengthen the arguments of those campaigning for the abolition of the death penalty. Some 50,000 signatures were appended to a petition for mercy sent to the Home Secretary and a tellingly cogent case against capital punishment was made by the *Daily Mirror* columnist 'Cassandra'. This squalid murder and the rather pathetic antics leading up to it proved to be of considerable importance in British criminal history. Ruth Ellis was the last woman to be hanged under process of law in the United Kingdom and the case was undoubtedly instrumental in securing the abolition of capital punishment for murder. After suffering traumas of terror at the prospect, Ruth died bravely enough at Holloway on 13 July 1955. Albert Pierrepoint officiated.

Sidney Silverman was an indefatigable campaigner against capital punishment and must have fancied his chances of success when he introduced the Death Penalty (Abolition) Bill in the House of Commons in 1956. It was later narrowly defeated in the Lords but in 1957 the Homicide Act was passed. This reserved the capital sanction to just five kinds of murder, as well as reiterating its availability for those found guilty of treason, piracy on the high seas and violence or arson in naval dockyards, arsenals and on the ships of the Royal Navy. Although the Crown could exercise the prerogative of mercy, under the Act it could also, in the case of treason, recommend beheading rather than hanging.

In 1971 the old Holloway Prison was demolished and replaced by a modern and greatly updated and improved building on the same site.

Pentonville Prison opened in 1842 and was intended to be a prototype of the modern custodial reformatory. At first it housed mostly prisoners who had been selected for transportation to Australia. These were unlikely to be hardened recidivists but rather people who might make a fresh start once removed from their criminal associations in this country. When Newgate finally closed in 1902 its gallows was re-erected at Pentonville, which then became the hanging prison for north London. Despite various proposals for its replacement, Pentonville continues to maintain its brooding, baleful presence just a mile or so north from King's Cross and St Pancras stations.

It is by no means unknown for those who work in financial services to be extremely incompetent when it comes to managing their own money matters. This was certainly true of Frederick Henry Seddon, who lived in Upper Holloway and let the top floor of his house to a moderately well-to-do unmarried woman called Elizabeth Barrow. She knew that Seddon worked for an insurance company and trusted him enough to place her financial affairs almost totally in his hands. Also, fatally, she thought him a very nice man. About two months after Elizabeth had moved in, she fell ill with chronic diarrhoea, and was looked after with admirable devotion by Seddon and his wife. They were at her bedside on the night she died. Her funeral was arranged with great haste and without her relations being informed of her death. When the news did get out, her relations' concern about Seddon's management of her finances deepened into a belief that he had killed her. They went to the police. Elizabeth was exhumed and her body was found to contain a lethal quantity of arsenic. This may have been obtained from fly-papers, which at that time could be bought openly over the counter of hardware shops. The arsenic was extracted by boiling the papers in water and a single paper was reckoned to produce enough arsenic to kill a healthy adult. The Seddons went to court charged with murder. Frederick was found guilty, but his wife was acquitted. He had a clear motive of financial benefit from murdering Elizabeth. He was hanged at Pentonville in 1910 amid concerns that the evidence that sent him to his death was purely circumstantial.

The year 1910 also saw the death by hanging at Pentonville of 'Dr' Hawley Harvey Crippen. This murder case, one of the most celebrated in British criminal history, has been told and retold on countless occasions but has never lost its ability to fascinate. Perhaps this is because of the way in which its elements came together to create a crime of such piquancy. Spare a thought for the cast. Crippen himself was a small man, self-effacing and mild-mannered, easy to ignore and hopelessly henpecked by his domineering wife, who was not only physically larger than him but also attractive in a somewhat blowsy way. She was extrovert and promiscuous. He was a medical man, not fully qualified as a doctor but with a professional knowledge of poisons. Despite his rather unattractive appearance, Crippen was cast in the totally unexpected role of a paramour able to win the affection and sexual favours of Ethel Le Neve, an attractive woman twenty years or so his junior. Crippen murdered his domineering wife, cut her up with a skill normally reserved only for experienced surgeons and buried her various parts in the coal cellar of the family house off the Camden Road, not far from Holloway Prison. He then fled with Ethel, who was disguised as a youth, on the steamship SS *Montrose*, hoping to carve out a blissful new life for himself and his elfin-like young consort in Canada. They were registered on the ship as father and son, but Crippen's indiscreet behaviour caught the attention of the ship's captain. News of the murder and photographs of the suspects had been widely broadcast and the captain contacted Scotland Yard, sure that these two passengers, masquerading as 'Mr Robinson and his son', fitted the descriptions of the wanted fugitives. Convinced that the couple were indeed Crippen and Ethel, detectives then embarked on a faster ship which reached its destination more quickly. Blissfully ignorant of what had transpired during the crossing, Crippen and Ethel found detectives waiting to arrest them as their ship docked. This was the first occasion on which wireless telegraphy was used in a criminal case. Crippen and Ethel were brought back to Britain to stand trial for murder at the Old Bailey. Crippen made it quite clear that Ethel had known nothing about his murderous intentions towards his wife and she was acquitted, eventually putting these experiences behind her and going on to live a life of relative obscurity. Crippen revealed the depth of his passion by asking for the right to be buried with a photograph of Ethel, probably the only woman he ever loved. His wish was granted.

Roger Casement was born near Dun Laoghaire in County Dublin in 1864 and was knighted for his public services as a consular agent in 1911, having attracted wide-ranging respect and regard among Britain's political and social elite. However, they were soon to show how capricious their respect actually was. Casement was a fervent Irish patriot and nationalist. When the First World War started, he toured Germany and the USA seeking support for the cause of Irish independence. In Germany he met captured Irish soldiers in prisoner-of-war camps and encouraged them to try to find ways to be taken back to Ireland in order to fight the British. By doing so, Casement was committing high treason because, like all other Irish citizens at that time, he was a British subject. He was arrested as he came ashore from a German submarine off the Irish coast early in 1916. He had been under observation for some time. As part of the investigation into his activities, his apartment at 50 Ebury Street, London SW1, was raided and a substantial amount of material was taken away. This made it clear that Casement was an extremely promiscuous homosexual, who had had affairs with innumerable men and boys during the various postings that had gone with his job. These private papers, which gained notoriety as the 'Black Diaries' (and may or may not have been genuine), gave salaciously lurid details of Casement's sexual activities.

The government regarded this material as heaven-sent for the purpose of discrediting Casement, given the general esteem in which he had previously been held. Indeed he was not only well thought-of in Britain but crucially was also admired in the United States, which was still theoretically neutral. Anything that put Casement in a bad light and simultaneously threw mud at the cause of Irish nationalism was gratefully received. The Home Office therefore, with cynical malice, started leaking selected gobbets of information, some would say disinformation, in places where it was felt they could do most damage. Homosexuality at that time aroused public expressions of revulsion and condemnation regardless of the extent to which it was actually prevalent in society at large. The government's 'spin-doctors' skilfully handled the dissemination of information in such a way as to build up a powerful moral case against Casement. This was intended to erode his support in left-wing and supposedly liberal circles and to undermine his record of unimpeachable integrity as a public servant. The authorities were successful in stigmatising Casement and he was hanged at Pentonville in 1916. The treatment Casement received for his treason was in marked contrast to that extended to Sir Edward Carson, a Unionist politician and former Solicitor-General in the Conservative government from 1900 to 1906. Carson made it clear that he and other Protestants in Northern Ireland would be prepared to use any means to prevent the implementation of the Liberal government's 1911 proposals regarding Home Rule for Ireland. Such means included armed uprising, in preparation for which weapons were obtained and military drilling took place. This treasonable statement and its associated subversive activity took place behind a screen of 'patriotism' and 'loyalty to the Crown', defence of the Empire and defence of the Protestant religion. Britain's establishment maintained a deafening silence about Carson's treason. He was, after all, one of their own.

On an October evening in 1917 central London was subjected to an aerial bombing attack that was probably more frightening than lethal. At 101 Charlotte Street, just to the west of Tottenham Court Road, lodged Louis Voisin, a giant of a man. Immensely strong, and a butcher by trade, he was not very bright, although sufficiently devious to run two mistresses, neither of whom knew that the other existed. One of them was a Belgian lady, Emilienne Gerard, aged 32, the wife of a French army chef. As soon as the air raid started, she made for the nearest tube station, as did many others living in London at the time. She was never again seen alive. A couple of days later a road sweeper found a parcel, which he opened to reveal a partially clothed, headless female torso and a scrap of paper bearing the enigmatic words 'Bloodie Belgiam'. A second package found nearby shortly afterwards contained the woman's legs.

The police identified the remains through a laundry mark and when they found a photograph of Voisin and an IOU signed by him, they swooped on his flat, where he was cosily occupied with Berthe Roche, his other paramour. In the kitchen, which contained a bloodcurdling collection of butcher's implements, they found splashes of human blood. An outhouse contained Emilienne's head and hands, covered in sawdust and ineffectively hidden in a wooden cask. Voisin was taken to a police station for questioning. Asked to write the words 'Bloody Belgian', he did so slowly and ponderously, rendering them as 'Bloodie Belgiam'. He produced a feeble story about going to Emilienne's flat only to find that she had been murdered and dismembered. Thinking (rightly) that the police might suspect him, he told them that he panicked and disposed of her body parts in a number of packages. The jury was unimpressed and the judge sentenced Voisin to death (in French, because as we have seen he had difficulties with the English language). He was hanged at Pentonville Prison. The exact truth about what happened was never fully established but it seems likely that the murder occurred when the two women confronted each other for the first time. Berthe had probably acted as Voisin's accomplice and so was sentenced to seven years, but she was soon certified insane and died later, still a prisoner, in a ward for mental patients.

On Friday 6 May 1927 a trunk was placed in the left-luggage office at Charing Cross station. A few days later the nauseating stench emanating from the trunk encouraged the staff to call the police. When the trunk was opened, five brown-paper parcels were found inside, each containing the dismembered parts of a female body. The famous Home Office pathologist Sir Bernard Spilsbury established that the woman was on the plump side and aged about 35. He also showed that she had been beaten severely before being asphyxiated. Soon the victim was identified as Minnie Alice Bonati, a prostitute. First-rate detective work pointed the finger at 36-year-old John Robinson, a rather unsuccessful entrepreneur, who had apparently taken Bonati back to his office in the Victoria district of London for sex. When she demanded money first a fight broke out, during which he shoved her and she fell, banging her head on a coal scuttle – or so he claimed. Frightened, he left the office, and when he returned he found to his horror that she had died. Panicking, he then carved her up, placing the pieces in the paper bags in a trunk. In an understandable state of agitation, he then popped into a pub for a fortifying drink and there enlisted the help of one of the patrons to help him load the trunk into a taxi to Charing Cross station. Robinson was identified by some crucial forensic evidence. During the hearing the public was amused to hear that not only was Robinson's office directly opposite a police station but that he had taken the empty trunk to Victoria by bus, bizarrely insisting on carrying it upstairs with the help of the conductor. Robinson was hanged on 12 August 1927.

It has long been fashionable to talk in glowing terms of the unity across all sections of British society that was engendered by the demands of the Second World War and how people pulled together to defeat the common enemy. Less frequently mentioned is the large increase in criminal activity which occurred during the war years. Not only were unscrupulous profiteers at work but the darkened streets of Britain's towns and cities provided many possibilities for opportunistic criminals, such as the two young men, both habitual offenders, who robbed an elderly pawnbroker in Shoreditch on 30 April 1942. Their names were Dashwood and Silverosa, and both were in their 20s. Their victim, Leonard Moules, was shutting up shop one evening when they seized him, dragged him back into the shop and hit him repeatedly and without mercy on the head, inflicting injuries from which he died several days later. They then grabbed the day's takings and ran, Silverosa leaving a perfect palm print behind him. In the course of the investigation a soldier came forward and told the police that he had seen two young men tentatively handling a gun in a café on the day of the robbery and assault. Dashwood and Silverosa were soon caught. Each tried to blame the other for the vicious attack but both were hanged at Pentonville in December 1942.

Another wartime case was the 'Cleft Chin Murder', so-called because of the victim's most conspicuous facial feature. Karl Gustav Hulten was a young American soldier serving with a parachute regiment in England. Going absent without leave, he had commandeered a large US army truck and spent several weeks driving round the country, committing various minor offences. It almost beggars belief that when he needed more petrol he simply drove into the nearest US base and filled up there – and no one questioned what he was doing. He met 18-year-old Elizabeth Marina Jones in a café in Hammersmith. She was a sad case. She had left home with the hopeless intention of following her father who had been drafted into the army. She got into trouble, was sent to what used to be called an approved school and ended up getting married. This last act reeked of desperation but at least it meant that she did not have to go back to the school. However, she was physically abused on the first matrimonial night and the couple went their separate ways immediately afterwards.

Elizabeth was lonely, vulnerable and confused when she met Hulten. His American accent and manners, his role as a paratrooper and the imposing truck that he drove all impressed the poor girl. She was thrilled when he said that back home he was a gangster and became even more excited when they took a ride in the truck. Hulten seemed to feed off Elizabeth's adulation. Soon the couple embarked on a series of assaults and robberies, many of them bungled. These culminated in the fatal shooting of the taxi-driver George Edward Heath on the Great West Road near Chiswick. It was a shocking and pointless murder, carried out by Hulten to impress the girl by taking his 'tough guy' image to the limit. Not surprisingly Hulten was quickly picked up by the police, but as an American serviceman he was handed over to the US authorities. It was agreed that the pair should stand trial for murder together at the Old Bailey in January 1945. Both were found guilty of murder, although the jury recommended mercy for the girl. There was widespread indignation in the United States that a British judge had sentenced an American citizen to death and there were demands for Hulten to be brought back home for trial. This protest was cut short when Hulten was hanged by Albert Pierrepoint at Pentonville on 8 March 1945. There was some resentment when Elizabeth obtained a last-minute reprieve. She spent nine years in prison and then, after changing her identity, went back to her native Wales.

Neville George Clevely Heath was a handsome young man of good education who possessed all the social graces. He was also a first-class rotter. He lived largely without paid employment, using a variety of aliases as well as claiming military ranks to which he was not entitled. He had a powerful but perverted sex drive and with his looks and charm had little difficulty in finding sexual partners. In June 1946 he took a room at the Pembridge Court Hotel in Notting Hill, signing the register as 'Colonel Heath'. He then picked up Mrs Margery Gardner in a club and brought her back for sex. Margery had a strong liking for pain-oriented sexual activity but the unfortunate woman could not have anticipated the explosion of sadistic violence which Heath unleashed. He beat her so severely with a whip that vivid bruises were left imprinted on her body, he almost bit off one of her nipples and he forced a poker into her vagina, inflicting awful injuries from which she would have died had he not suffocated her first. Heath then calmly took himself off to Bournemouth, where he registered under the name 'Group-Captain Rupert Brooke' at the Tollard Royal Hotel. There he met 21-year-old Doreen Marshall, whom he murdered with possibly even greater violence. He was duly charged with the murder of Margery, but the most contentious issue before the court was really whether or not he was insane and thus not fit to plead. The judge, Mr Justice Morris, pointed out that the manifestation of uncontrollably violent sexual lust did not qualify as insanity. The jury took his point and Heath was found guilty of murder. He was executed at Pentonville on 26 October 1946.

On the night of 9 March 1954 two young men from Fulham, Kenneth Gilbert and Ian Grant, set out to rob a small hotel in Harrington Gardens, London SW7. They broke in through the coal cellar and overpowered the hotel's porter, leaving him bruised, gagged and bound. He suffocated during the night. The men stole £2 in cash and some cigarettes. Both were stupid, and at work the next day could not resist talking about the 'job' they had done the night before. They were quickly arrested and charged with murder, and duly appeared at the Old Bailey on 10 May 1954. The main issue was whether or not they had intended murder when they embarked on the crime. The jury had no hesitation in finding them guilty. These two pathetic small-time villains, who created so much misery for so little reward, managed to get themselves into the annals of criminal history as their executions constituted the last double hanging in Britain, on 17 June 1954. The executioner was Albert Pierrepoint.

Just as the United Kingdom is now infamous for the large number of criminals incarcerated in its prisons, so in earlier times England gained some notoriety for the eagerness and frequency with which it hanged its erring citizens. It was often considered appropriate for executions to take place close to where the crime itself had been committed as it was felt that such executions had a particularly salutary effect, impressing on those who lived in the vicinity that they were within the effective ambit of the law. This means that scattered around London are innumerable sites where perhaps no more than a single execution was ever carried out, and for which in many cases no historical record exists. A further complication is that sometimes a place where a gibbet was located is confused with the actual place of execution.

An example of the authorities responding by using multiple sites for executions occurred in 1517 when serious riots took place in the city, incited by the singularly xenophobic preacher Dr Beal, encouraged by John Lincoln. Angry crowds of apprentices, not a few priests and others attacked the homes and businesses of a number of foreign settlers and the authorities retaliated by making hundreds of arrests. After due consideration Lincoln and thirteen others were sentenced to death at the sites of their offences. Thus individual hangings occurred in such places as Aldgate, Aldersgate, Gracechurch Street, Leadenhall Street and Bishopsgate. (Lessons were perhaps learned about the time-consuming task of erecting and dismantling so many gallows. Therefore in 1595, when large-scale outbreaks of violence once more threatened the city, the Provost Marshal was presented with an easily portable gallows which could presumably be moved from one trouble-spot to another quickly and economically.)

Many years later Leadenhall Street was to witness another execution. A crowd of between 12,000 and 20,000 spectators turned out to witness the execution of the highwayman and housebreaker Colonel Turner in 1662. He had tied up and gagged a rich merchant and then ransacked his house, carrying away a large amount of money and some gemstones. Turner greatly tried the patience of the crowd as he poured forth an apparently endless last dying speech in the hope that he would survive long enough to receive the reprieve that he clearly thought was on its way. On this occasion Samuel Pepys had hired a viewing place on the wheel of a cart so that he could see over the heads of the crowd. He endured severe cramps because he dared not dismount while Turner was delivering his tedious peroration for fear that he might miss the hanging itself, which of course he had paid good money to view. Greatly irritating the choleric Pepys as well as everyone else in the crowd, Turner droned on with a protracted description of his family background, his gallant service in the civil war just ended, the lack of moral fibre that had brought him to this pretty pass and even a disparaging description of conditions inside Newgate. With the consummate ease usually displayed only by politicians, he brushed aside repeated reminders that he should finish. Eventually he ran out of words but continued to play for time by saying his prayers at great length and distributing alms among the crowd. Eventually he accepted the inevitable. Just before he was turned off, he spied a comely woman at a nearby window and called out, 'Your servant, mistress' – so the odds are that he was still talking as he swung in mid-air. The clothes in which a prisoner was hanged were always regarded as one of the perquisites of the hangman. Turner, however, insisted that his clothes should go to his relations but he compensated the hangman by paying him 50s, with a half-crown tip for drinks.

In Cheapside stands the church of St-Mary-le-Bow (of 'Oranges and Lemons' fame), and within earshot of its great bell true cockneys are born. Not far from the church was a fountain known as the Standard and a number of executions took place at this conspicuous landmark. The first were two fishmongers executed in 1340 or 1351 (depending on which account is believed) for striking the person of the Lord Mayor of London during a riot. Wat Tyler used this site for a number of 'executions' during the Peasants' Revolt in 1381. These hangings were more in the nature of lynchings, and it is unlikely that the services of an official public executioner were required. In 1450 Jack Cade, leader of the Kentish Rebellion, had Lord Saye and Sele and other unpopular courtiers executed here. He himself was later beheaded in King's Bench Prison.

In 1685 Henry Cornish was executed in Cheapside for high treason, having supported the Duke of Monmouth's uprising. The crowd was comparatively muted as he was executed because he had been a well-liked sheriff of the city. He was probably a scapegoat and the fact that his execution went ahead contributed to the resentment felt towards James II. Other types of punishment were also inflicted in Cheapside. In 1269 foreign merchants who refused to use the official weights had to watch while their own weights were smashed and then burned. In 1293 three men had their right hands cut off for rescuing prisoners. The heads of rebels and traitors were often displayed briefly in Cheapside before being taken to London Bridge. At a later date there was a pillory in Cheapside and Daniel Defoe spent some time there for publishing a scurrilous pamphlet called *The Shortest Way with the Dissenters*.

Another location for executions was the street known as St Paul's Churchyard, adjacent to the cathedral. In 1441 Roger Bolingbroke, a necromancer or sorcerer, was hanged, drawn and quartered here and there is a reference to this event in Shakespeare's *Henry VI*. A number of executions also took place here during the religious persecutions of Tudor times.

Four of the conspirators in the Gunpowder Plot – Sir Everard Digby, Robert Winter, John Grant and Thomas Bates – were executed at the western end of the churchyard in January 1606. They had been dragged on wicker hurdles from their places of confinement, the Tower in the case of the first three, and in spite of the fact that it was a decidedly cold morning a sizeable crowd had turned out. It included relations of the condemned men, offering last-minute encouragement, but by far the majority vented their spleen on those they loathed as Papists and would-be regicides. Digby was the first to mount the scaffold and he used the opportunity to declaim about his faith and conscience, insisting that he indissolubly cleaved to these while readily admitting that he had broken the law as it stood. He was still alive when he was cut down and eviscerated. It is said that when the executioner held his heart up to public view and declared it to be the heart of a traitor, Digby's detached head unexpectedly snarled that the man was a liar. Winter went quietly to his death while Grant gave a wholly unapologetic valedictory speech, but Bates rather cringingly and at some length tried to assure the crowd that although he had done wrong he had done it for the right reasons and he begged their forgiveness.

The Jesuit priest Father Henry Garnet was accused of complicity in the Gunpowder Plot. A man of formidable intellectual acumen, he used his trial to highlight the weak legal and theological arguments of the prosecution case. His execution attracted a huge and hostile crowd, but there was some admiration for his courage. Some onlookers even prevented the hangman from cutting Garnet down while he was still alive to disembowel him, and later, when the hangman held up the severed head, the act evoked nothing more than uneasy murmurings and groans among the spectators. Zealous Catholics subsequently averred that fragments of the scaffold on which Garnet died were found to be displaying miraculous portraits of the man himself.

There are numerous lesser-known locations around London where executions occasionally took place. One of these was St-Giles-in-the-Fields, where Sir John Oldcastle was executed in 1417. A personal friend of Henry V and a guardian of the Welsh Marches, Oldcastle fell from favour when he embraced Lollardry. The Lollards – the word is a mocking one suggesting that they droned on at great length – were followers of John Wycliffe and early critics of what they considered to be impious and corrupt practices on the part of the Church. The king, however, was determined to stamp out all manifestations of heresy. Oldcastle not only refused to recant but went on the attack, stridently denouncing the hierarchy of the Church. The king went out of his way to help Oldcastle but his best intentions were put to naught when Oldcastle escaped from the Tower and attempted to raise a rebellion in 1414. After three years in hiding he was recaptured and, still unrepentant, was put to death close to the present-day junction of Oxford Street, Charing Cross Road and Tottenham Court Road.

Clerkenwell Green was the location of a number of executions. It is recorded that in 1538 a crowd of 20,000 turned out to watch three simultaneous hangings, one of the victims being a hangman himself. This was one Cratwell, who had robbed a booth at nearby Bartholomew Fair. His presence on the gallows must have added some spice to the proceedings. Lincoln's Inn Fields is said to be London's largest square and it was here that fourteen conspirators in the Babington Plot were hanged, drawn and quartered in 1587. The plot was the brainchild of Sir Anthony Babington, a zealous Roman Catholic. The intention was to murder Queen Elizabeth and, with support from the Papacy and from Spain, to replace her on the throne with Mary, Queen of Scots, who Catholics believed was the only person with a true claim to the English throne. As might be expected in these turbulent times, the ranks of the conspirators had been penetrated by Sir Francis Walsingham's spy network. As ringleader, Babington was hanged first and had the misfortune still to be conscious when his penis was cut off and he was eviscerated. In an unusual show of mercy Elizabeth then issued an order that care was to be taken to ensure the other conspir- ators were already dead before they were mutilated. The discovery of this plot effectively sealed Mary's fate. She was executed later the same year at Fotheringhay Castle near Peterborough in Northamptonshire.

The year 1683 saw William, Lord Russell, executed in Lincoln's Inn Fields for his part in the Rye House Plot to assassinate Charles II. His wife pleaded vehemently for mercy but Charles is reputed to have argued with inexorable logic that if the wretched man was reprieved, it would only be a matter of time before he tried to kill him again and next time he might succeed. Russell bore his death sentence stoically, even defiantly, remarking that the pain of the axe would be fleeting and no worse than having a tooth extracted. Unluckily for him, he had not reckoned on the incompetence of Jack Ketch, who had to employ three strokes of the axe to remove his head, using the limp excuse that his lordship had moved at the critical moment. Not surprisingly, ghostly pain-racked screams have been reported as emanating from Lincoln's Inn Fields in the witching hours.

Many of those involved in the Gordon Riots of 1790 were executed close to where they had committed their offences. Two, for example, were hanged in Aldersgate Street opposite the house they had set on fire. In 1817 a sailor by the name of Cashman, who had committed a robbery, was hanged in Skinner Street in the Finsbury district off St John Street. In 1715 John Price lost his post as public hangman because he had been imprisoned for debt. Conditions were not too onerous for him because he was allowed to leave prison during the day on condition that he returned at night. However, in early 1718 he went absent without leave and on a Sunday in April got gloriously drunk, and found himself wandering through fields close to Moorgate. Hucksters had set up stalls in the area in the hope that the lovely weather would attract Londoners to leave the city's fetid streets for a spot of recreation in the open country round about. Price found one of these hucksters, a woman, minding her stall alone and raped her. She put up a fight which so annoyed him that he broke her arm and knocked out one of her eyes before he was overpowered. He was hanged in Bunhill Fields close by.

The demagogic MP John Wilkes was ejected from the House of Commons in 1763 and thrown into the Tower of London because of an article he had written for the *North Briton* newspaper. This article was considered to be seditious libel and it was ordered that the offending issue, no. 45, should be symbolically burned by the common hangman in front of the Royal Exchange. The hangman on this occasion was Thomas Turlis. As he approached the fire, he and the other officials present were showered with stones thrown by a sizeable and extremely hostile crowd. Braving these missiles, Turlis somehow managed to thrust the *North Briton* into the fire, whereupon someone in the crowd rushed forward and pulled it out. The mood became uglier and Turlis and the sheriff's men had no alternative but to withdraw in confusion.

In 1767 John Williamson was executed for starving his wife to death. His first wife having died prematurely, he then married a much younger woman. She had some money but was unprepossessing and was regarded by some at the time, rather unkindly, as an idiot. The law at the time directed that the wife's property became the husband's on marriage. Williamson, having got his hands on her money, proceeded to abuse her cruelly, locking her up in a darkened room, torturing her and only providing the minimum of food and water. Eventually she died from this treatment. Williamson was convicted of murder at the Old Bailey and in January 1767 he was hanged in Chiswell Street, Moorfields, close to where he had lived. It was only with some difficulty that the crowd was prevented from lynching Williamson.

Thomas Venner was hanged, drawn and quartered in Coleman Street in the city, having briefly achieved a degree of notoriety as the leader of a 'Fifth Monarchist' uprising. The Fifth Monarchists were a fanatical sect based on an interpretation of the Bible which argued that there had been four great empires in the past but the next was to be the 'Fifth Monarchy' of Christ. It would exist for a thousand years until the Last Judgement and would be controlled on Christ's behalf by 'saints' – who were naturally the Fifth Monarchists themselves. The job of the 'saints' was to prepare the way for Christ by purging the world of every semblance of carnality. Such aspirations inevitably brought them into conflict with the forces of law and order and led to their persecution. The revolt was small-scale but surprisingly troublesome. It was led by Venner, who paid the price with his life but doubtless thought it was worth it. He died in 1661.

Thomas Savage, a youth of 17, was a wastrel, much given to whoring, drunkenness and petty crime. He was employed at the Ship tavern in the disreputable district of Ratcliffe, east of the Tower of London, and spent much of his free time with a prostitute called Hannah Blay. She put pressure on him to rob his master and thereby obtain some ready money. He was reluctant to try this because the maid was always in the house. Hannah was determined, however, and in October 1668 she got Savage so drunk and fighting mad that he beat the maid to death with a hammer and robbed his master of £60. Nemesis was inevitable for such a vicious but poorly thought-out offence and after conviction and temporary lodgings in Newgate, Savage was taken to Ratcliffe Cross, close to the scene of the murder. He took some time to die when he was turned off the cart but eventually he appeared to be dead and was cut down. Soon afterwards, however, he showed signs of recovering, breathing and opening his eyes – but he did not remain in this state for long because the sheriff's men quickly took him back to be hanged again, this time successfully.

The Ratcliffe Highway murders caused an enormous stir in 1811. They occurred in a densely packed part of the East End, close to the Pool of London. It was a lively, cosmopolitan area full of seamen looking for a good time, brothels, drinking houses, violence and crime. A mother and her baby, a young apprentice and a serving girl were all found dead, having been attacked with a savagery that appalled even the most hardened of the authorities. Shortly afterwards the murderer struck again, breaking into a pub and killing the landlord, his wife and another serving girl. A lodger managed to escape the carnage and partly as a result of his information a sailor by the name of Williams came under suspicion. The dingy garret in which he lived contained a number of possibly incriminating items. But Williams, if indeed he was the murderer, evaded justice by taking his own life, after which his body was buried with a stake through the heart at the junction of Cannon Street Road and Cable Street in what is now London E1.

Doubtless there were other locations in London north of the Thames where executions and other punishments took place occasionally, but the records for such events are meagre or non-existent.

NINE

Execution Dock, Wapping

> . . . privateers in time of war are a nursery for
> Pirates in time of peace.
>
> *Charles Johnson (probably Daniel Defoe),*
> Lives of the Most Notorious Pirates

'Execution Dock' was the nickname given to the spot on the north bank of the River Thames where pirates and others who had committed capital offences on tidal waters (or waters under the jurisdiction of the Admiralty) were executed. It stood between Wapping New Stairs and King Henry's Stairs off Wapping High Street, about a mile east of the Tower of London.

Wapping has for centuries looked to ships and the sea. It is likely that its origins go back to Saxon times, when much of the area was marshy. The land was reclaimed in a piecemeal fashion, and at the end of the sixteenth century the great Londoner chronicler John Stow (1525–1605) described it as 'filthy' and remarked that it contained many tenements and cottages occupied by sailors' victuallers. The district earned a reputation for raunchiness and Samuel Pepys recorded at some length the goings-on of the sailors of the Royal Navy who inhabited the district during the reign of Charles II. The area remained semi-rural in the eighteenth century, when Dr Johnson recommended a visit to Wapping as an eye-opener for those who had led a sheltered life. It is recorded that in 1750 the High Street contained no fewer than thirty-six taverns.

As the volume of shipping on the Thames built up, Wapping found itself at the heart of the Pool of London and it attracted a host of nautically based industries such as block-making and boat-building. In the nineteenth century the area around the High Street came to be dominated by tall and gaunt warehouses. Wapping was always a noisome place. London's air was fouled by the burning of ever increasing amounts of seacoal, and the sooty fog that resulted usually blew eastwards with the prevailing winds and settled like a grimy pall over Wapping and its environs. The area was hit hard during the bombing of London's docklands in the Second World War. For some years afterwards much of the area was semi-derelict but towards the end of the twentieth century Wapping underwent a process of gentrification and many of the warehouses have been converted into luxury riverside apartments with views to die for.

Looking at the Thames in central London today, with commercial shipping almost non-existent and riparian traffic dominated by pleasure-craft, it is hard for us to visualise the intensive use that was made of the river in earlier times, especially when London Bridge was the only crossing available. The Thames was a major highway. The watermen, yesteryear's equivalent of today's taxi-drivers, ferried travellers across the river or between various parts of the developing capital. The river offered a safer and quicker way of moving around London than the teeming streets with their slow-moving traffic and threatening criminal presence. The Pool of London was London's main port from Roman times until the building of the enclosed docks in the nineteenth century, and was always a sea of masts and a hive of activity. Wapping was at the centre of it.

Public executions and gibbetings were meant to be looked at. The banks of the Thames therefore provided an obvious place for the public execution and gibbeting of felons who had committed offences on tidal waters. Thus substantial numbers of pirates were executed at what became known as 'Execution Dock'. Further down the widening river the remains of many erstwhile pirates were displayed on gibbets at the water's edge. Their gory remains often lasted a surprisingly long time. The skeletal remains of Captain Smith, hanged at Execution Dock in 1708 and then gibbeted downstream, were still gazing sightlessly out over the dismal margins of the Thames five years later. Crows and other birds had long since had the fleshy bits.

The best-known pirate to be hanged at Execution Dock was the immortal Captain Kidd. Opinions have long been divided on Kidd's role in history. For some he is the absolute epitome of the swashbuckling and bloodthirsty buccaneer. For others his reputation is out of all proportion to his deeds and real significance, and he no more deserves to be portrayed as the role model of piracy than Dick Turpin deserves fame for his breakneck ride to York to establish an alibi, a ride that he made only in the pages of popular fiction. So who was the real Captain Kidd, what did he do and how did he come to end his days at Wapping in 1701? Was he, as some have asserted, a scapegoat and a stooge in complex political shenanigans?

William Kidd was born in Scotland around 1645 but little is known of his early life. He was certainly an experienced mariner and became the master of a number of small merchant vessels. In 1689, however, he became captain of the privateer *Blessed William*, operating from the Nevis Islands in the West Indies. He was ashore when his crew decided to seize the ship and go off in search of fresh prey, but now as pirates rather than privateers. Kidd was given another ship, *Antigua* and set off in hot pursuit of the *Blessed William*. He never caught it. He arrived in New York and put down temporary roots, marrying a rich widow in May 1691 and making a number of influential contacts among local business leaders, including one by the name of Robert Livingston. In 1695 Kidd took *Antigua* to England, hoping to get a licence for privateering from the Admiralty Court. While in London he and Livingston made the acquaintance of the Earl of Bellomont, who was just about to take up duties as Governor of New York and Massachusetts. Together the three men concocted a scheme to capture pirate ships and seize their booty, but instead of returning the goods to their rightful owners, they would sell everything for their own profit. In other words, they decided on piracy rather than privateering. They then brought in as sleeping partners four men who would provide financial sponsorship and receive a substantial share of the profits. Not surprisingly, these arrangements were kept secret, since the sponsors included a secretary of state, several senior judges and Admiralty officials. Even William III was apparently going to pocket 10 per cent of the profits!

Kidd then sailed in the 300-ton, 34-gun *Adventure Galley* with a royal commission to attack French shipping tacitly; he was also to seek out and capture a number of specified pirates and to keep captured ships and their cargoes without submitting them to be examined and assessed by the usual authorities. Instead Kidd was to submit his booty to Governor Bellomont at Boston. These arrangements meant that Kidd risked all the hazards of the sea and took on ships that were often able to give a good account of themselves. In return he received only a very small proportion of the profits in relation to the risks involved. Kidd may well have thought this too as he took unilateral action. He promised his crew 60 per cent of the profits although the initial agreement had stated that Bellomont was to receive 60 per cent. Kidd also decided to turn pirate.

For about four years Kidd cruised the Indian Ocean with only mediocre success. A degree of caution was necessary because it was often difficult to assess the fighting capability of strange vessels when they were first sighted. Kidd, however, tended towards the timorous rather than the sensibly cautious. Unfortunately for him, the only language his motley crew understood was resolute leadership resulting in bold and successful plunder. When Kidd repeatedly refused to take on ships he felt unsure about and only captured small and relatively worthless prey, the crew became increasingly restive. One crew member, Moore, was bolder than the others and remonstrated with Kidd when he allowed a well-found Dutch vessel to escape unscathed. It was an acrimonious confrontation which ended when Kidd smashed a heavy bucket over the man's head and killed him. Such decisive action elicited grudging admiration from his crew of murderous brigands.

Kidd's only substantial capture was that of the *Quedah Merchant*, sailing under a French flag. This vessel was leased by a number of important officials connected to the very influential East India Company. Kidd added insult to injury when he renamed the vessel *Adventure Prize* and used her as his main patrolling ship. Kidd's continued reluctance to chance his arm against unknown ships frustrated his crew so much that when the ship stopped at Madagascar most of them deserted and joined Robert Culliford, a particularly notorious pirate, whose powerful and well-found ship just happened to be in port and whose leadership they thought was likely to prove more productive. They took with them much of the loot from the *Quedah Merchant*. According to Kidd, they also destroyed the log of the *Adventure Galley*. He insisted that this would have helped to exonerate him but its disappearance weighed against him at his trial.

Kidd was now officially recognised as a pirate rather than a privateer and a manhunt was launched to seek him out and capture him. His sponsors meanwhile must have viewed Kidd's activities with mixed emotions. Doubtless they were eager to make him pay for breaking the agreements under which he was employed to go off freelancing. At the same time they must have been dreading his capture in case he revealed the terms of the original privateering commission and named the people behind it. The best thing would be for Kidd to be killed while attempting to evade arrest – if it could be arranged.

Kidd learned that the authorities were after him when he put in at the Caribbean island of Anguilla in April 1699. He decided to head for Boston, hoping that Governor Bellomont would provide him with support. He was therefore horrified when he was seized and thrown into prison; soon he was placed in irons and sent by sea to stand trial in London for piracy and for murdering the seaman Moore. Kidd now unwittingly found himself embroiled in the bitter squabbles between the Tory and Whig factions. The Tories had found out about the Whig sponsors of Kidd's activities and heaped pressure on him to reveal all, but Kidd's only concern was to prove that he was not a pirate and that Moore's death was justified because he was a mutineer. Sadly for him, Kidd was found guilty of both piracy and murder. He was executed at Wapping on 23 May 1701 and his body displayed in chains in a gibbet further downstream where it would be seen by those on board the innumerable ships making their way to and from London.

The case of Captain Kidd, the ruthless pirate of legend, has attracted interest ever since. That he killed Moore and embarked on a career as a pirate cannot be denied. Controversy tends to centre on whether he had a fair trial. Was he a stooge? Did those in high places, threatened by what he might possibly reveal, decide to ensure his silence by having him framed, prosecuted and judicially hanged? Certain evidence that might at least partially have exculpated Kidd went missing and could not be produced in court. The only two witnesses used by the prosecution had deserted Kidd early on, and although both had later engaged in piratical activities they each received pardons as a reward for their evidence against Kidd. There are also unanswered questions about why Kidd accepted the agreement under which he sailed as the front man for his rich and influential sponsors. His financial rewards under this agreement were far less generous than was normal. Is it realistic to suppose that Kidd would not turn pirate? He and his sponsors would all have known that the potential reward from piratical activity was far greater. Why sponsor a privateering commission of dubious provenance when a pirate cruise would be likely to generate a far greater income? How could it happen that Kidd, despite having official letters of marque as a privateer, was boarded as he sailed down the Thames estuary by a Royal Navy vessel which impressed eighty of his hand-picked crew? Why was no one ever called to account for this illegal act? It left Kidd with little option but to replace them with a motley collection of shifty villains and murderous scapegraces.

A further mystery concerns the fate of Kidd's treasure. There is not a shred of real evidence to prove that it ever existed, but millions of words have been written about this hoard and several expeditions have sallied forth determined to locate and claim it. Fifty years ago this treasure was valued at £1 million. Kidd himself would only have made the merest fraction of this sum as a result of his activities. For those who have tried to find it, it has proved an expensive holy grail.

Hard facts have never been allowed to stand in the way of the creation of myths and the emergence of legends. Kidd is still probably the first name that comes to mind when pirates are mentioned. His exploits, largely imagined, have appeared in countless comics and penny dreadfuls, in fiction and on the silver screen. Numerous contemporary ballads and broadsheets commemorated his activities with a mixture of envious admiration and moral indignation. Here is a sample from one such ballad:

I murdered William Moore, as I sailed, as I sailed,
I murdered William Moore, as I sailed.
I murdered William Moore and left him in his gore,
Not many leagues from shore, as I sailed, as I sailed,
Not many leagues from shore as I sailed.

My name was William Kidd, when I sailed, when I sailed,
My name was William Kidd, when I sailed,
My name was William Kidd, God's laws I did forbid,
And so wickedly I did, when I sailed, when I sailed,
And so wickedly I did when I sailed . . .

I'd ninety bars of gold, as I sailed, as I sailed,
I'd ninety bars of gold, as I sailed,
I'd ninety bars of gold and dollars manifold,
With riches uncontrolled as I sailed, as I sailed,
With riches uncontrolled as I sailed . . .

Condemned pirates were usually housed in the Marshalsea Prison in Southwark and brought in procession across London Bridge, through the city and past the Tower to be executed at Wapping. Others were brought from Newgate. The procession might draw large crowds as it passed through the streets, and for particularly notorious pirates the multitude of spectators at Execution Dock would be augmented by more crowds on the water in boats, or indeed on any other perch which offered a good vantage point. Large numbers would crowd around the gallows, which meant that some would be standing on or even partly sinking into the oozing, vile-smelling Thames mud. The procession was not dissimilar to those which travelled from Newgate to Tyburn because the condemned man rode in a cart accompanied by the prison chaplain. The procession was preceded by the Admiral Marshal or his deputy, bearing the silver oar that symbolised the authority of the Admiralty. The whole was accompanied by two city marshals and a posse of guards.

The condemned man was allowed to address the crowd at Execution Dock and could say more or less whatever he wished. Some harangued the authorities and others held forth on the injustice of the situation in which they found themselves, reiterating their innocence even at this late stage. Some pirates had discovered God at the eleventh hour and spoke piously to the crowd about the wages of sin. Such speeches were greeted with catcalls and abuse, as were those pirates whose reserves of fortitude had run out, leaving them crying hysterically and quaking with terror as they were assisted on to the gallows.

The gallows at Execution Dock was made of wood and consisted of two uprights joined at the top by a crossbeam from which the hangman's rope was suspended. A ladder was placed against the gallows and the prisoner, now with a hood over his head, was assisted up the ladder by the executioner, who then put the noose around his neck. When the marshal gave the signal, the executioner pushed the prisoner off the ladder. This did not cause instant death and sometimes friends or relations of the victim would rush forward to pull on his legs in an effort to end his agonies as quickly as possible. Until the beginning of the nineteenth century the body of the executed man was left to be submerged by the rising tide three times, this seemingly curious ritual emphasising that the offences had been committed on tidal water and therefore within the jurisdiction of the Lord High Admiral rather than the land-based authorities. The body was then taken away either for interment in an unmarked grave, for dissection at Surgeons' Hall or for hanging in a gibbet at some conspicuous spot further downstream on the banks of the Thames. Kidd himself was displayed in a cage hanging from a gibbet at Tilbury Point.

The Ordinary, Paul Lorrain, had found it impossible, in spite of his persistent efforts, to extract a confession or even a statement indicative of remorse from Kidd. He continued to declare his innocence of piracy and murder right up to his last moments, which were more than usually unpleasant because the rope snapped as Kidd was turned off the ladder and he plunged into the glutinous mud below while still conscious. He was extracted like a cork from a bottle and taken back to the gallows. Such was Lorrain's zeal that he climbed halfway up the ladder as the wretched man was being prepared to be relaunched into eternity. He was still intoning prayers and remorselessly exhorting penitence as Kidd was hanged once more, this time successfully. He was probably glad to get on his way.

A pirate who rather more closely conformed to the popular stereotype was the Scotsman John Smith, better known by his alias, John Gow. He was the ringleader of a particularly bloody mutiny on board the merchant ship *George Galley* off the coast of north-west Africa in November 1724. Several officers, including the captain, had their throats cut, some while they were asleep. Gow was then elected captain after the rest of the crew had been persuaded, occasionally with threats of violence, to turn pirate. An experienced seaman, it had not taken him long to realise that the *George Galley*, well found and equipped as it was with twenty guns, would make a fine pirate cruiser.

The ship was renamed *Revenge* and Gow and his men met with some success plundering merchantmen off the coasts of Spain and Portugal. Gow then persuaded his crew to head for Scapa Flow in the Orkney Islands to shelter for the winter and re-equip the ship. However, when they got there things started going badly wrong. Several members of the crew deserted and informed the authorities of the presence of a pirate ship in the vicinity.

Others plundered local settlements and abducted a number of women. *Revenge* ran aground and the remaining pirates were easily captured by a Royal Navy ship. Gow and his men were transported to London and placed in the Marshalsea. When Gow refused to plead, his thumbs were bound together and squeezed with whipcord – but he stayed resolute despite the awful pain. Next he was taken to Newgate and threatened with the *peine forte et dure*. This horrible torture was otherwise known as pressing, and is translated as 'strong, hard pain'. This was enough to persuade him to enter a plea of 'not guilty'. But it did him little good and he and his right-hand man, Williams, were hanged at Execution Dock early in 1725. Their bodies were displayed in chains, one near Deptford, the other at Greenwich. It was probably John Gow who inspired Sir Walter Scott's hugely popular novel *The Pirate*, published in 1821.

In 1738 John Richardson and Richard Coyle were hanged at Execution Dock. Richardson in particular had had a remarkable career. A native of New York, he devoted a quite extraordinary amount of energy to the relentless pursuit of sexual conquests. He was still only a teenager when it became expedient for him to go to sea because he had made his employer's daughter pregnant. He sailed to Amsterdam, where he made the first mate's wife his mistress. An enterprising fellow, Richardson was always on the alert for criminal opportunities and in Amsterdam he stole valuable goods from a warehouse before sailing back to America. A youth of considerable charm, he became friendly with a family whose household contained three pretty daughters and four toothsome maidservants. Here were riches indeed! It is likely that he wooed all seven of them and won their favours. Each of the three daughters entertained hopes of marriage to Richardson, but he had already set his sights on the daughter of a well-to-do local magistrate. The forthcoming marriage was soon announced. When the banns were read in church, a dumbfounded congregation was treated to the astonishing sight – and sound – of all seven young ladies objecting to the marriage on the grounds that Richardson had made them pregnant. Richardson slipped away from the church with as much insouciance as he could muster. The magistrate promptly withdrew his consent to his daughter's marriage – only to implore Richardson to marry her shortly afterwards when his daughter confirmed that she too was pregnant.

Richardson had some nerve. His seven earlier conquests were now pursuing him for maintenance. The magistrate and Richardson, for entirely different reasons, wanted to avoid any further scandal and therefore reached an agreement. The magistrate gave Richardson all the money that would pass to his daughter on her marriage (which was to go ahead), while Richardson for his part signed an undertaking that he would not abscond with it. Drawing once more on his charm, he then persuaded one and all that he could put the money to immediate and effective use by going to Boston and investing it in the building of a merchant trading vessel. He earnestly promised that he would return within three months. Inevitably, perhaps, they never saw him again.

Some young men might have found all this excitement too much for them and reined back somewhat on their amorous activities, but not Richardson. In Boston he seduced the wife of a Quaker and then stole £70 from her husband before moving to Philadelphia, where he found lodgings with an attractive widow and her two lovely daughters. Readers will probably not be surprised to learn that he seduced all three and then obtained a considerable dowry from the mother in return for marrying the younger of her two daughters, who was now, of course, a fallen woman. Adding bigamy to his various other misdemeanours, Richardson took the money and vanished once more.

Richardson eventually ended up in England, where he seduced a wealthy heiress from Kent. She fell desperately in love with him, as indeed they all did. The promise of marriage was enough to persuade the lady to make over all her considerable fortune to him – whereupon once more he vanished. This time he made for Venice and decided to sign on as a crew member on an English ship which had just arrived with a cargo of pilchards. Now he made his first mistake. He was persuaded to play a leading role in the crew's mutinous plan to murder the captain and seize the ship. This they did. Richard Coyle took over as captain and Richardson assumed the duties of first mate. The ship eventually put into Tunis, where the British consul accepted Richardson's convincing explanation that the captain had been lost during a storm. The authorities even provided the crew with some money, but Coyle got drunk and started boasting about the mutiny and murder. He was arrested but Richardson, slippery as ever, got away. However, news of the brutal murder soon began to circulate around the Mediterranean, along with a description of the wanted Richardson, and he was soon captured. Sent back to England, he was hanged at Execution Dock with Coyle on 25 January 1738.

Hangings ceased at Execution Dock in 1831 but few had taken place in the preceding decades. Among them was the hanging of Captain John Sutherland in 1809. He had stabbed his young black servant while in a drunken rage. Despite a show of contrition and fear, which the crowd usually treated with contempt, he was given a hero's send-off. This was because most of the spectators did not think that the killing of a black youth constituted a serious enough crime to warrant the death sentence; they considered that Sutherland was the victim of a miscarriage of justice.

In Wapping High Street stands the well-known riverside pub, the Town of Ramsgate. It is still possible to sit at the rear of this historic building overlooking the Thames and observe the place where the executions were carried out. There is even a mock gallows complete with a noose on the site. Execution Dock, incidentally, never was a dock in the normal sense of the word; instead the name derived from cockney gallows humour. A much newer pub, opened since the area has become gentrified, is called the Captain Kidd. Thus are myths perpetuated.

Execution Dock was not just used for the hanging of pirates. In 1754 Captain Lancey was executed for scuttling the brig of which he was master, and in 1802 William Codlin, master of the brig *Adventure*, was executed for destroying his ship by boring holes in her hull in an attempt to defraud the insurers. James Lowry was hanged in 1752 for flogging a seaman to death and John Smith and Robert Mayne were hanged for mutiny in 1762. In 1771 another ship's master was hanged for murdering a cabin boy.

The Pool of London extended downriver from London Bridge as far as Rotherhithe and Wapping. The plundering of ships' cargoes, both on the water and on the quayside, was perhaps the greatest single criminal enterprise in a city always noted for lawbreaking, and it reached its peak in the eighteenth and early nineteenth centuries. By 1797 more than 10,000 coasting vessels and 3,500 ocean-going ships were using the Pool annually. London was the richest, largest and busiest port in the world at this time and vast numbers of thieves, both professional and amateur, took full advantage. It was all too easy. The quays and jetties could not cope with the sheer volume of shipping and so the river was cluttered with vessels waiting to be unloaded. Large numbers of ships were moored in the river and their cargoes transferred into lighters and then left on the quayside or stored in nearby warehouses. Supervision and security were almost non-existent and at every stage there were opportunities for theft, both systematic and casual. Even after the docks were built, Joseph Conrad wrote in 1879 of his experiences as a seaman: 'London, the oldest and greatest of river ports, does not possess as much as a hundred yards of open quays upon its river front. Dark and impenetrable at night, like the face of a forest, is the London waterside.' It is likely that most of the port's workforce boosted their income by engaging in pilfering. Additionally, professional criminal networks creamed off so much that shipping companies often complained that they might lose as much as half their cargo to theft while their vessels were in the Pool of London.

Most of the more professional plundering was neither more nor less than piracy. The most determined river pirates operated at night. Known as 'night plunderers', they were well armed and they boarded lighters and barges that they knew contained worthwhile and easily portable cargoes. These were seized, taken ashore and then sold through a sophisticated network of receivers, who themselves put up the finance for these operations and often colluded with the ships' officers and the revenue men. 'Heavy horsemen' were quayside workers who wore baggy clothing to conceal the goods they systematically filched. 'River pirates' cut lighters adrift and pillaged their goods as they drifted. 'Mudlarks' threw goods overboard and retrieved them from the mud at low tide. It was to tackle the predations of these people that the London River Police force was established in 1798 and soon afterwards the enclosed and more easily secured docks began to be built.

Ashore there was a ready market for almost any kinds of goods stolen from the ships and an army of crooked businessmen bought and sold this bounty. Nowadays goods of dubious provenance being sold cheaply are often said to have 'fallen off the back of a lorry'. In the nineteenth century they were said to have 'dropped off a ship in the Thames'. The Pool of London was in effect a vast floating warehouse containing a range of goods so enormous as to be able to satisfy the wants of each and every Londoner. Goods sold at a fraction of the price they would have fetched had they gone through the normal channels of business (and if customs and excise duties had been paid). This then was Wapping and the environs of Execution Dock.

The authors were unable to establish when the first executions took place at Execution Dock or to obtain information as to the number of miscreants who ended their lives there. There seems a surprising dearth of archive material and they feel sure that many more than those mentioned must have died at Wapping. If any readers could provide more information or pointers in the right direction, they would be most grateful.

TEN

Executions South of the Thames

London seems to me like some hoary massive
underworld, a hoary ponderous inferno.
D.H. Lawrence (1885–1930)

Kennington is a low-lying district in the London
Borough of Lambeth. The origins of its name may
indicate that in Saxon times it was in royal hands. A
palace existed there in the fourteenth century belonging to
Edward of Woodstock, Prince of Wales (1330–76), better
known as the Black Prince. Royalty continued to reside in
the district sporadically until the seventeenth century.
Kennington Common, now Kennington Park, was the
principal place of execution on the Surrey bank of the
Thames, where those convicted of capital crimes at
St Margaret's Court in Borough High Street were put to
death. The area witnessed very much the same kinds of
revelry among the crowds that was such a feature of the
processions from Newgate to Tyburn and the same
jostling and jollities around the scaffold.

London, and indeed the whole of England, was in a
state of turmoil in 1746 because of fears of a Jacobite
uprising. The Jacobites sought to restore the Stuart
dynasty to the throne after James II had been deposed in
the Glorious Revolution of 1688–9. Concerns about the
danger they posed were probably exaggerated and the

threat more insubstantial than it appeared. Thus rebels and sympathisers were quickly taken up by the authorities. Among them were Francis Townley, George Fletcher and James Dawson. They were held in Horsemonger Lane Gaol and then dragged on hurdles to be executed at Kennington Common on 20 July. Townley, regarded as the ringleader, was dealt with first. He was cut down while still alive and then decapitated. His heart was extracted and then burned while his body was quartered. Townley had ordered an expensive new velvet suit especially for the occasion and met his death with courage. The others then received similar treatment. The body parts of these men were parboiled and pickled and sent for display not only on Temple Bar in London but as far afield as Carlisle and Manchester, as a gory warning of the perils of committing treason.

In 1749 Richard Coleman was hanged at Kennington Common. A young girl called Sarah Green was returning from a party in the early hours when three men attacked her. Later, lying seriously injured in hospital, she declared that she had heard one of them addressed by the name 'Coleman'. A few days later Coleman was sitting, rather drunk, in a Southwark pub when he got into a row with a stranger who suggested that he had had something to do with the attack on Sarah. He was arrested and brought to the hospital. After twice declaring that she could not be sure that Coleman was one of her attackers, she then said that she did indeed recognise him. She died shortly afterwards from her injuries. Coleman escaped but a warrant was issued for his arrest and a reward was offered to anyone apprehending him. From a secret hiding place Coleman took the unusual step of announcing his innocence in the *London Gazette* and declaring his confidence in the judicial system. He then gave himself up, only to find that his confidence was sadly misplaced. In spite of the fact that witnesses came forward to say that he was elsewhere when the attack had taken place, he was found guilty. Later it was proved that three other men had perpetrated the murderous attack and poor Coleman had been innocent all along.

Jerry Abershaw was a beguiling criminal. Dashing, courteous and insouciant, he very much fitted the mistakenly glamorous image of Britain's highwaymen, or 'Knights of the High Toby' as they were known in the seventeenth and eighteenth centuries. He was born in 1773 and took to the road when only 17 years of age, Putney Heath and Wimbledon Common being his favoured hunting grounds. Little is known about his personal life, although he was unusual in not being given to roistering with the easy-going doxies who liked to cluster around a liberally spending 'gentleman of the road'.

Abershaw's partner in crime was Richard Ferguson, known appreciatively as 'Galloping Dick'. Ferguson seemed to have a natural affinity with horses, as well as powerful libidinous urges towards the opposite sex. The former often secured him employment, the latter was frequently the cause of his losing it.

Ferguson's usual work was as a postilion and it was when driving a gentleman along the Great North Road that he was stopped by two highwaymen working together, one of whom he recognised as Jerry Abershaw. For his part, Abershaw knew he had been recognised but he and his partner made off quickly when they heard the sounds of approaching travellers. Soon afterwards their paths crossed again in a wayside inn. Ferguson probably hoped to try a little blackmail, given what he knew about Abershaw, but he found himself entranced by Abershaw's company, his generosity (he paid for their food and drink) and the ripping yarns he told about his adventures on the road. Cleverly Abershaw brought in and landed his catch. He flattered Ferguson, expressing astonishment that he was 'only' a postilion and suggested that the two of them could work together for their mutual financial benefit. Ferguson's employment and contacts would enable him to provide Abershaw with information about travellers, any valuables they were likely to be carrying with them, and the routes and times of their journeys.

This proposal appealed to Ferguson's innate greed and for some time his new working relationship with Abershaw prospered. However, he was not smart enough to conceal his new-found wealth and he soon drew attention to himself with his liberal spending and his relaxed attitude to work – which meant that he frequently did not bother to turn up. The result was that he was sacked from one job after another until he decided to take to the road as a highwayman – ironically at almost exactly the same time that Abershaw was arrested, charged and found guilty of robbery on the highway.

Abershaw was apprehended in Southwark, in the process shooting one of the Bow Street Runners involved. The man died. Abershaw got away but was soon retaken and brought to justice. He showed no signs of remorse and even mimicked the judge as he placed the black cap on his head to pronounce the death sentence. He decorated the walls of his condemned cell with sketches (using the juice of black cherries as ink) depicting him carrying out his robberies. In the cart travelling to his execution he maintained a stream of cheerful banter with the guards and exchanged salutations with acquaintances in the throng. A large, approving crowd turned out to witness his execution at Kennington Common in August 1795 after which his body was gibbeted at Putney, attracting tens of thousands of visitors over the following weeks. Abershaw was just 22 when he died. 'Galloping Dick' was himself caught and hanged in 1800.

Kennington Common as such no longer exists, except for a fragment which is now Kennington Park. St Mark's Church close to Oval Underground station is thought to stand on the spot where the executions took place. It is claimed that the base of the gibbet has been found under the church.

Also in Southwark is St Thomas Waterings at the junction of the present Old Kent Road and Albany Road. Centuries ago this site was used for executions and a number of Catholic martyrs died there, including John Jones on 12 July 1598. A Catholic priest who had been ordained abroad, he returned to England to minister illicitly to covert groups of Catholic worshippers. Heretics were regarded as traitors at that time and so they suffered the punishment for treason, which was hanging, drawing and quartering. Unusually John Pibush had to wait six years for his execution after he had been convicted of treason in 1600. In 1593 John Penry was executed here for sedition. From the point of view of the authorities St Thomas Waterings was an advantageous site because it was distant enough from the densely populated parts of Southwark and the city to attract only small crowds. It is likely that many people died at this spot because it was a recognised place of execution for Surrey felons before Horsemonger Lane Gaol came into use. In 1603 Valentine Thomas, convicted of treason, was hanged and disembowelled at an unrecorded location in the Old Kent Road.

Horsemonger Lane Gaol was the common name for the Surrey County Gaol built in Southwark in the 1770s. It had the usual unattractive exterior of such places and usually housed only petty offenders and debtors, but felons from Surrey were executed on the roof of the gatehouse. The occupiers of nearby houses used to rent out their front windows at exorbitant rates on execution days, much as they did in Old Bailey, north of the river. Occasionally executions took place outside the gaol.

Colonel Edward Marcus Despard was one of the most notorious offenders to be hanged at Horsemonger Lane, in his case for 'treasonable conspiracy'. Something of a scoundrel, Despard had hurriedly left his army post in Honduras after questions began to be asked about various unsatisfactory aspects of his conduct. Although official inquiries later cleared him, his military career was finished and he was left nursing a sense of grievance. He began to associate with political dissidents and consequently came to the attention of government spies, who decided it was expedient for him to be placed in custody during the Irish Rebellion of 1798. This only furthered his feelings of disaffection and soon after his release in 1800 he was arrested in a Lambeth pub with a large number of confederates, on information once again provided by undercover government agents. It seems that Despard was at the centre of a crazy plot to assassinate the king and seize the Tower of London and the Bank of England. Among the many witnesses called to attest to the honour of Despard's character was none other than Horatio, Lord Nelson. Although the jury found Despard guilty, they recommended clemency in view of his military service. It was all to no avail, although he was spared the agony and indignity of being drawn and quartered. He died bravely in 1803. For many years the hurdle on which Despard was drawn to his execution was preserved but it has since disappeared.

Richard Patch was a Devonian who was hanged on top of Horsemonger Lane Gaol in 1806. Unable to make his farm in Devon a paying proposition, he moved to London and bought himself into a partnership with Isaac Blight, a ship-breaker who was in some financial difficulty. It is likely that Patch did a secret deal with Blight to assist him in getting off the hook, at least as far as his money troubles were concerned. But perhaps Patch became greedy and tried to get away without paying Blight the whole amount promised. Perhaps Blight objected and Patch therefore decided to kill him. However it came about, the unfortunate Blight was shot through the window of his house and died of his injuries the following day. The case attracted considerable interest at the time. Although there were some anomalies in the evidence – including the fact that the shots were fired from outside the house but Patch was present inside the house immediately afterwards – he was found guilty.

Mr and Mrs Manning were hanged in 1849 for murdering her former lover, Patrick O'Connor. The motive was identified as revenge for substantial losses the couple had incurred as a result of bad financial advice given by O'Connor. The latter was attacked with a chisel and also shot fatally, after which he was buried under the kitchen floor. The Mannings, although partners in this crime, were by no means the closest of married couples and the nervous and physical energy expended in killing O'Connor seems also to have destroyed their relationship. They fell out, this time permanently. Manning tried to sell some of their assets and then absconded to Jersey, while Mrs Manning went to O'Connor's lodgings and stole a number of items which she proceeded to sell before decamping to Edinburgh. It had been an ill thought-out murder and these subsequent foolishly greedy acts soon aroused the suspicions of the police, who duly discovered O'Connor's body. In court the Mannings each tried to fix the blame on the other. Mrs Manning treated the court to a scathing tirade about the shortcomings of the English judicial system, after which she threw some of the aromatic herbs traditionally scattered around the court at the judge as he was pronouncing sentence. A strikingly handsome woman of Swiss extraction, she appeared on the scaffold wearing a black satin dress. In so doing, she provoked a wave of revulsion against that particular material which lasted for up to thirty years. It is testimony to the theatrical and pervasive effect of hangings on spectators and on popular culture as a whole that fashion could be affected in this way. The execution of the Mannings also had a profound effect on Charles Dickens, who watched the event and observed the animalistic behaviour of the crowd as they bayed for the blood of this singularly repulsive pair of murderers. Dickens did not know which was worse, the appearance of the Mannings in their death throes or the expectant voyeuristic faces in the crowd. The sight only made him even more determined to work for the end of the system that made a public spectacle out of the deaths of such unpleasant people.

The execution of the Mannings was the first in England since 1700 of a married couple and it attracted enormous interest both for that reason and because of the histrionics in court of the spirited and fiery Mrs Manning, who somehow managed to be both tantalisingly attractive and repulsive at the same time. The balladeers and broadside publishers did especially well and here is an example of their efforts, quoted in D.D. Cooper's book *The Lessons of the Scaffold*:

> See what numbers are approaching
> To Horsemonger's fatal tree
> Full of bloom in health and vigour
> What a dreadful sight to see.
> Old and young pray take a warning
> Females lead a virtuous life
> Think you of that fateful morning
> Frederick Manning and his wife.

On 16 April 1862 James Longhurst was hanged at Horsemonger Lane for murdering a girl of 7. The heinousness of his crime ensured an especially large and hostile crowd. As usual, numerous handbills were sold at the scene. These verses give a flavour of the typical doggerel such handbills contained:

> Good people all I pray draw near,
> And my sad history you soon shall hear
> And when the same I do relate,
> I trust you will a warning take.
> At Horsemonger-lane on the scaffold high,
> For a cruel murder I was doomed to die.

> James Longhurst, it is my name,
> I've brought myself to grief and shame,
> Through the dreadful deed that I had done,
> At Churchill-field, near Guildford town.

It was in last June, the twenty-eighth,
I did this deed as I now state;
An innocent child I there did slay,
And with a knife took her life away . . .

The Judge said, James Longhurst you are guilty found,
You will go from here to London town
And there you'll die a death of shame,
And meet your fate at Horsemonger-lane . . .

Horsemonger Lane Gaol closed in 1878 and was demolished in 1880. Its site is now covered by Newington Recreation Ground.

Wandsworth Prison was originally planned to replace Brixton but as so often happens intentions were overtaken by events. It usually housed prisoners serving short sentences but in 1878 it took over from Horsemonger Lane as the south London location for judicial hangings. It is situated in south-west London close to Wandsworth and Clapham Commons.

Catherine or 'Kate' Webster, also known as Catherine Lawler, was born in Ireland and migrated to the London area in search of work. She found honest employment but it did not provide sufficient income for her perceived needs and so she turned to crime, specialising in robbing lodging houses. Rather more ambitiously, she then decided to rob and murder her employer, Mrs Thomas, a comfortably off widow in Richmond-on-Thames, and to sell whatever of her assets she could lay her hands on. She attacked Mrs Thomas with a meat cleaver, killed her, made a bodged job of dismembering her and then boiled her body parts, selling the fat to neighbours to use as dripping. The head of the unfortunate Mrs Thomas was never found, although bits of her body were found as far away as Twickenham and Barnes. Although Kate fled to Ireland, she was swiftly arrested and brought back to London. She was convicted of murder and hanged at Wandsworth on 29 July 1879.

When perusing lists of murderers, it is interesting to note that many of them are members of the medical profession. Medical men and women have a uniquely trusted role in society and their knowledge of and access to potentially lethal substances has made their path to crime a little more slippery. George Henry Lamson was a general practitioner who found himself in financial difficulties because he was a morphine addict. He took to murder in the hope of ending his financial problems, although it is not clear quite how he thought this would be achieved. When his father-in-law died he left Lamson's wife and her two brothers very considerable sums of money. Lamson chose as his victim one of the brothers, Percy, a disabled youth of 18, and administered a lethal dose of poison in a piece of Dundee cake. It was a clever move because at that time there was no way to detect scientifically the poison used, aconitine. Lamson then fled to Paris but the chemist who had sold him the poison had read about the murder in the newspapers and contacted the police. Lamson was quickly brought back to England and convicted of murder. He was hanged at Wandsworth Prison on 28 April 1882.

A little medical knowledge can go a long way and so it was with Severin Klosowski, alias George Chapman, who was born in Poland and trained as a barber-surgeon. He emigrated to London in 1888 where he married bigamously, living with both 'wives' in the East End. Eventually the first wife disappeared. A serial philanderer,

Chapman had many affairs, sometimes involving cohabitation, but three of his relationships ended abruptly when the women concerned fell ill with vomiting and diarrhoea and then died. The police became suspicious and when the bodies were exhumed they showed traces of antimony poisoning. Antimony is a metallic substance and one of the classic murderers' poisons. It is usually administered in the form of a white powder in small quantities over a protracted period and causes sickness, abdominal pain, loss of appetite and diarrhoea. All these symptoms are entirely compatible with – and thus mistaken for – common diseases of the stomach, but they led inevitably to death. Chapman was convicted of one murder and was hanged at Wandsworth in April 1903. Some historians believe that Chapman was Jack the Ripper, based on his surgical knowledge and the fact he knew his way round the Whitechapel and Spitalfields areas of London so well, having lived there for some years.

Before his retirement, Sir Henry Wilson had reached the rank of Chief of the Imperial General Staff without at any time particularly distinguishing himself as a professional soldier. A Protestant, he was a vehement opponent of the Irish Republican movement. On 22 June 1922 he unveiled a war memorial at Liverpool Street station and was returning to his house in Eaton Square in all his military finery when he was shot dead by two Irish nationalists. Police were on the scene very quickly and gave chase. A running battle developed in the street and two police officers were seriously wounded before the assassins were overpowered. Both were hanged at Wandsworth a few months later.

In 1927 PC Gutteridge was cold-bloodedly shot down and murdered in the execution of his duty. Frederick

Browne was a career criminal, strong and violent, a nasty piece of work who habitually carried a gun. He had served time in prison for a considerable variety of offences but his main criminal enterprise was receiving and selling stolen cars. His partner was a shifty little ne'er-do-well called Pat Kennedy, who dealt in stolen bicycles and also had a string of criminal convictions. Their operations were based in a private workshop/garage in the Clapham district of south-west London. One cold night in September 1927 they were driving around rural Essex in a car stolen from a house in Billericay when they attracted the attention of PC Gutteridge, who was on night patrol duties. He signalled them to stop. His dead body was found the next morning. He had been fatally shot through the head. The most chilling aspect of the crime was that, while still alive, he had been shot through each eye.

The next morning the stolen car was recovered in Brixton. Examination by forensic experts revealed bloodstains and a spent cartridge case. So far so good – but then the trail went cold. Some months later Browne was arrested after a car accident in Sheffield. The police raided the garage in Clapham, where they discovered not only a number of stolen vehicles but more importantly cartridges of the sort that had killed PC Gutteridge. Meanwhile Kennedy had fled to Liverpool, and it was typical of this little man's overblown image of himself as a gangster that he took out and brandished a gun when confronted by the police. It was equally typical of his general ineffectuality that when he pressed the gun against the officer's body and squeezed the trigger, it failed to fire because he had left the safety catch on. Kennedy quickly grassed and the police were able to put together a full reconstruction of events on that fateful night in Essex.

Not surprisingly, it was Browne who had fired the gun on that occasion but the court found both men guilty of murder and both were hanged, Kennedy at Wandsworth and Browne at Pentonville.

Harry Dobkin had 'loser' written all over him. In 1920 he married Rachel Dubinski but it was clearly less than a love-match because the couple split up after just three days. Sadly a child was conceived as a result of their union. Dobkin was hardly a loving father and wanted nothing to do with the child. He was steadfastly pursued by Rachel to ensure that he paid maintenance, and when he failed to do so, she saw to it that the authorities were told. The result was that Dobkin spent several short periods in prison. He grew to loathe Rachel, especially as she repeatedly sought him out and made embarrassing scenes, publicly upbraiding him for his many inadequacies. Then in 1941, while London was reeling under the Blitz, Rachel disappeared. Dobkin was a fire-watcher but he attracted some criticism for failing to report a fire in the crypt of the church next door to the building where he was on duty. This lapse on his part was quite understandable because just over a year later the body of a woman was found in this crypt. It had been mutilated in an attempt to prevent identification but the head, which had been severed from the body, lay close by and was soon identified as that of Rachel Dobkin. It was clear that she had been strangled. Dobkin's patience had obviously run out after yet another acrimonious confrontation and he had murdered her. On 27 January 1943 Dobkin was hanged at Wandsworth Prison.

The much-derided voice of 'Lord Haw-Haw', broadcasting from Germany, boomed out of the radio sets of the British nation for five years during the Second

World War. With his marked nasal intonation and exaggerated 'Oxford' accent, he regaled the British public with regular news bulletins consisting almost entirely of a catalogue of British setbacks and disasters. Sometimes his listeners would roll around helpless with mirth as he announced the total annihilation by bombing of the town in which they were living at the time or the sinking with all hands of a naval vessel that had entered harbour just five minutes earlier. However, for much of the war things did not go Britain's way and with wild rumours already circulating Lord Haw-Haw was just plausible enough to encourage the large-scale sapping of morale that was, of course, precisely his intention.

William Joyce, for that was his name, was small of stature. He had a prominent jawline, severely cropped hair and a noticeable scar on his right cheek, probably made by a razor during a street brawl in the days when he was a member of Oswald Mosley's 'Blackshirts'. He has to be given some credit for his apparently genuine and wholehearted, if misguided, belief that Britain needed an extreme right-wing political regime in order to restore its fortunes. In the aftermath of the First World War, with the decline of her staple industries, growing unemployment and economic recession, Joyce was by no means alone in advocating such a drastic solution. Many establishment figures in Britain had more than a lingering admiration for the way that Hitler and Mussolini approached their problems – not least in dealing with the trade unions and left-wing political organisations.

Joyce was eventually arrested near the Danish border in 1945 as the German Reich that he so admired was collapsing all around him. He was born in New York in 1906 but had obtained a British passport by telling the authorities that he had been born in Ireland before the Partition. The issue of his nationality was only one of the interesting points thrown up by his case and led to intense legal wrangling as to whether a British court was entitled to try him at all. His fate was sealed by the fact that, whether it was strictly legal or not, he had possessed a British passport at the time he started making his propaganda broadcasts. His activities on Germany's behalf 'gave comfort to the king's enemies' and therefore constituted treason. Joyce was hanged at Wandsworth on 3 January 1946.

Few murder cases have ever grabbed the public's attention in quite the way that the 'Acid Bath Murder' did in 1949. Britain was slowly emerging from the cares and austerities of the war years when along came John George Haigh to provide a stark reminder that evil in human form still existed even after Hitler's death in the bunker in Berlin. Accused of murder, Haigh pleaded insanity on the grounds of being a vampire! He was, however, not the first known acid bath murderer. Like his predecessor, the French murderer Georges Sarret in 1925, Haigh thought he had found the perfect solution to the crucial problem facing all murderers, that of how to dispose of the remains of his victim. He harboured the comforting but mistaken notion that murder could not be proven against a suspect if the body of the victim no longer existed.

Haigh was glib, garrulous and dapper and possessed of a certain superficial charm. He was the kind of man once aptly described as a 'lounge lizard'. He was also a ladies' man and confidence trickster, who had served a number of prison sentences for offences involving fraud. He spent much time inhabiting second-rate hotels in the Kensington and Bayswater districts of London, where he exercised his charms on the wealthy widows who constituted a significant part of such hotels' residents. He spun beguiling yarns about how he was an inventor with a portfolio full of good ideas but who needed cash in order to bring these inventions to fruition and market them. In exchange for immediate financial support he could promise generous future profits to those who could provide him quickly with funds up front. Although this was the con-man's classic line, he found a number of elderly ladies who were only too happy to provide him with financial backing. Gratefully pocketing the cash, Haigh would then disappear in search of fresh victims, while the ladies were left to rue their gullibility. Most were reluctant to go to the police or make any kind of fuss for fear of further humiliation.

At the Onslow Court Hotel in Kensington Haigh met Mrs Olive Durand-Deacon. She was a wealthy, lonely widow, flattered by his attentions. Hardly understated in appearance, Olive wore large amounts of expensive jewellery and had a fondness for decking herself out in costly furs. Haigh had noticed these and to him they suggested 'instant cash'. She was very impressed when he evinced great interest in an idea she had come up with for manufacturing artificial fingernails for cosmetic purposes. Haigh, having made due preparations, suggested that she accompany him to his factory at Crawley in Sussex. There he shot her. Taking off her rings, trinkets and most of her clothes, he placed her body in a large iron tank which he then filled with a highly corrosive acid. He quickly sold some of her jewellery locally and then returned to Kensington, where it soon became evident that Olive had gone missing.

Haigh now showed himself too clever by half. With profound but misplaced egotism, he then told the police that he had not only destroyed Olive with acid but that he had also previously murdered five other people in a similar fashion. He directed the police to his 'factory' – in reality little more than a workshop – in Crawley and even offered to accompany them there and show them round. Unfortunately for him, first-rate pathological work on the fatty sludge recovered from the bottom of the tank produced sufficient evidence to make a positive identification of Olive, whereupon Haigh found himself charged with murder, having of course already made a confession. Understandably put out by this turn of events, Haigh then went on to advance in his defence the astounding revelation that he had been driven by compulsive urges to drink his victims' blood. The media of course instantly dubbed him the 'Vampire Killer', but Haigh hoped that these disclosures would convince the court he was insane. They did not and Haigh was executed at Wandsworth Prison on 6 August 1949. Although by this time pressure was building for the abolition of capital punishment, Haigh went to his death unlamented.

Further strengthening the arguments of those campaigning for the abolition of capital punishment was the celebrated case of Craig and Bentley in late 1952 and early 1953. This controversial case has been revisited time and time again via both the printed word and the visual image, so only a summary of the germane points will be given here. Christopher Craig was a youth of 16 who fancied himself a tearaway. Derek Bentley was 19, although with a mental age of only 11. Craig's elder brother had just been sent to prison for armed robbery. In the family tradition Craig was carrying a revolver and a knife when he and Bentley decided to break in to a warehouse in Croydon. Bentley, who already had a criminal record, was equipped with a knuckleduster and a knife.

The break-in was not planned with any real care and the pair were observed from across the road by a woman householder. She called the police who arrived on the scene while the young men were still inside the building. Aware that they had been rumbled, they tried to escape. Bentley was caught on the roof by a police officer and it was at this point that he allegedly shouted to Craig, who was brandishing his gun, 'Let him have it, Chris!' These words were certainly ambiguous, although Bentley staunchly denied having said them anyway. Craig fired several times and a police officer was hit in the head and killed. Armed police were soon on the scene and the youths arrested. At the Old Bailey both men were found guilty of murder. Craig was ordered to be detained at Her Majesty's pleasure because he was a minor, while Bentley, who had apparently done no more than shout encouragement, was sentenced to death. A massive campaign was launched to obtain a reprieve for him but without success, and he was hanged at Wandsworth on 28 January 1953. Abolitionists and Bentley's relations continued to agitate for abolition. In 1992 the Home Secretary Kenneth Clarke published the findings of his review of the case. His conclusion – which seemed unlikely to have satisfied anyone – was that had he been Home Secretary at the time, he would have recommended a reprieve, although he was not prepared to grant a posthumous royal pardon.

Richard Noble was an attorney, albeit not a very enthusiastic or successful one, who found that philandering offered a far more rewarding and congenial outlet than legal work for such talents as he possessed. John Sayer was a Buckinghamshire landowner with a promiscuously errant wife called Mary, who was also a spendthrift. Seeing his financial affairs spiralling out of control, Sayer engaged Noble's services as an attorney. Perhaps inevitably, Noble joined the roll call of Mary's lovers but his sexual appetite was considerable and so he took her mother as a lover as well. He used his knowledge of the law to persuade Sayer, whose love for Mary seems never to have wavered, to sign most of his assets over to her. He also managed to get him to put his signature to a document in which he agreed not to divorce Mary even if he had evidence of her adultery. In 1710 Mary, having stolen a large sum of money from her long-suffering husband, left him and set up home with Noble. Sayer, who up to this time seems to have been remarkably gullible, or perhaps simply easy-going, was now in such serious financial straits that he had to take refuge from his creditors by entering the Fleet Prison. Maybe this turn of events caused Sayer to realise how he had been duped and he placed a notice in the newspapers alerting readers to the activities of his wife and her lover. As a result they were forced to take slum lodgings in seamy Southwark. When Sayer and the magistrate's men went there in order to take her back to the marital home Noble stabbed Sayer with a sword, killing him instantly. Noble was tried at the Kingston-on-Thames Assizes, convicted and executed in the town on 28 March 1713.

George Webb and Richard Russell were a couple of low-life characters who combined occasional low-paid and unskilled, if honest, employment with opportunistic criminal activity. They burgled premises in the New Cross and Deptford areas but were taken up by the authorities and executed in August 1805 at Shooters Hill near Blackheath.

About half a mile to the east of Tower Bridge on the south bank of the Thames is a small inlet that used to be used by barges loading and unloading at the nearby wharves. Often called St Saviour's Dock, it is actually the mouth of a small stream called the Neckinger. Rising not far from the site of the large and important Cluniac monastery of Bermondsey Abbey, this short river runs largely forgotten beneath the streets, but it is the only one of central London's 'hidden' rivers to have a mouth that is easily accessible by people on foot. The river gets its curious name from the fact that River Thames pirates were once executed there, the rope that was used to do the job being known as the 'Devil's neckcloth' or 'neckinger'.

Doubtless legal executions were also carried out elsewhere in that part of London lying south of the Thames. These places and their victims have largely been forgotten.

ELEVEN

Executioners and Hangmen of London

> Ye hangmen of Old England,
> How sturdily you stood,
> A-smoking pipes by Tyburn Tree,
> A-swigging pots in the Old Bailee,
> And strung up all you could.
>
> *Old Ballad*

Judicial hanging was probably introduced by the Anglo-Saxons and saw limited use in Norman times. The profession of hangman as such did not exist, executions being carried out by men who offered their services as and when needed or who were carrying out instructions given by others. Bizarrely, hangings were also sometimes performed by the victims of offences if they could not find anyone else to do it for them. Where miscreants were hanged rather than decapitated, death would have been by strangulation, which was both slow and exceptionally painful as no drop was employed to break the neck.

Being an executioner even on an ad hoc basis may have brought financial rewards and in some cases fame. This fame, however, was often more akin to notoriety and did not usually confer popularity or social status. Eventually professional executioners appeared on the scene. They tended to come from what we now describe as the lower-middle and working classes, like the majority of their victims. They were frequently reviled by the rest of society. Understandably resenting being cast in the role of pariahs, executioners sometimes justified their work by arguing that it rid society of its worst malefactors and therefore made people feel safer and more secure. As Alfred Marks, author of *Tyburn Tree*, said about the role of the executioner:

> Selected by the State to carry out its decrees, it would seem that he should have been invested with a dignity but little inferior to that of the judges who pronounced the sentence carried out by him in co-partnership. Without the practical assistance of the executioner, the solemn sentence of the robed, ermined, full-bottom-wigged judge would be of no effect. Nevertheless, this officer of the State, practically inculcating on the scaffold the great truths of morality impressed on the public from the bench . . . never received the homage due to him . . .

The concept of the professional hangman or executioner seems to have emerged in early modern England, and in Tudor times, with political and religious persecution rampant, there was plenty of work available for such men, who also needed to be able to turn their hand to floggings, brandings and burnings and various other methods of torture. Executioners seem to have been regarded as a necessary evil but many were indeed evil men in their own right. Some were criminal offenders or sadists deriving great satisfaction from their work; others were extremely incompetent or simply inept. It was well known that some could only perform their duties, properly or otherwise, when drunk. So what kind of man took on the role of executioner? In this chapter we will take a look at the careers of a selection of executioners who plied their trade in London and its environs.

In 1553 an anonymous executioner removed the Duke of Northumberland's head but drew the attention of the crowd because he had a peg-leg. Was there ever another one-legged hangman? A very early hangman to be specifically named was Derrick, who plied his trade in the last decade of the sixteenth century. In 1601 he executed the Earl of Essex, a man who allegedly had earlier spared his life when he had been condemned to death for rape. Derrick appears under that name in Sir Walter Scott's novel *The Fortunes of Nigel*, published in 1822. It is said that Derrick gave his name to a type of crane which resembled the gallows he had designed.

Gregory Brandon was Derrick's assistant for many years. In 1616 he was granted a coat of arms by accident because of a practical joke played on the Garter King of Arms. This unwontedly elevated Brandon to the rank of gentleman and allowed him to be addressed as 'Esquire', a privilege he greatly relished.

Richard Brandon succeeded his father. Whereas most boys of that time whiled away their childhood days playing 'tiggee', hide-and-seek or the Jacobean equivalent of 'doctors and nurses', young Brandon sought out and seized all the cats and dogs he could lay his hands on. Anxious to prove his credentials as the right person to succeed his father, he practised assiduously by beheading his luckless captives. His juvenile experiments bore fruit because he gained the position he so much coveted and later he executed the hated Earl of Strafford; he may also have executed Charles I. Rumour had it that he was extremely unwilling to execute the king but was forced into the job, and that he was so full of remorse that he fell into a terminal decline and died four years later. Some say that he died much sooner.

Edward Dun was mentioned in the novel *Hudibras* by Samuel Butler and it may well have been he who severed the heads from the exhumed bodies of the regicides Cromwell, Ireton and Bradshaw in 1661. It was probably Dun who in 1660 publicly burned *The Tenure of Kings and Magistrates*, John Milton's defence of the execution of Charles I. Dun died in 1663.

Charles II was the 'Merry Monarch' and his restoration to the throne encouraged a return to the unalloyed enjoyment of those simple sexual and sensuous pleasures that had been so vigorously suppressed during the puritanical days of the Commonwealth. For all that, during Charles's reign many heads rolled. Jack Ketch was executioner from 1663 to 1686, acting as both a hangman and a headsman as required. He gained a reputation as a brutal incompetent for the manner in which he bungled the executions of Lord Russell in 1683 and the Duke of Monmouth in 1685. In 1686 he was briefly deposed for making offensive comments about his employers but was later restored to office. He is perhaps unique in the annals of executioners for having successfully gone on strike to secure better wages. It was Ketch who inflicted multiple floggings on the odious little perjurer Titus Oates. A number of men implicated by Oates in the so-called Popish Plot were hanged, drawn and quartered by Ketch in 1679. Jack Ketch's name lived on after his death in 1686 as a generic (and often abusive) name for all hangmen. He even became a bogeyman, his name being used to threaten fractious children. Years later he emerged as a character in Punch and Judy shows and is so repulsive that he ends up being hanged himself.

Imagine how the habitués of a good hanging must have relished watching the death throes of John Price. After all, he had once been the chief executioner so it was a case of the biter bit! Born in 1677 in the Soho district of London, Price was just 7 when his father died. His mother was left destitute and young Price was forced to go out and seek a living, initially as a pickpocket. He went from job to job, including a spell as a seaman in the newly emergent Royal Navy. In 1713 he applied to be hangman, a post requiring sobriety, honesty and industriousness, and he certainly appeared to be the ideal candidate. His knowledge of knots, gleaned from his time at sea, proved useful and he soon gained a reputation for competence in his new calling. He was respectful to those who employed him and never other than professional in his dealings with his victims, but sadly for him he had too much of a liking for women and drink. He was, of course, by no means the first man to discover the pitfalls engendered by a weakness for such things. He got into debt and on one occasion he was stopped and arrested by the bailiffs while travelling with a prisoner in the procession to officiate at Tyburn. Although he was able to discharge this particular debt, others piled up and he was imprisoned in the Marshalsea as a debtor. He was in prison for over two years and the experience seems to have brutalised him. In 1718 he escaped. Shortly afterwards, inflamed by drink, he attacked, raped and fatally injured a woman at Moorfields. He was found guilty and condemned to death. He whiled away the intervening time in Newgate getting drunk and fighting mad before being hanged at Bunhill Fields, near the spot where he had committed his offence. Vast hostile crowds turned out to scream their hate at the rapist and murderer, grateful for the chance to see a hangman hanged. His corpse was then placed in a gibbet near Holloway.

William Marvell replaced Price after he had been imprisoned for debt. He was a brawny blacksmith but an incompetent hangman and executioner. It was Marvell who in 1716 beheaded the Earl of Derwentwater and Lord Kenmure, rebel aristocrats, at Tower Hill. Marvell dispatched the earl swiftly enough but his nerve seems to have failed him and two strokes were required to end Kenmure's life. As with Price, women and wine proved to be Marvell's downfall and he was arrested for debt while travelling to officiate at a triple hanging at Tyburn in 1717. A fight broke out between the bailiffs trying to seize Marvell and people in the crowd who hated the bailiffs more than they despised the hangman and were bent on stopping them taking him away. The crowds also resented this interruption to the anticipated entertainment on the gallows. Marvell was pulled to and fro and manhandled so roughly that he was too badly injured to carry out his duties. The procession eventually continued to Tyburn, where an appeal was made for a volunteer hangman. A bricklayer who indicated his willingness to stand in was set upon and almost beaten to death, and a long and embarrassing wait followed. No further volunteers came forward and eventually the authorities had no option but to take the three condemned prisoners back to Newgate, much to the amusement of the crowd who delighted in the confusion of the authorities, even though the hangings had not taken place. In this case the prisoners were reprieved and transported, but one escaped, returning to England and carrying out a robbery for which he was hanged at Tyburn in 1721. Marvell, discharged from his duties, fell into bad ways and in 1719 was arrested for theft and sent to penal servitude in the American colonies, where presumably he died. He featured in Harrison Ainsworth's wildly inaccurate historical novel *Jack Sheppard*, published in 1839.

John Hooper, otherwise known as 'Laughing Jack', was a man of a very different kidney. He found life immensely amusing and, despite having the facial features of a grotesque gargoyle, was loved by the crowds for the fund of witticisms and verbal japes with which he regaled them while going about his business. Even those waiting to be hanged may have found some solace in the coarse but good-natured raillery generated around the gallows when Hooper was at work. Possibly it was while working as a turnkey at Newgate that Hooper recognised his calling and set his sights on becoming a hangman. He achieved his desire in 1728 and only nine days after being appointed he demonstrated his skills as a hangman to the total satisfaction of all, except perhaps his victim, a robber named James Haddock. A determination not to let the job get to him must have been required in 1731 when he was required to cut off the ears and slit the nostrils of a forger named Japhet Crook. The latter bore what must have been excruciating pain with great stoicism and followed his ordeal with a bout of heavy drinking with admiring friends before being taken away to spend the rest of his life in confinement. Hooper's career probably reached its climax when he executed Sarah Malcolm in 1733. She was a young woman who had murdered her employer and two fellow servants with quite extraordinary brutality. The execution was performed in Fleet Street close to the scene of the atrocities she had committed and it excited enormous interest, the crowds screaming their hatred of her and their support for Hooper's handiwork. After this Hooper seems simply to have faded away, and he had either retired or died when his role was taken over in 1735 by John Thrift.

Thrift's tenure of office was a long one. He took his duties very seriously and always attempted to be as humane as his job allowed. He was highly strung, often trembling like an aspen while working. His debut was especially nerve-racking. It took place at Tyburn in March 1735 and he was required to hang no fewer than thirteen felons. In his nervousness he forgot to cover their faces, an oversight that earned him a sharp reprimand from the under-sheriff. In 1736 Thrift hanged a highwayman called Reynolds. All signs of life had apparently been extinguished and the man was cut down and placed in his coffin. But no sooner had this been done than the coffin lid was unexpectedly pushed open and a bewildered Reynolds sat up, gazing around him with understandable confusion. The crowd cheered Reynolds good-naturedly but the mood turned nasty when Thrift set about hanging him once again. This offended the crowd's sense of fair play and some of them climbed the gallows and attacked Thrift, giving him a very severe beating. He was only saved from possible death by a troop of musketeers. Thrift was certainly very squeamish for a man of his trade and was extremely put out in 1746 when he was required to hang, draw and decapitate nine Jacobite rebels on Kennington Common. But worse was to follow when it fell to him to decapitate lords Kilmarnock and Balmerino at Tower Hill. He cried and shook visibly, and the crowds were treated to the extraordinary sight of the headsman being comforted by one of the very men he was about to execute! He dispatched Kilmarnock quickly but required three blows to sever Balmerino's head from his body. He made a better job of decapitating Lord Lovat, the rapist, in 1747. His head was removed with a single blow. He was the last person in England to be beheaded while alive (as opposed to being decapitated after death, like the Cato Street conspirators in 1820).

Thrift seems to have been an obsequious man who was easily overawed in his professional dealings with those of 'gentle' birth. By now his nerves had been shredded by his experiences and he often found himself being spat at or threatened as he went about his private business in the streets. In 1750 a jeering and hostile crowd followed him to his house off Drury Lane. They provoked him so far that, quite uncharacteristically, he seized a sword and chased some of them down the street. What happened next is unclear but Thrift was charged with murdering one of his pursuers. Now the poor man found himself being used as a cat's-paw in the politics of the time. He was judged guilty, but the Whig faction was determined that he should not die because the dead man was an avowed Jacobite. The execution was first postponed, and then he was given a free pardon and restored to his duties. Always a somewhat haunted man, Thrift never recovered his equilibrium and died on 5 May 1752. There were angry scenes at his funeral as the undertaker's men were pelted with stones and offal. One is left wondering why Thrift ever became an executioner, let alone why he stayed in the job for so long, given his highly emotional nature. Perhaps he simply did it for the financial rewards. Hangmen received an official salary well above the income of their social peers and there were many perks that went with the job.

Thomas Turlis was a hangman of some stature. He held office from 1752 to 1771 and gained a reputation for zeal, efficiency and imperturbability, none of which, however, was enough to make him popular with the public or, of course, with his victims. His working life was full of incident. In 1763 he accompanied a formidable virago by the name of Hannah Dagoe to Tyburn where she was due to be executed. On arrival she tore off her restraints and threw most of her clothes – which were always regarded as one of the hangman's perks – into the crowd. Turlis then engaged in an unseemly tussle with Dagoe, who dealt him such a blow that she nearly knocked him out. Egged on by a jubilant crowd – this was just the kind of thing they loved to see – she continued to taunt Turlis, who eventually managed to pinion her once more. Dagoe continued to show spirit and hurled herself out of the cart before Turlis was ready. She died quickly. In the same year Turlis had the unusual duty of publicly burning edition no. 45 of the *North Briton* newspaper, edited by the turbulent John Wilkes. He was immensely popular with the London crowds and so a large contingent of constables was deployed in case of trouble. They were needed. Turlis was showered with filth and more solid missiles, and no sooner had he placed the offending publication on the fire than part of it was pulled out again by an unknown rescuer, who then vanished into the crowd. The mob now charged at Turlis and the constables, forcing them to flee.

Like the other hangmen, Turlis was also responsible for corporal punishment for a variety of non-capital offences. In June 1767 he carried out six whippings, earning himself £2 in addition to his executioner's stipend. Perhaps the apogee of his career came in 1760 when he hanged the highly disagreeable Lord Ferrers at Tyburn for the murder of his steward. Ferrers rode to his hanging in his private landau attended by liveried servants. He was dressed in a white satin wedding suit. Some of the largest crowds ever to attend a hanging turned out that day because there was intense interest in the aristocratic Ferrers, who had been found guilty of such a gratuitously brutal murder by his peers in the House of Lords. As befitted his social position, he had been lodged in the Tower while awaiting execution. He was also the first felon to be hanged on a new form of gallows and the crowds were keen to view the working of this new contraption. From the entertainment point of view they must have been gratified that it did not work well, Turlis and his assistant having to heave on the earl's legs in order to complete the job. Subsequently the crowds watched enraptured as Turlis and his assistant fought for the rope used in the hanging. Turlis won and his assistant burst into tears.

Turlis's other victims included Dr Archibald Cameron, hanged in 1753 for complicity in the Jacobite uprising of 1745, and Theodore Gardelle, executed in 1761. The latter had developed a passion for his landlady and entered her bedroom with evil intent. But not only did she reject his advances, she knocked him across the room. The scorned and humiliated Gardelle then hit her with a poker, knocking her out. In a panic, and thinking he had killed her, he stabbed her, began to dismember the body and started a fire. Not surprisingly, he was quickly apprehended. In 1767 Turlis officiated at the execution of Elizabeth Brownrigg. This would have brought him some temporary popularity with the crowds around the scaffold because she was widely hated for her cruelty to the servant-girls she employed. Turlis died in 1771 while returning from an assignment at Kingston-on-Thames.

Edward Dennis enjoyed a lengthy tenure as hangman (1771–86), gaining the unique distinction of officiating at executions at both Tyburn and Old Bailey. Where Thrift was histrionic and Turlis coolly efficient, Dennis was stolid and uninspiring. It is unlikely that he allowed the stresses of the job to get him down. He simply did not have sufficient imagination. One of his most colourful victims was 'Sixteen-String' Jack Rann, a modish, even dandyish highwayman who earned his curious nickname through his habit of wearing breeches with sixteen strings attached to the knees (and, on occasion, a hat with sixteen strings on it). He was a likeable and cheerful chap with a roguish eye for the ladies. He was probably too good-natured to make a success of highway robbery, but his sartorial elegance was only one part of his general extrovert personality. He went to his death at Tyburn chatting to anyone within earshot, smiling and acknowledging the felicitations of the crowd and dressed in a brand-new pea-green suit made especially for the occasion – with sixteen strings on the breeches.

Dennis hanged the celebrated Revd Dr William Dodd at Tyburn in June 1777 before one of the largest crowds ever seen there. Dodd was nicknamed the 'Macaroni Parson' on account of his foppish appearance, 'macaronis' being dandies. Dodd was hopelessly extravagant. He fell into debt and out of desperation uttered a forged bond. Although tried and convicted, he had offered full restitution and with his reputation for good works it was thought that a reprieve would be brokered. The law, however, proved inexorable. As the day of execution approached, plans were made to bribe Dennis to place the noose in such a way that Dodd would survive the hanging, although appearing to be dead. The idea was that his friends would then spirit him away to receive the best possible medical attention. Now Dennis may well have been paid to ensure that Dodd did not die, but such was the mêlée around the scaffold as the requirements of the law were carried out that it was very difficult to extricate the condemned man and indeed he proved to be beyond the reach of any medical attention. In 1779 Dennis hanged another man of the cloth. This was the Revd James Hackman, who, finding his love unrequited, had shot and killed the object of his desires, a lovely young woman called Martha Ray, the mistress of Lord Sandwich, First Lord of the Admiralty. Once more Dennis operated in front of huge crowds for they all loved to see clergymen with feet of clay get their comeuppance. The notorious anti-Catholic Gordon Riots took place in London in 1780 and it seems that Dennis became involved in the opportunistic looting of a shop close to Lincoln's Inn Fields. Witnesses came forward and, with a malevolence that would probably only be accorded to a hangman, testified against Dennis, who had to be housed for his own safety in a single cell in the bridewell at Tothill Fields. He was condemned to death only to be reprieved and restored to his duties, going on to hang many others who had been involved in the riots. Dennis survived in office long enough to perform a few executions outside Newgate and he died in 1786.

His successor William Brunskill was a rather cringing, obsequious fellow who was not always on top of his job. For all that, he dispatched a number of eminent felons. In 1786 and 1789 he officiated on the last two occasions at which women were burned at the stake. Until 1790 women could be executed in this barbarous way for the murder of a husband and for coining or debasing the coinage, all of which were regarded as a form of treason. In 1797 Brunskill was about to hang two criminals outside Newgate when, owing to carelessness on his part, the trapdoor on the scaffold opened prematurely. The felons were precipitated to their deaths but two priests who were offering solace on the scaffold followed them and were severely injured as other officials tumbled down on top of them. This event was regarded with superstitious awe because it was widely believed that the two felons had been wrongfully convicted. Brunskill hanged Governor Wall in 1802, thoroughly botching the job so that the wretched man took fifteen minutes to die. Another of Brunskill's especially notorious victims was Colonel Despard, hanged for treason at Horsemonger Lane in 1803. After he had been hanged, a masked man appeared and dextrously removed Despard's venerable head. The last famous felon to be hanged by Brunskill was John Bellingham, the man who had assassinated Prime Minister Spencer Perceval in 1812. By this time the nature of his work and the crowds' constant derision had begun to affect Brunskill, and like others of his trade he had turned to drink for solace and Dutch courage.

By the time James Foxen became hangman in 1820, London executioners were often asked to provide their services in assize towns up and down the country. The 'Newgate Practitioner', as London executioners were often called, was without question the doyen of the country's hangmen and so Foxen and one or two of his predecessors often found themselves travelling considerable distances to carry out executions in the provinces, making a useful addition to their income in the process. Foxen hanged Henry Fauntleroy, the celebrated banking fraudster, outside Newgate on 30 November 1824, and three years later faced what was probably his most difficult assignment when he was required to hang Charles White. This man ran a successful bookselling business in Holborn but had tried to burn down his premises in order to defraud the insurance company. Arson was a felony and White was condemned to death. Few prisoners responded with such obvious trauma and terror. While in Newgate he had made several unsuccessful attempts to escape. When the day for his execution arrived, he struggled frantically as Foxen tried to put the cords around his limbs, and on the scaffold he managed to get free and tear his cap off. With the greatest difficulty Foxen and his assistants managed to restrain him again, but when the signal was made for the drop White somehow contrived to be partly stuck in mid-air but with one foot on the platform. With a superhuman strength born of utter desperation, he got his hands free and struggled to loosen the cord around his throat even as he slowly choked to death. Even the most hardened members of the crowd stood transfixed with horror as White's face and body contorted with agony. Foxen eventually managed to terminate White's prolonged sufferings by pulling on his legs. This appalling incident bolstered the developing movement of opinion against public execution.

On 4 April 1829 William Calcraft was sworn in as executioner for London and Middlesex. He went on to become one of the most celebrated of London's executioners. As a young man he had a number of casual jobs, including hawking meat pies around the crowds at public hangings; here he made the acquaintance of the executioners and decided that it was his life's mission to follow in their footsteps. His first official duty was to hang Esther Hibner. She, like the egregious Mrs Brownrigg and others before them, had abused and tortured the young girls who worked for her. Calcraft was physically strong and of a stolid, equable temperament, uncommunicative and undemonstrative while working. On 31 December 1829 he executed Thomas Maynard, the last person to be hanged for forgery, and three other miscreants in Old Bailey. Calcraft had his own theories about the technique of hanging and used a short drop. Although Maynard and his fellows were seen to suffer unnecessarily, no one in authority saw fit to instruct Calcraft to use a longer drop in the future. Calcraft performed his duties for no less than forty-five years and his trademark seems to have been that most of his victims took an inordinate time to die. He was responsible for executing some of the most illustrious criminals of mid-nineteenth-century London. Among them were John Bishop and Thomas Williams, who in 1831 murdered a boy in order to sell his corpse to the anatomists, who used it to demonstrate to medical students, James Greenacre, who murdered Hannah Brown in 1837, and François Courvoisier, a superior servant who murdered his master in 1840 by slitting his throat. In 1849 he put an end to the lives of Mr and Mrs Manning, who had brutally murdered the latter's former lover for financial gain, in 1864 he ended the life of Franz Muller, who was found guilty of the first murder on a railway train, and in 1868, in the last public execution in England, he disposed of the life of Michael Barratt, the Irish nationalist who tried to blow up the Clerkenwell House of Correction in order to let fellow Fenians escape.

During his long career Calcraft had never become inured to the insults that came his way as a hangman, and as he got older he became increasingly worried that associates of his victims would seek him out to extract revenge. He had a particular fear of vengeance-seeking Irish nationalists. If anything, he became more taciturn and introspective as he got older, although he remained very reluctant to give up his position. He was eventually pensioned off and died in his eightieth year. Executioners of course inflicted corporal as well as capital punishment and many were the floggings that Calcraft administered, and for which he received useful additional payments. In May 1829, for example, he inflicted seventy lashes on a young silk-weaver in Bethnal Green, whose offence is not recorded. Sometimes Calcraft was asked to do work outside London and then he charged a considerably higher fee for the specialist services he provided.

If any hangman achieved true celebrity it was William Marwood, who officiated from 1874 to 1883. He was born in the small Lincolnshire town of Horncastle, where he traded as a cobbler. He developed an interest in execution and sent many letters to the authorities condemning the way in which hangings were performed. It seemed to him that the death throes of the victims were needlessly cruel and prolonged. He suggested making a careful calculation adjusting the length of the rope to the weight of the body. By doing so, when the bolt was withdrawn enough force would be created to dislocate the neck and bring about instantaneous death. Among those he bombarded with correspondence was the Governor of Lincoln Prison, who in 1871, perhaps in the hope of simply shutting him up, invited him to perform an execution. He did so using his own system of calculations and with very satisfactory results. News of his efficiency spread and Marwood was asked to carry out further hangings. His system clearly worked and it was perhaps no surprise that Marwood was offered Calcraft's post when the latter was pensioned off.

Marwood took immense pride in his professional skill, arguing that he was a real public benefactor because his method of execution was quick and therefore more humane. He was fond of saying that whereas his predecessors hanged their victims, he executed them. He found that his developing fame was good for his main business as people flocked to have their shoes soled and heeled by the public executioner. His shop in Horncastle became a museum of execution, festooned with memorabilia such as coils of rope, each labelled with the name of the particular miscreant whose life it had ended. He was happy to hold forth about his work to anyone who would listen. Whereas executioners were usually hated, Marwood was well liked, not because of any evident relish for executing people per se but for the evident pride and skill he brought to his calling, which was generally thought of as a necessary evil.

Marwood's first prominent victim was Henry Wainwright. On the surface a respectable tradesman and a pious, even unctuous, church-goer, Wainwright's alter ego seduced women with single-minded zeal. When his business began to fail, the expense involved in keeping his mistresses led him to murder and dismember one of them in 1875. Perhaps Marwood's most celebrated victim was the legendary Londoner Charlie Peace, who was hanged in 1879 at Armley Prison in Leeds for a murder he had committed at Sheffield. A man of immense personal charm although extraordinarily ugly, Peace was a talented musician who ran a picture-framing business and was a pillar of respectable society. He was also a master of disguise and a very skilled cat burglar who carried firearms and was prepared to use them to evade arrest. If that wasn't enough, he was also an inveterate womaniser. After his death his activities were celebrated and exaggerated in penny dreadfuls which were read avidly by generations of children and less discerning adults.

Women servants who murder and cut up their employers have always attracted voyeuristic curiosity and Marwood had the job of hanging Kate Webster at Wandsworth Prison in 1879. Her big mistake had been to throw various body parts of her victim into the Thames, where, instead of being swept away on the outgoing tide, they remained stubbornly visible and were quickly recovered. In 1882, also at Wandsworth, Marwood ended the life of Dr Lamson, who had poisoned his young brother-in-law with aconitine, a deadly alkaloid derived from monkshood, a common garden perennial and probably the most dangerous of all British plants.

Marwood died in Horncastle on 4 September 1883. Rumours circulated that he had been mysteriously poisoned, perhaps by Irish nationalists, of whom he had hanged a number. So persistent were these rumours that the local coroner exhumed Marwood's remains to demonstrate that his death was due to pneumonia and liver disease. Marwood was one of the few public executioners to be accorded a place in the *Dictionary of National Biography*.

When a hangman left the trade, for whatever reason, there was never any shortage of applicants for the vacancy. Many applicants were so keen that they offered to do the job without payment. Among those who applied to act as Marwood's replacement was James Berry, a shoe salesman and later police constable from the West Riding of Yorkshire. His first application was unsuccessful but his patience was eventually rewarded and he got the job in 1884. Unlike other holders of the office, Berry was always sober and well behaved, although not always as efficient as he might have been. He was, however, keen to minimise the suffering of his victims and he tried to develop a table of optimum drops based on the weight and build of each prisoner. He also took to placing the hood over the prisoner's head before he reached the scaffold, so that he was saved the additional horror of seeing the waiting noose.

Berry was busily occupied travelling the length and breadth of Britain in his professional capacity. He charged £10 per execution plus travelling expenses but was prepared to accept £5 plus expenses in those cases where a late reprieve arrived after he had already set out. He carried out relatively few hangings in London but did officiate at the execution of Mary Eleanor Wheeler, known as Mrs Piercey, who murdered the wife of one of her lovers by battering her with a poker and cutting her throat. The execution took place inside Newgate just before Christmas 1890. Berry was rather egotistical and in retirement published a ghosted autobiography and then went on the lecture circuit, talking about his professional experiences. He soon developed some skill as an entertainer and his talks became choreographed and accompanied by magic lantern slides. However, eventually the nature of his work and the 134 people he had executed niggled at his conscience and he turned to drink. Late in life he took up Christianity and went out on the road again, this time speaking against the death penalty.

He died in 1913, by which time he looked far older than his 60 years.

James Billington knew his vocation when he was only 10. He wanted to be a hangman and proved it by building a model gallows and experimenting with dummies. A Lancastrian, he had a roving remit, but in 1896 carried out the last triple execution at Newgate, also precipitating his assistant through the trapdoor when he pushed the lever accidentally. This faux pas did not prevent him officiating the following morning at the execution of Amelia Dyer, the 'Reading baby-farmer'. 'Baby-farming' involved the placement of unwanted babies and children with women who fostered them for as long as required, sometimes until adulthood, in return for payment. The egregious Amelia killed at least seven children in her care but it is likely that the number who died at her hands was much higher than that. Baby-farming was illegal and Amelia (who, incidentally, was a member of the Salvation Army), served a short prison sentence for the offence in 1880. She also spent time in what were then known as lunatic asylums because of her suicidal tendencies. Amelia looked every inch a respectable and kindly late middle-aged woman. The court, however, heard how she had murdered the children and then deposited their remains in packages in the River Thames. Most if not all had been strangled, presumably to save the costs of feeding and looking after them. The oddities of the case aside, Amelia attracted attention because at 57 she was the oldest woman to be hanged in Britain since 1843. She was executed on 10 June 1896.

William Billington followed in his father's footsteps and carried out the first execution inside Pentonville Prison when it took over from Newgate as the place of execution for male prisoners in London north of the Thames. This took place on 30 September 1902 and employed the scaffold previously used at Newgate, which was regarded by those who knew best, the executioners, as the finest in Britain. Previously it had been the practice to raise a black flag on the roof of prisons when an execution had taken place. Now a bell was tolled instead. In March 1903 at Wandsworth, Billington junior hanged Edgar Edwards, alias Owen, who had murdered a married couple and their child in the course of a robbery. He dismembered their bodies and buried them in his garden at Leyton. Having failed to persuade the jury that he was insane, Edwards seems to have become resigned to his fate and mocked the judge when he put on the black cap to pronounce sentence of death. In both these executions, Billington's assistant was Henry Pierrepoint – the first mention of what was to become a very familiar name in the annals of execution. In April 1903, also at Wandsworth, the same combination hanged George Chapman, a remorseless philanderer and murderous poisoner. It has been claimed, on somewhat flimsy evidence, that Chapman was Jack the Ripper.

A disproportionate number of hangmen at this time came from south Lancashire. Of the seven hangmen on the Home Office's approved list in 1929, four were from Lancashire. John Ellis was a Lancastrian. Like one or two others of his calling, he suffered from stage fright. It was Ellis who dispatched Dr Crippen at Pentonville on 23 November 1910. He also hanged the Irish patriot Roger Casement in 1916, and afterwards he wrote that he had never known a prisoner show such bravery and composure while facing imminent death. Less well known was his hanging at Pentonville in 1918 of a Frenchman called Voisin, a butcher by trade, who used his professional skills to carve up and dismember a young woman he had murdered. In March 1918 Ellis hanged Henry Jacoby at Pentonville. An 18-year-old pantry boy in a West End hotel, he had battered a female guest to death with a hammer. The case was controversial because Jacoby claimed that his confession had been extracted under extreme duress. There was a widespread feeling that he should be reprieved for this reason and also because he was simple-minded, but appeals on his behalf were unsuccessful. Ellis always claimed that he had been very upset by having to carry out this particular execution.

Henry (or 'Harry') Pierrepoint was a Yorkshireman, who like many others of his kind had first aspired to the hangman's role while just a schoolboy. His elder brother Tom also acted as a hangman. Extremely partial to drink and notoriously garrulous when in his cups, Henry Pierrepoint is a familiar figure because he kept a particularly comprehensive diary of his activities as well as detailed notes about the physical and mental characteristics of his victims. He hanged Arthur Devereux at Pentonville in 1905 for the murder of his wife and twin sons. Noted for his unflappability, Henry Pierrepoint was fond of sucking sweets when working. He hanged two young men at Wandsworth in 1921 for the murder of a woman while committing a robbery. In 1924 he returned to Wandsworth to execute Jean-Pierre Vacquier, who had killed his lover's husband with strychnine. Soon afterwards, also at Wandsworth, he hanged Patrick Mahon. A married man but an inveterate womaniser, Mahon had murdered Emily Kaye, one of his many paramours, in a bungalow love-nest he had rented at

Eastbourne. Mahon had had enough of Emily because she was becoming too possessive. He may also have known that she was pregnant, which would have caused him various unwanted complications. This case caused an extraordinary sensation at the time because of the methods Mahon used to dispose of Emily's body. He cut her legs and head off so that her body would fit into a trunk, and then decided to burn parts of her body. In this case he was only partially successful so he then tried, again without much success, to boil them. Some small pieces he wrapped in brown paper and threw out of a train. Items of Emily's bloodstained underwear and a knife were placed in a Gladstone bag and deposited in the left-luggage office at Waterloo station. Mahon's preposterous initial explanation that he used the bag for carrying fresh meat for his dog was soon disposed of, and as his world collapsed around him he made a full confession. He horrified even hardened police officers with his graphic and gruesome detail. Further physical evidence of the crime was found at the bungalow. One significant outcome of this affair was the creation by Scotland Yard of a standard kit to be used by forensic officers at the scene of crime. This became known as the 'Murder Bag'.

In 1928 Robert Baxter and his assistant hanged Frederick Browne and Pat Kennedy for the cold-blooded killing of PC Gutteridge. These two recidivists and ne'er-do-wells stole cars for a living. These then had their number plates changed, were resprayed and otherwise superficially 'serviced' before being sold to those who simply wanted a cheap jalopy, no questions asked. They had been waved down in an Essex lane by PC Gutteridge while driving a car just stolen in Billericay. Gutteridge was shot at close quarters and then shot again through the eyes as he lay dying on the side of the road. They were hanged at Pentonville and Wandsworth respectively.

Those men approved of for the purposes of carrying out hangings had a thin time of it in the 1920s and 1930s because hangings were few and far between. Rather distastefully the surviving hangmen were forced to tout for work across the whole of the United Kingdom and the manner in which they did this sometimes incurred Home Office disapproval. Pressure was now developing more strongly for the abolition of hanging.

The third and best-known member of the Pierrepoint dynasty was Albert, who carried out a large number of executions during his very long career. At school he was asked to write an essay around the well-worn theme of what he wanted to do when he grew up. His teacher, probably bored to tears with the normal juvenile ramblings and fantasies involving engine drivers, dictators, explorers, lion tamers and owners of chocolate factories, may well have recoiled with revulsion when he read young Albert's opus which stated with brutal honesty that his ambition was to follow the family tradition and become an executioner. He cut his teeth, as it were, by acting as the hangman's assistant, and his first full commission came in 1940 when he was 35 years of age. He was given the job of hanging a gangland hoodlum at Wandsworth Prison. Pierrepoint was kept busy during the war executing enemy spies, such as the woebegone German parachutist and would-be fifth columnist who landed near St Albans while London was being blitzed and was captured within minutes of touchdown. He was hanged at Wandsworth, a locale for which Pierrepoint seemed to have a particular penchant. Among his most celebrated victims was William Joyce, known to all as 'Lord Haw-Haw', who was hanged at Wandsworth on 3 January 1946. At Pentonville in October 1946 Pierrepoint hanged the murderer Neville Heath, a handsome, debonair man whose crimes seemed all the more appalling for the complete sangfroid with which he conducted himself in court. A former RAF airman, he quipped shortly before he was hanged, 'It's just another op. Only difference is that I know I'm not coming back from this one.' Back at Wandsworth in 1949 Pierrepoint officiated at the hanging of John George Haigh, the 'acid bath murderer', who claimed that he was a vampire and needed human blood in order to sustain himself. Returning to Pentonville in March 1950 Pierrepoint hanged the pathetic Timothy John Evans, found guilty of murdering his wife and baby. Evans went to his premature death constantly but hopelessly reiterating his innocence, and it was revealed later that he almost certainly did not commit these murders. John Reginald Christie, a seedy little man who resided at 10 Rillington Place in North Kensington, and who was only capable of sexual intercourse if his partner was unconscious or dead, admitted a few years later that he had killed Mrs Evans. He also murdered other women in the pursuit of this peculiar form of sexual gratification. On 15 July 1953 Pierrepoint ended Christie's life at Pentonville.

Pierrepoint was on familiar territory when he hanged Derek Bentley at Wandsworth early in 1953. This execution caused an outrage at the time. Bentley was a simple-minded if nasty young waster who, while carrying out a bungled burglary, was already under police restraint when he supposedly shouted the words 'Let him have it!' to his under-age accomplice, who then shot and killed a police officer. The apparent injustice of this case was seized upon by the growing lobby of those determined to see the end of capital punishment in the United Kingdom.

On 13 July 1955 Albert Pierrepoint hanged Ruth Ellis at Holloway Prison. Her execution was particularly contentious given the furore that was developing around the future of the death penalty. It may be significant that Pierrepoint, who thought of himself as the consummate professional carrying out a regrettably necessary public office, resigned shortly afterwards. He had been an executioner for twenty-four years. Almost twenty years later he wrote a best-selling autobiography in which he stated that in his opinion capital punishment was no deterrent to murder and achieved nothing for society except a vicarious sense of revenge.

Hangings continued sporadically after Pierrepoint retired. By now substantial pressure was developing among influential, liberally minded people for the legal abolition of capital punishment. Their arguments were strengthened by a number of apparent miscarriages of justice, such as the execution in 1962 of James Hanratty for the 'A6 Murder' which he almost certainly did not commit. On 13 August 1964 two hangings took place simultaneously, one at Walton Prison in Liverpool and the other at Strangeways in Manchester. The men concerned had been found guilty of murder. They were the last two people to be executed in Britain.

So the role of public executioner in Britain has faded into history. Will it ever be revived? For hundreds of years the law chose to inflict death on certain of its citizens who were thought to have committed particularly heinous offences. Juries of upright citizens assessed the evidence and found men and women guilty of crimes carrying the death sentence, while judges uttered the awful words which consigned the offenders to the place of execution. But in a way the actions of judges and juries were a step away from the punishment. It was the executioners who implemented the decisions of the court. The execution brought the hangman and his victim into a brief but very intimate and fraught relationship. There was no hiding place around the scaffold.

Many of the men who acted as executioners were mentally damaged by their experiences. We need not feel too sorry for them. They volunteered to be hangmen, and they did so for financial reward or whatever other gratification their role may have brought them. They were in the business of killing and, despite some of them stating that they were simply public servants implementing the rule of law, the killing they did was entirely premeditated. This alone marked them out from some of their victims. Mind you, the job always had its perks. Some undoubtedly enjoyed the feeling of power and the sense of notorious celebrity that went with it.

More concrete was the money that could be made unofficially from selling relics associated with hangings. A host of superstitions surrounded the gallows. It was believed that the hangman's rope had curative powers for a wide range of ailments. Bound round the head it could cure headaches and toothaches. Even a single strand was reckoned to ward off a variety of fits and fevers when, somewhat ironically, it was worn around the neck. The hangman could do a brisk trade selling pieces of the rope to members of the crowd, while items of the condemned felon's apparel also sold well for their alleged magical properties. The touch of a dead man's hand, preferably a man who had met an untimely death – those who had just

been hanged were perfect for the purpose – was believed
to work wonders for such complaints as goitre, cysts,
scrofula and ulcers. As soon as death was pronounced,
there was often a horde of women who pressed forward
in an attempt to seize the still-warm hand of the deceased
and press it to their bosoms in order to absorb its
prophylactic qualities. Occasionally a mistake was made
and the felon had not actually expired. What greater
incentive to revival could the felon have had than to find
his hand in direct contact with a rapid succession of
female bosoms?

Even more highly prized was the detached hand of an
executed criminal. Known as the 'Hand of Glory', it was
severed while the body was still on the gallows. It was
then pickled for about fifteen days, causing it to dry out
and become hard. A candle composed of wax with fat
from a hanged man and a dash of sesame was then fixed
between the fingers of the hand. It was believed that a
burglar who carried such a hand, so long as the candle
was lit, was immune from discovery when he broke into a
house. This was because the presence of the candle put all
the house's inhabitants into a deep slumber which lasted
as long as the intruder was on the premises. Burglars were
known to carry these gruesome objects as late as the
nineteenth century. If this practice seems a trifle odd, even
more bizarre was a preventative measure which could be
taken by the householder. This was to smear all possible
points of entry with an ointment, the ingredients of which
included the gall of a black cat, the fat of a white hen and
the blood of a screech-owl. Was it trial and error that
enabled them to fix on this particular combination of
substances or would other equally outré and diverse
ingredients have done just as well? After this, the idea of

people rubbing a splinter from the gallows on their gums as a cure for toothache seems positively mundane. The rope, incidentally, could also act as a talisman and a section of it, especially one with a knot in it, was thought to be particularly helpful to those who gambled with cards.

This all enables us to understand how the perquisites and the cash bonuses that went with them helped to attract men to an occupation which most people would consider an uncongenial and unnatural one. Doubtless any restoration of the death penalty in the future would see no shortage of applicants for the role of hangman or executioner.

TWELVE

The Carnival of the Scaffold Crowd

> Carnivals . . . were entertainment, a welcome
> respite from the daily struggle to earn a living, they
> gave people something to look forward to. They
> celebrated the community . . . displaying its ability
> to put on a good show; and perhaps the mocking
> of outsiders . . . the excitement of the occasion and
> the heavy consumption of alcohol meant that
> inhibitions against expressing hostility to the
> authorities could be explosive.
>
> *P. Burke,* Popular Culture in
> Early Modern Europe *(1994)*

Many of the features of carnivalesque ritual were
recognisable in the behaviour of scaffold crowds.
Carnivals in early modern Europe took place in early
February before the period of Lent and offered an
opportunity for people to let off steam. People dressed up,
ate and drank to excess and stuck their fingers up to
authority. Carnival has been called the second life of the
people because it allowed a break from the day-to-day
drudgery and routine of life. Behaviour at carnivals was
irreverent and offered the people an opportunity to
display both individual and collective expressions of their
feelings before the austere restrictions of Lent were
imposed. Figures of authority who demanded respect and

reverence were often reduced to the lowest level by mocking and parody. However, carnivals should not be romanticised. There was entertainment, enjoyment and a holiday atmosphere – but the participants could also, on occasion, be violent and more than capable of isolating and bullying social minorities or individuals. Carnivals combined both humour and savagery.

Britain did not have the large-scale carnivals seen in Europe, but there was an abundance of festivals, wakes and revels which embraced similar elements. These events could be robust, sometimes bizarre, grotesque, anarchic, violent, and sometimes imbued with ritual and meaning. The largest public gatherings for centuries took place on execution days when people assembled around the scaffold to witness the death of the condemned. London, with its huge population, inevitably saw the largest crowds. However, the word 'witness' suggests a rather narrow interpretation of what they actually did at these events.

The whole ritual surrounding the execution – the procession to the gallows, the selling of food, drink and broadsheets, the opportunities for pickpockets, the drunken revelry and fights, the last dying speech followed by the agonising death throes of the condemned, the undignified scramble for the dead body by agents of the anatomists and the family of the deceased – was part of the performance. This image is vividly portrayed by William Hogarth in his *Idle 'Prentice executed at Tyburn*, which depicts a scene that goes well beyond the idea of a crowd of spectators awed into submission or passivity by this demonstration of the power of the state. That is not to say that crowds displayed the same carnival behaviour at all executions but the potential was always there. The theatre of the crowd was a familiar part of London's history and sites of execution such as Tyburn and Smithfield were as familiar to the population as the famous landmarks of St Paul's Cathedral, London Bridge or the Tower.

At Tyburn on execution days a crowd would assemble hours in advance. The food and drink vendors would be doing a roaring trade, as would the thieves and pickpockets. Seats could be hired in viewing platforms known as 'Tyburn pew openers', with admission prices carefully calculated to take account of the fame and notoriety of the condemned felon or felons. The most famous of these grandstands was known as 'Mother Proctor's Pew' after its original owner. This would fill up early in the day if the occupants thought they were in for a good show. This structure proved to be an excellent investment. It was first used in 1724, and when Lord Ferrers was executed in 1760 the grandstand netted its owner an estimated £5,000!

Like carnivals, public executions took place at particular times and in particular places. The radical Francis Place, a tailor, wrote that 'a hanging day was to all intents and purposes a fair day'. The authorities mostly tolerated the behaviour of the crowd but there were occasions when unruliness created a threat to order, as was often the case in places such as Tyburn, the May Fair and Bartholomew Fair. Unruly behaviour, particularly in an expanding fashionable residential area, contributed to the transfer of executions from Tyburn to Newgate in 1783. In 1798 the question of abolishing Bartholomew Fair was raised as it was considered to be the 'haunt of amusement, riot and dissipation'. The May Fair, which was held during the first fortnight in May, was considered to be 'the chiefest nursery of evil'. Agitation for its suppression increased until it was finally closed in 1809, largely as a result of the growth of Mayfair as a high-class residential area.

The output of cheap print in the sixteenth and seventeenth centuries whetted the appetite of an audience avid to read the gory details of an execution. Broadsides provided information on a single sheet with an illustration at the top followed by a popular narrative about the person to be executed. Along with the alehouses, taverns and coffee-shops, broadsides and ballads contributed to a culture of gossip and tales about executions within a population always eager for cheap titillation.

Black humour was an essential feature of public executions and various slang terms emerged to describe the many aspects of the hanging day: 'hanging match', 'collar day', a 'hanging fair' or the 'Paddington Fair', to 'dance the Paddington frisk', 'jammed', 'collared', 'twisted', 'nubbed', 'backed', 'stretched', 'cheated', 'crapped', 'tucked up' or 'turned off'. Also common were sayings such as 'a man hanged will piss when he cannot whistle' and 'there is nothing in being hang'd, but a wry neck, and a wet pair of breeches'. The term 'pulling his/her leg' was a reference to the hastening of the death of the condemned by pulling on their legs immediately after they had been dropped. Relatives or friends usually carried out this act of 'mercy'.

London teemed with elements of the carnivalesque and the pleasures of sex, eating and drinking to excess were not the preserve of a particular class as both high and low society revelled in such activities. The mixing of classes was still evident by 1770 at the celebrated release of the radical John Wilkes. The crowd was described as composed of 'half-naked men and women, children, chimney-sweepers, tinkers, Moors and men of letters, fishwives and females in grand array'. Violence and hooliganism were as common among the aristocratic classes as they were among street urchins. Against this rich fabric of life, London has been compared to the Gargantuan carnival monster, in its gigantic, fleshy and voracious form growing fat upon its appetite for 'people and for food, for goods and for drink; it consumes and it excretes, maintained within a continual state of greed and desire'.

All social classes in London had attended executions but the participation of the more 'well-to-do' declined from the late eighteenth century. London's population approached one million during the eighteenth century, accompanied by an alarming increase in crime. The novelist and magistrate Henry Fielding drew attention to the 'vast addition' to the suburbs as well as the city and the 'immense number of lanes, alleys, courts and Bye-places' which he felt had almost been contrived to conceal the criminal: 'A thief may harbour with as great security, as wild Beasts do in the Deserts of Africa or Arabia.' The writer William Makepeace Thackeray described an execution crowd in 1840 as including 'all ranks and degrees – pickpockets and peers . . . tickled by the sight . . . and the lust of blood'. The rich might be seated, as at Tyburn, while the poor jostled for places among the huge crowd viewing the event from rooftops, trees and windows. Despite such concerns, fewer people were executed in the eighteenth century than in the sixteenth. Transportation to America, and after 1787 to Australia, siphoned many away from the scaffold but it was predictably the poor that constituted the majority of the victims of execution, as well as the bulk of the spectators.

The main function of public executions, as far as the authorities were concerned, was to demonstrate to the assembled spectators the dire consequences of breaking the law. Executions served as a demonstration of the power of authority and acted, or so it was hoped, as a deterrent to the populace not to embrace a life of crime. This was reinforced by the practice of allowing the condemned prisoner to make a last dying speech, a practice that developed during the sixteenth century. Almost always included in the speech was a plea for forgiveness for the prisoner's crime, which was an offence not only against the victim but also against the monarch and the state. The speeches varied from pious religious utterances to long-drawn-out stories which provided unintended entertainment and titillation, although their main intention was to serve as serious reflections on the nature of sin and its consequences. In 1676 one of the condemned at Tyburn warned 'the multitude [not to] spend their time in idleness, or disobedience . . . or be seduced and drawn away by lewd women'.

The crowd responded in different ways to the speeches, depending on the condemned person, their crime and their behaviour on the day. Needless to say, the gallows crowd often thoroughly enjoyed what was intended by the authorities to be a sombre event. The sixteenth-century artist Pieter Bruegel the Elder captured this sense of irreverence in his painting *The Magpie on the Gallows* (1568). It shows a landscape with meadows and fields and a castle overlooking a village. In the foreground is a gallows where people are dancing. In the bottom left-hand corner a man is defecating, acting out the proverb 'to shit at the gallows' – meaning that he is unconcerned about death and the power of the authorities, which are symbolised by the gallows.

There were always some who questioned the effectiveness of public executions as a means of deterrence. The English colonial politician Edward Gibbon Wakefield (1796–1862) wrote: 'You want to frighten the people . . . [but] you will hear sighs and groans, and words of rage and hatred . . . and then laughter . . . of an unnatural kind [enough] to turn you sick.' Henry Grattan (1746–1820), the MP and campaigner for legislative reform, offered a similar sentiment: 'The more you hang, the more you transport, the more you inflame, disturb, and disaffect.' Henry Fielding (1707–54), the novelist and legal reformer, also highlighted the general disregard that many showed towards the scaffold. When the execution of eleven felons at Tyburn in the mid-eighteenth century was followed by a spate of street robberies on the following night, Fielding wrote: 'In real truth, the executions of criminals, as at present conducted, serve, I apprehend, a purpose diametrically opposite to that for which they were designed; and tend to inspire the vulgar with a contempt of the gallows rather than a fear of it.'

Many critics felt that the regular displays of violence in the pillory, stocks and gallows only hardened the attitudes of onlookers. Frequent exposure, it was thought, would 'harden the heart: those who see life taken in so careless a manner, will not have a proper value for their own lives or the lives of others', wrote John Scott in 1773. Others asked whether repeated viewings of such violence would make a person 'become indifferent to the spectacle'. The Gentleman's Magazine in 1784 commented that those who attend hangings 'go with the same ease and indifference they would go to a race'. The fact is that many Londoners were inured to images of death, and not just at the point of death. Rotting bodies on gibbets and spiked heads on poles were commonplace sights.

Although the number of executions declined during the eighteenth century and reduced still further in the nineteenth, large crowds still turned out. In 1847 J. Ewing Ritchie stated that: 'We have seen every execution for the past ten years, and boast how on one day we saw one man hung at Newgate and took a cab to Horsemonger-Lane in time to see another.'

Writing in the *London Journal* in 1763 James Boswell reflected on his reasons for visiting Tyburn, as well as his reactions to what he saw there. 'My curiosity to see the melancholy spectacle of the executions was so strong that I could not resist it.' He described how he visited the scene with a friend and managed to obtain a good view despite a 'most prodigious crowd of spectators': 'I got upon a scaffold very near the fatal tree, so that we could clearly see all the dismal scene.' Afterwards he recorded how he was 'most terribly shocked, and thrown into a very deep melancholy'. The evening after the execution he lamented that he was 'haunted with frightful imaginations' and admitted that he was 'too easily affected . . . It is a weakness of mind. I own it.'

The authorities controlled public executions – they approved them, managed them and eventually withdrew them from the public gaze. This was not surprising given the activities and antics of the scaffold crowds, who adamantly refused to play the role expected of them. They came in their thousands and frequently appropriated the event for their own purposes. They protested, scoffed, mocked and expressed vulgar displays of irreverence and at times alarmed the authorities by their riotous behaviour. The state might have controlled the theatre of punishment but it had little hold over what happened during the performance.

The performance itself became a stage from which the condemned could manipulate the spectators to their own advantage. For religious martyrs in the sixteenth and seventeenth centuries it became the ideal means to preach their beliefs, while political radicals could gain sympathy for their cause and the criminal could play to the crowd. In many instances the crowds cheerfully lent their support to those who had challenged authority, as described by the poet Shelley in his *Essay on the Punishment of Death* (1813). He wrote that those who die for political crimes 'make death appear not evil but good. The death of what is called a traitor, that is, a person who, from whatever motive, would abolish the government of the day, is as often a triumphant exhibition of suffering virtue as the warning of a culprit.'

Many radicals found themselves at the gallows for protesting about their working conditions and they often gained sympathy from the crowds, particularly from their fellow workers. In the late eighteenth century the working conditions of the silk-weavers of Bethnal Green were deplorable and led to disturbances and the destruction of looms. Two men, John Doyle and John Valline, gained much support from the crowd when they were hanged at Bethnal Green in 1769 for the crime of 'silk-cutting' – destroying the half-woven cloth on another weaver's looms as a protest against working conditions in the industry. The *Gentleman's Magazine* indignantly reported that 'the mob on this occasion behaved outrageously, insulted the Sheriffs, pulled up the gallows, broke the windows, destroyed the furniture, and committed other outrages'.

Some condemned prisoners 'cheated' the crowd and escaped the public humiliation of execution by committing suicide. The murderer John Williams hanged himself in the House of Correction in Cold Bath Fields in 1811. The following day his corpse, dressed in blue trousers and a white-and-blue-striped waistcoat, was placed on an inclined platform on a cart and taken through the streets of London. Thousands turned out to view the procession, which ended at the intersection of St George's Turnpike and Cannon Street. There the body was lowered into a grave and a stake driven through it. This incident shows that crowds were even prepared to flock in vast numbers just to see the bodies of dead men. After an execution the bodies were sometimes laid out for display, as happened to three executed street robbers in November 1728. They had been hanged at Tyburn and were laid in state in an alehouse where 'vast numbers of people resorted to see them'. They were later buried at a church near Smithfield.

Large crowds could be both dangerous and intimidating, and people were warned by placards and notices about the dangers of entering the crowd, particularly the risk of being crushed. A *Foreigner's Guide to London* of 1740 offered Tyburn as one of the sights to visit but advised that 'executions are always well attended with so great mobbing and impertinences that you ought to be on your guard if curiosity leads you there'. Many accidents occurred in the huge masses of people on execution days, often with fatal results. One boy and a sheriff's officer were killed and many others wounded when the scaffold collapsed at East Smithfield in 1700. In June 1698 the prison cart set off from Newgate for Tyburn and stopped at St Sepulchre's, where a large crowd had congregated. Such was the press that the wall at the corner of the churchyard collapsed, killing one man and injuring up to forty others, four of whom died later. Such was the confusion at the scene that the cart had to take a detour from the usual route.

Thousands of people gathered for the execution of the Babington conspirators in 1586, when there was 'no lane, street, alley, or house in the suburbs of London or in the hamlets bordering the city out of which there issued not some of each sex and age'. Those who were not fortunate enough to see the actual executions crammed into the fields to watch the burning of the victims' entrails. In 1676, when four men and one woman took their final journey to Tyburn, 'vast numbers of people [followed] the carts to behold the last sad scene'.

Long speeches on the scaffold provoked the wrath of the eager crowds. In January 1664, for example, Colonel James Turner was executed for stealing from a merchant a quantity of precious stones – diamonds, rubies and sapphires – to the value of nearly £6,000. He was executed at the end of Lime Street in Leadenhall. Pepys described him on 10 January: 'Colonel Turner, (a mad, swearing, confident fellow, well known by all, and by me,) [is] now in Newgate for which we are all glad, so very a known rogue he was.' When Turner appeared on the gallows he spoke for an hour, probably hoping that a last-minute reprieve would appear. This incensed the large crowd which became tired of waiting and started to shout insults at him.

Unpopular criminals had to run the gauntlet of abuse and were pelted with stones and garbage as they made their way toward the scaffold. One description of a hanging day from the early eighteenth century conveys a perverse mixture of awfulness and the curiously intriguing. Five prisoners were taken from Newgate to Tyburn where a 'prodigious' mob' had assembled along the route, including traders, ballad-sellers, hawkers, fruit-sellers and entertainers such as jugglers and tumblers. As the condemned approached the gallows the crowd swelled in number and the prison Ordinary became a target of ridicule and insult. The singing of psalms was drowned out by the crowd, who responded with curses and shouting and descended into a 'barbarous kind of mirth'. Friends rushed forward to hasten the death of the prisoners by pulling their legs. Undignified fights broke out between the surgeon's agents and relations who were trying to claim the bodies. As the writer left he reflected on the event, adding that the whole scene had been one of 'confusion, noise, swearing, praying and singing'.

Many writers echoed this image, including a ballad in *Punch* in 1839 which commented on an execution at Horsemonger Lane Gaol:

Thicker flocked the crowd apace, louder grew the glee,
Thence was little kids a dancin, and fightin for a spree . . .

Charles Dickens attended the execution of François Courvoisier, the valet who had murdered Lord William Russell, and subsequently wrote that the crowd displayed 'no sorrow, no salutary terror, no observance, no seriousness; nothing but ribaldry, debauchery, levity, drunkenness, and flaunting vice in fifty other shapes'.

The Swiss traveller Cesar de Saussure wrote in the 1720s that criminals were given several days to prepare for death, during which time they might ask for anything they required either for the soul or for the body:

The chaplain of the prison does not leave them, and offers every consolation in his power . . . On the day of execution the condemned prisoners, wearing a sort of white linen shirt over their clothes and a cap on their heads, are tied two together and placed on carts with their backs to the horses' tails. These carts are guarded and surrounded by constables and other police officers on horseback, each armed with a sort of pike. In this way part of the town is crossed and Tyburn, which is a good half-mile from the last suburb, is reached, and here stands the gibbet.

Saussure added that it was common to see criminals going to their deaths unconcerned, while others 'are so impenitent that they fill themselves full of liquor and mock at those who are repentant'. On reaching the scaffold the prisoners were made to mount a very wide cart made for the purpose where 'a cord is passed round their necks and the end fastened to the gibbet, which is not very high'. The chaplain, also on the cart, 'makes them pray and sing a few verses of the Psalms'. At this stage relatives 'are permitted to mount the cart and take farewell'. After approximately fifteen minutes 'the executioner covers the eyes and faces of the prisoners with their caps, lashes the horses that draw the cart, which slips from under the condemned men's feet, and in this way they remain all hanging together'.

Saussure also noted that friends and relations tugged at the condemned men's feet to hasten death and that the:

bodies and clothes of the dead belong to the executioner; relatives must, if they wish for them, buy them from him, and unclaimed bodies are sold to surgeons to be dissected. You see the most amusing scenes between the people who do not like the bodies to be cut up and the messengers the surgeons have sent for the bodies; blows are given and returned before they can be got away, and sometimes the populace often come to blows as to who will carry the bought corpses to the parents who are waiting . . .

Relations and friends added to the free-for-all around the scaffold when they fought with the surgeons' agents for the bodies of the condemned. The *London Magazine* of October 1749 reported on the execution of fifteen sailors who had been involved in a riot in the Strand. At the gallows had gathered a 'multitude of spectators', which included a vast body of sailors armed with bludgeons. The men had not intended to mount a rescue but were there to make sure the surgeons' agents did not take the bodies of their friends. In the last execution on the 'Triple Tree' at Tyburn in 1759, the mob sternly opposed the agents and a riot ensued in which several persons were wounded. The mob won the day and carried away the body in triumph. The surgeons also resorted to using the mob to seize bodies. The *Daily Journal* of 31 August 1724 recorded that the body of Mr Davis was carried off by a mob, employed for the surgeons, who, 'under the specious pretences of opposing them, drew in many others to join with them, and thereby frustrated the charitable and generous intention of his friends'.

The streets and sites of execution and pillory were thronged with crowds who turned out to partake in the theatre of punishment. They would vent their anger against those criminals they despised and offer sympathy and support to those they liked or admired. Charles

Hitchen, a former Marshal of the City of London, was convicted in 1727 for attempting to commit sodomy. Expecting a rough reception, Hitchen wore armour when he was placed in the pillory but he still had to be rescued by constables. The Catholic martyr John Shert, who was executed at Tyburn in 1582, was foolish enough to admonish the crowd by wagging his finger at them. He then made the mistake of losing his nerve as the rope was placed around his neck and struggled with the hangman to stop the execution. His action predictably drew a flood of sarcastic comments from the executioner and laughter from the crowd. However, another martyr, Edmund Campion, suffered his torture and execution in 1581 with such courage and dignity that he won the crowd's sympathy. In the case of the Catholic Edmund Gennings, the executioner was requested to show the spectators pieces of his flesh 'so their curiosity might give censure whether he was fat or leane, blacke or fayre'. To satisfy the morbid curiosity of the crowd, the hangman 'tooke up one of his [Gennings's] forequarters by the arme, which when he had shewed to the People, he contemptuosly flung it downe into the baskets agayne wherin it lay, and tooke up the head that they might see his face'.

There was little respect for the dead. In 1601, after the priest Mark Barkworth had been quartered, it was noticed that constant kneeling had hardened his knees. Someone in the crowd picked up one of Barkworth's legs after the quartering and called out, 'Which of you Gospellers can show such a knee?' In 1820 the Cato Street conspirators were executed at Newgate, and had the rather grisly misfortune of being the last people to be publicly decapitated. Afterwards the executioner raised one of the severed heads to show the crowd but then dropped it. They responded by shouting, 'Ah, butterfingers!'

There were occasions when the tragedy of execution turned to comedy. Gallows humour could be both cruel and sympathetic, as in the case of John Davis in May 1733. Davis did what many prisoners must have contemplated doing, and that was to escape despite the difficulties involved. On his way to Tyburn Davis claimed that he felt sick and pleaded not to be tied to the cart. As he approached the gallows he leapt vigorously from the cart and fled across two fields, cheered on by the watching crowds. However, he was eventually caught and returned to suffer his inevitable fate.

Two years later, in 1735, the behaviour of three criminals, Gregory, Sutton and Hughes, brought a predictable response. Gregory and Sutton brazenly laughed at those watching, while Hughes was described as entirely stupefied. All three were pelted with dirt and whatever other objects the crowds could lay their hands on. While they were hanging from the rope a man in the crowd took advantage of the distraction and attempted to pick the pockets of a spectator. Unfortunately for him he was caught and was 'hurried to a pond, where he underwent the usual discipline of the populace'. Samuel Roberts and Thomas Bacchus were drawn to Tyburn on hurdles in May 1772 for the crime of coining. On the journey from Newgate to Tyburn they sobbed and implored the crowds to respect the law and abjure all criminal temptations. This, however, simply provoked the scorn and rage of the crowd, who showered them with verbal abuse and urged the hangman to dispatch them quickly.

If deterrence and example were the *raison d'être* of public punishment there were many occasions when it backfired and the crowd were quick to make their feelings known about what they perceived as the rights or wrongs of the sentence. The bookseller John Williams was a popular figure who had sold prints ridiculing the Earl of Bute. When Williams was placed in the pillory in 1765 he was not pelted in the customary manner; instead the crowds cheered him and collected £200 for him. Daniel Defoe was another who received the acclaim of the crowd for his anti-authoritarian views. When he was placed in the pillory at Charing Cross in 1703 it was garlanded with flowers and large crowds turned out to express their solidarity and support.

Criminals could achieve immediate popularity by their actions on the scaffold. The murderer William Borwick had the crowd in fits of laughter with his theatrical performance. He inspected the rope and shouted that he hoped it would be strong enough because he would hate to think he might break any bones. The thief Tom Austin asked a woman in the crowd if he could have one of her tasty-looking tarts, as he did not know if he would have the chance to try them again. However, for every criminal who displayed bravado there were many more who trembled in abject terror at the sight of the scaffold. Many accounts describe how the condemned had to be helped to the gallows because they were so weak through fear; some were rendered speechless with terror so that they could not utter their last dying words. Many fainted, screamed, cried or tried to resist their fate with a futile struggle. Some went with dignity, others with a degree of showmanship. However, in a reassuring and optimistic tone the sixteenth-century observer William Harrison was certain that 'our condemned persons do go so cheerfully to their deaths; for our nation is free, stout, haughty, prodigal of life and blood'. This was easy for Harrison to say, as he did not have to face the agonies of the gallows.

Heroes and villains were in plentiful supply for the crowds to jeer and cheer. John Felton, who had assassinated the hated Duke of Buckingham, was fêted and cheered on his way to the Tyburn gallows in 1628, and was publicly blessed by the crowd for delivering them from the despised duke. Felton became a national hero.

The crowd was quick to pass judgement and to express its views on the crimes committed by certain individuals. This was particularly so in the case of anyone who had been instrumental in sending innocent people to their deaths in order to gain a reward. In June 1732 the robber-turned-informer John Waller was sentenced to stand twice in the pillory at the Seven Dials, bareheaded, with his crime written in large characters. He did not live to see his second stint in the pillory. Such was the indignation of the populace that they pelted him to death. The next day the coroner's inquest gave a verdict of 'Wilful murder by persons unknown'. Barney Carroll and William King received a hostile reception on their way to Tyburn in July 1765. Their crime of 'cutting and maiming' had involved robbing a man on the highway and cutting him across his eyes and nose. They were hanged 'amid the execrations of an offended multitude'. The patience of the crowd could also be tested if the condemned spent too long over their prayers. The Catholic John Nelson was heckled during his prayers with shouts of 'away with thee'. Likewise, the same demands were aimed at William Sherwood and Thomas Woodhouse, with cries of 'hang him, hang him'.

It is difficult to know whether the catcalls were signs of religious disapproval or simply a response to the performance of the condemned. None the less the power of the last speech could be convincing, as the Venetian ambassador acknowledged at the execution of Henry Garnet. He recorded that Garnet was a man of 'moving eloquence' and the power of his speech could 'produce just the reverse of what they [the crowd] desire'. Sometimes the crowd would respond with mockery and hostility, especially if the condemned showed signs of cowardice or arrogance on the scaffold. Twenty years into the reign of Elizabeth the London crowd was largely anti-Catholic but would still respond favourably to a 'good performance' by a condemned Catholic on the scaffold. John Roberts, for example, won the applause of the many Protestants in the crowd for his courage.

This was not the case with the Revd Benjamin Russen, who was executed in December 1777 for the rape of a young girl, Anne Mayne. Russen had admitted to 'taking liberties with the child which were highly unbecoming'. At Tyburn, Russen made the mistake of being sanctimonious with the crowd. After saying a long prayer, he exhorted the surrounding multitude to take warning by his fate. He then proceeded to censure the indecency of the people near the gallows who had kept their hats on while prayers were said. He lectured them piously about the place where wrongdoers were to suffer the sentence of the law and abjured them to show respect. Russen had been on the receiving end of insults from the crowd throughout his journey from Newgate to Tyburn, and as a result of his hectoring increasingly acerbic catcalls and insults were hurled at him.

Anti-Semitic feelings ran high when Levi Weil, Jacob Lazarus and Solomon Porter were executed at Tyburn in December 1771 for murder. They were among a gang of eight who had broken into a house, terrified the household and murdered a labourer who came to the help of the family. The rabbi who had visited them in prison refused to accompany them to their place of execution. When they arrived at Tyburn immense crowds were waiting, 'anxious to witness the exit of [these] wretches'.

Patrick Maden was saved from the scaffold and carried away 'amid the acclamations of the people' in 1774. His life was saved at the last minute by Amos Merritt, who himself became a victim of the scaffold in the following year. Merritt burst through the crowd shouting to the executioner that he had an important communication regarding Patrick Maden, who was just about to have the noose placed around his neck. Maden was carried back to Newgate. Merritt was taken into custody and confessed that he himself had committed the robbery of which Maden had been convicted. Maden was then officially pardoned. Despite his confession, Merritt escaped justice owing to a lack of evidence. However, later in the year Merritt was indicted for breaking and entering the dwelling-house of Edward Ellicott and robbing him of plate, a gold watch and other valuable articles. Ironically he was executed at the place where he had saved Maden's life.

Popular prisoners often gained sympathy from the crowd and this proved to be the case in 1720 when the 18-year-old printer John Matthews appeared at the gallows. He had been charged with printing a seditious publication entitled *Vox Populi Vox Dei*, which asserted that the Pretender had an hereditary right to the Crown.

Matthews had also encouraged people to rise up against the government. Two witnesses who gave evidence against him were fellow workmen. On 6 November 1720 Matthews was executed at Tyburn, but his case had excited considerable public sympathy. Six months after his execution one of the printers who had been a witness against him died, and was to be buried at Islington. A mob gathered in the churchyard,

> and in a vile brutish manner, opposed his being put into the ground, cursing and damning the poor dead man in a most execrable degree; till at length growing most impudent and outrageous, they filled up the grave with earth, and throwing the boards about, that lay round it, threatened to sacrifice the persons whose duty 'twas to attend him to the grave . . .

The mob caused so great a tumult that the next night a detachment of soldiers was sent from Whitehall to make sure the corpse was buried in peace. The crowd had been so determined that the body should not be buried they 'got fiddles and drink into the church yard, and kept guard there till day light, dancing and rioting, till some of them were too drunk to move off in the morning'.

William Stayley, who was hanged, drawn and quartered for treason in 1678, provides another example of the crowd's conduct at the graveside. He had specifically requested that his quarters should not be placed on the city gates. As he had conducted himself in an exemplary manner throughout his trial and execution his request was granted and his quarters and head were placed in a coffin and buried in St Paul's churchyard. However, his Catholic friends carried out a funeral ceremony with great pomp and said Masses at his grave. The authorities were incensed by this and ordered the sheriff to have the remains of the body dug up and set on the gates and his head placed on London Bridge.

Many of the condemned were clearly aware that this was to be their last and possibly finest moment. It was also an opportunity for the more composed to receive some attention and play up to the crowd. If the performance was entertaining, the crowd reciprocated by cheering. Hannah Dagoe gave good value for money when she arrived at the Tyburn gallows in May 1763. She came from Ireland and worked in Covent Garden until she was arrested for robbery. Hannah was particularly strong and had proved to be the terror of her fellow prisoners; she even stabbed one of the men who had given evidence against her. When she arrived in the cart beneath the gallows, she managed to loose her hands and arms; seizing the executioner, she gave him such a violent blow on the breast that she nearly knocked him down. She then taunted him by daring him to hang her. The spectacle did not stop there. In order to cheat the executioner of her clothes, she took off her hat, cloak and other garments and tossed them to the cheering crowd. After a struggle the hangman managed to get the rope about her neck, but Hannah resisted him to the end. Pulling out a handkerchief, she bound it over her face and threw herself out of the cart before the signal was given. She leapt with such violence that she broke her neck and died instantly.

Dressing for the occasion was not uncommon. Roderick Audrey was executed at Tyburn in 1714 at the age of 16 for committing many robberies. Trembling with fear on the way to the scaffold, Audrey had pinned his hopes on a last-minute reprieve but it did not come and he gained neither sympathy nor pity from the crowd. None the less, either in anticipation of his reprieve or just dressed up for his final parting, Audrey was attired in a white waistcoat, clean napkin and white gloves, and was holding an orange in one hand. Jack Rann, who was executed at Tyburn for highway robbery in November 1774, had established a reputation as a flamboyant dresser. At his execution he was dressed in a new suit of pea-green clothes, a hat bound round with silver strings and a ruffled shirt. As he stared at the gallows it was said that he looked at it as an object which he had long expected to see, but not as one that he dreaded. In January 1765 John Wesket went in some style when he was hanged at Tyburn for the murder of his master, the Earl of Harrington. He wore an eye-catching blue and gold frock coat and, as a symbol of his innocence, a white cockade in his hat. On the journey to the scaffold he stood up in the cart eating oranges and casually throwing the peel into the street. This show of nonchalance won the approval of the crowd, who cheered and applauded him. The French observer Henri Misson wrote that when some condemned persons were to be executed great attention was given to getting 'handsomely dressed'. Itemising the apparel, he added that, 'When his suit of clothes, or night gown, his gloves, hat, perriwig, nosegay, coffin, flannel dress for his corpse, and all those things are brought and prepared . . . his mind is at peace and then he thinks of his conscience.'

The legal system had its own sense of theatricality, as Hogarth depicted in his illustration *The Bench*, which shows judges as indifferent and pompous thugs in wigs and ermine. The central figure is Sir John Willes, Chief Justice, lecher and scourge of rioters, while other judges in the background are falling asleep. The theatre of punishment in London had its own script, following the accused from courtroom to scaffold journey and then to the spectacle of execution. The whole event might be compared with a huge, cruel pantomime or a Punch and Judy show. The character of Punch symbolises a carnival tradition with its mixture of entertainment, audience participation and its associations with violence.

The 'world as a stage' analogy can be made with other places of popular carnivalesque pleasures. The behaviour exhibited by the crowd on execution days was not dissimilar from its response in the theatre or alehouse, or at blood sports such as cockfights, bear- and bull-baiting, badger-baiting and bare-knuckle fights. In 1727 Bernard Mandeville described the environment of an alehouse with its 'vile obscene talk, noise and ribaldry discourses together with . . . belchings and breakings of wind . . . [which] are enough to make any rational creature amongst them ashamed of his being'. Theatre audiences were criticised for 'blasphemy, impiety, indecency and riotous behaviour'. The poet Robert Southwell wrote of 'the fools, the drunkards, the madmen, the monsters, the pickpockets' and the various areas of 'lewdness and impurity, at Bartholomew Fair'.

Bernard Mandeville wrote in 1725 that the crowds at Tyburn had become very volatile. There were often fights beneath the gallows when elements of the 'mob' attempted to stop a hanging. Fights between other parts of the crowd, the officials and those rowdy elements resulted in the most 'terrible blows that are struck, the Heads that are broke, the Pieces of Sticks, and Blood, that fly about, the Men that are knock'd down and trampled upon, are beyond imagination'.

Booths and carts were set up around the area of the scaffold selling food, souvenirs and pornographic literature. A painting of an execution at Newgate in the late eighteenth century shows the scene crammed full of people who have turned up to watch the hanging of three prisoners. They lean out of windows, they perch on one another's shoulders and on the roofs of buildings. Street traders hawk their wares. It was usual to make the gallows as conspicuous as possible. At Horsemonger Lane Gaol the condemned were hanged from the roof in order that the crowd could see as much of the event as possible. In June 1612 the authorities had arranged for the missionary priests William Scott and Richard Newport to be executed between six and seven o'clock in the morning in order to deter the anticipated multitude. However, the plan failed and huge crowds turned out in force, along with members of the nobility and gentry in their coaches, to see the executions. It was said of the execution of Peter Lambert at Tyburn that it attracted more in 'number than ever attended any man to that place before, some of them being Earles and of the nobilitie'.

Such large gatherings were a magnet for pickpockets, drunkards and rogues, who prospered with almost complete immunity during these horrific events because controlling and policing the crowd was virtually impossible. If the function of public execution was to deter people from committing crime, then what was achieved was precisely the opposite of what was intended. Hangings were also supposed to bear witness to the visible power of the law and the state, but the ribaldry and irreverence on show totally undermined this.

Between the Restoration in 1660 and the mid-nineteenth century there were significant changes in criminal law and punishments. The introduction of lawyers as prosecuting and defence counsel was a significant development. However, it was in the system of punishments that the biggest changes were seen. As prisons grew in number, and with them the concept of custodial sentences, the use of whipping, branding and the pillory declined. The system of transporting convicts to America and from 1787, after the American Revolution, to Australia relieved the overcrowding in prisons and saw a reduction in executions.

By the late eighteenth century the association of hanging days with drinking, revelry and Dickens's 'fifty other types of vices' began to alarm those people whose tastes and sensitivities had been changed and refined by religious revival and moral reform. The professional classes and the urban poor had largely made up the London mob as well as the scaffold crowd. However, in the late seventeenth century anxieties about the behaviour of the working population began to engage the energies of moral campaigners, such as the Society for the Reformation of Manners. Imposing social discipline and morality became the concerns of such groups, as well as the propertied classes of London. It was the ascendance of this middle class, combined with changing attitudes towards public spaces as residential areas, that began to weaken the attraction of public executions. The Gordon Riots of July 1780 marked a watershed for the large-scale actions of the London mob. This began when a crowd of some 50,000 people protested against proposals for Catholic emancipation. The demonstration turned into a riot and for the next five days many Catholic chapels, private houses and buildings were destroyed, including the Bank of England, King's Bench Prison, Newgate and

Fleet Prisons. The army was called out but could not prevent the destruction of property estimated at over £185,000; some 285 rioters died and another 173 people were injured. In all, 139 arrests were made; 25 of the rioters were hanged and 12 imprisoned.

Evangelicalism and Methodism attempted to improve the manners and morals of the lower orders, who were thought to be the main spectators at public executions and who appeared to enjoy them far more than was thought acceptable. The authorities were clearly not happy about ordinary people enjoying morbid pastimes such as a 'good hanging'. The *Daily Telegraph* reinforced the gulf between the middle classes and public executions when it reported on the composition of the crowd at the last public execution in England in 1868: 'The beggars were coming to town . . . there was the wretched raggedness, there was the dirt, sloth, scurvy, and cretinism of rural vagabondage, trooping over the bridge.'

Clearly these voices had chosen to ignore Lord Byron's comments in the House of Lords some years earlier. In a speech arguing for the abolition of public executions, Byron reminded the privileged class in Parliament about the contribution of this 'wretched raggedness of humanity':

It is the mob that labour in your fields and serve in your houses, that man your navy, and recruit your army – that have enabled you to defy all the world, and can also defy you when neglect and calamity have driven them to despair! You may call the people a mob; but do not forget that a mob too often speaks the sentiments of the people . . . Will the famished wretch who has braved your bayonets be appalled by your gibbets? Are these the remedies for a starving and desperate populace?

However, the uncomfortable visibility of the mob fuelled the debate on the need to end public executions, although not yet for the outright abolition of the death penalty. The argument shifted to the need for privacy in order to prevent the disorder caused by the gallows crowd. Charles Dickens wrote many letters to newspapers such as the *Daily News* and *The Times* condemning not only public executions but the behaviour of the scaffold crowd. His position on execution changed from outright abolition to supporting private executions, a point he made in a letter to the editor of *The Times*: 'I simply wish to turn this dreadful experience to some account for the general good . . . that the Government might be induced to give its support to a measure making the infliction of capital punishment a private solemnity within the prison walls.'

After witnessing the execution of Courvoisier, Dickens had hoped never again to see such a thing. However, he did reluctantly attend the hanging of Frederick and Maria Manning at Horsemonger Lane Gaol in 1849. They had killed a lodger and buried him under the flagstones of their kitchen floor. Dickens wrote that he 'went there with the intention of observing the crowd'. His observation of the immense crowd at the execution led him to conclude that 'the sight [was] . . . inconceivably awful [in its] wickedness and levity'. He was appalled at the language, the shrillness, the laughing, the howls and the strong chorus of parodies on Negro melodies, with substitutions of 'Mrs Manning' for 'Susannah'. As the day progressed:

. . . thieves, low prostitutes, ruffians, and vagabonds of every kind, flocked on to the ground, with every variety of offensive and foul behaviour. Fightings, faintings, whistlings, imitations of Punch, brutal jokes, tumultuous demonstrations of indecent delight when swooning women were dragged out of the crowd by the police, with their dresses disordered, gave a new zest to the general entertainment.

At the moment of execution Dickens noted that 'thousands upon thousands of upturned faces, so inexpressibly odious in their brutal mirth or callousness' looked on at the 'two miserable creatures who attracted all this ghastly sight'.

A *Times* editorial disagreed with Dickens and commented:

The scene is doubtless the most horrid, and apparently the most hardening, that can be imagined. We are not prepared, however, to follow Mr. Dickens to his conclusion. It appears to us a matter of necessity that so tremendous an act as a national homicide should be publicly as well as solemnly done. Popular jealousy demands it . . . The mystery of the prison walls would be intolerable, for, besides mere curiosity, popular indignation would ask to see or learn the details of the punishment.

A correspondent to *The Times* in November 1849 also took issue with Dickens:

The bad passions elicited by the concourse of the scum (as regards character) of London may be mischievous, and to be deprecated, but I much doubt that the execution itself has had an evil effect; indeed, I am satisfied that it has a contrary tendency . . . It is no proof of inefficacy that many murderers have been in the habit of witnessing executions, but who can venture to say how many may have been prevented from committing the crime, not even by witnessing, but by merely reading the horrid circumstances of an execution?

The abolition of public hanging came after the report of a royal commission of 1864–6 which led to new legislation in 1868 – twenty years after Dickens's letter to *The Times*. The behaviour of the crowd at public executions was the subject of debates in the House of Commons:

> The intention of these executions was . . . to be a deterring example to others. They all saw the kind of people who usually attended these public executions. They were, generally speaking, not the intelligent or reflecting, but, on the contrary, of the lowest and most criminal classes. They were of the classes most hardened, and who could witness executions without being in the least moved or deterred by them.

A similar view had been expressed over seventy years earlier by the *Gentleman's Magazine*, which in 1791 acknowledged the ineffectiveness of public hangings, commenting that 'instead of damping the feelings of the lower orders of people . . . [public hangings] only served to heighten their wickedness'.

Parliamentary debates recognised the undesirability of a mob congregated around the gallows:

> Public executions . . . appeared to cause unmitigated evil by bringing together masses of people who, for reasons of policy and morality, should be kept isolated

and dispersed. They knew that a place of execution was a scene of debauchery of the grossest nature. They knew that when the unfortunate criminals were brought on the scaffold men whistled and behaved as though in the gallery of a theatre, and while the attention of the spectators was attracted to what was going on their pockets were picked.

The Liberal MP Sir Francis Crossley added that 'there could be no doubt that the spectators at such scenes did not belong to a very refined class, and that much coarseness and want of feeling were displayed by them'.

The momentum for legal reform had been growing since the eighteenth century and during the nineteenth century individuals such as Charles Dickens and Elizabeth Fry and the Quaker movement were to lend their voices to the argument in favour of abolition, and with some success. Demands for reform and the abolition of public executions from the eighteenth century to the 1850s and 1860s achieved their aim when the last public execution was held outside Newgate Prison on 27 May 1868. Two days later Parliament passed the 'Act to Provide for the Carrying out of Capital Punishment in Prisons', which was hailed as 'consistent with the humane legislation of the [previous] thirty years'. However, this 'humane legislation' had only removed executions from the public gaze and the death penalty continued within the confines of the prison walls. Abolition would have to wait another ninety years.

Glossary of London Prison and Gallows Slang

Akerman's Hotel – Newgate, after one of its well-known custodians.

Banged up – Safely installed in prison.

Bates' Farm – Cold Bath Fields, a reference to one of its most infamous governors.

Burdon's Hotel – White Cross Street Gaol, named after one of its custodians.

Canary – A prisoner (like a canary in a cage).

Con – A convict.

Downs – Tothill Fields House of Correction.

Ellenborough Lodge – King's Bench Prison, Southwark. The spikes that topped its walls were known as Ellenborough's Teeth after an early nineteenth-century Lord Chief Justice.

Fillet of Veal – rhyming slang for Cold Bath Fields, a particularly notorious prison.

Flowery – Cell. From the rhyming slang 'flowery dell' = cell.

Lagging – Transportation to Australia.

Limbo – A prison.

Mill Doll – Bridge Street Gaol, Blackfriars.

Never-Wag – Fleet Prison.

Newman's Hotel – Newgate, after a well-known custodian.

Number 9 – Fleet Prison. (Its address was 9 Fleet Market.)

Old Horse – Horsemonger Lane Gaol.

Salt Box – The condemned cell at Newgate.

Screw – Prison officer, after an early slang word for key.

Tea Garden – Tothill Fields House of Correction.

Traveller at Her Majesty's Expense – A transported felon.

Ville – Pentonville Prison.

Wallflower – Planning an escape (derived from the term for a person at a dance who wants to get away from the crowd).

Wells – Clerkenwell House of Detention, after the many wells in the area.

Whitt or Whittington College – Newgate Prison, after its associations with Sir Richard Whittington.

Bibliography

Primary Sources

The Confession of Thomas Pits executed at Smithfield,
   12 October 1644
*The Dying Speeches and Behaviour of the Several State
   Prisoners* . . . (London, 1720)
*An Exact and impartial Account of the Indictment,
   Arraignment, Tryal, and Judgement (according to Law) of
   Twenty Nine Regicides, the Mutherers of His Late Sacred
   Majesty of Most Glorious Memory*, London, 1660
Fielding, H. *Enquiry into the Causes of the Late Increase of
   Robbers*, London, 1751
A Full Relation of the Behaviour and Confession of . . .
   London, 1676
Fraser's Magazine, 2 August 1840
Glasgow Herald, 9 April 1956
Hansard, 23 February 1864
Harleian Miscellany, iii, 1809
Intelligencer, no. 288, 1649
London Journal, 18–25 June 1720
London Post, 19–22 July 1700
Old Whig, 12 June 1735
Post Man, 21–3 June 1698
State Trials, no. 4, 1649. National Archives (Public Record
   Office), SP 16/517
The Times, 13 November 1849, 17 November 1849
The Truest News from Tyburn, 12 December 1674
Ward, Ned, *London Spy*, 1, pt 2, 1698

Weekly Journal or the British Gazetteer, 16 November 1728
Weekly News, 31 January 1606

Secondary Sources

Abbott, G. *Mysteries of the Tower of London*, Nelson, Lancashire, 1988
—— *Severed Heads; British Beheadings through the Ages*, London, 2003
Ackroyd, P. *London: The Biography*, London, 2000
Anon. *Hanging not Punishment Enough for Murtherers, Highway Men and House-Breakers*, London, 1701
Aykroyd, P. *Evil London*, London, 1973
Babington, A. *The English Bastille, A History of Newgate Gaol and Prison Conditions in Britain 1188–1902*, New York, 1972
Bakhtin, M. *Rabelais and His World*, Indiana, USA, 1984
Barber, S. 'Charles I: Regicide and Republicanism' *History Today*, 1996, vol. 46, no. 1
Barker, F. *Greenwich and Blackheath Past*, London, 1999
Barker, F. and Silvester-Clarke, D. *The Black Plaque Guide to London*, London, 1987
Barton, N. *The Lost Rivers of London*, London, 1992
Beattie, J.M. *Policing and Punishment in London, 1660–1750, Urban Crime and the Limits of Terror*, Oxford, 2001
Benson, T. *London Immortals*, London, 1951
Birkett, Lord (ed.) *The New Newgate Calendar*, London, 1960
Bland, J. *The Common Hangman: English and Scottish Hangmen before the Abolition of Public Executions*, Westbury, Wiltshire, 2001
Bleackley, H. *The Hangmen of England*, London, 1929
Bloom, C. *Violent London; 2000 Years of Riots, Rebels and Revolts*, London, 2003
Brandon, D. *Stand and Deliver: A History of Highway Robbery*, Stroud, 2001
Brooke A. and Brandon, D. *Bound for Botany Bay: British Convict Voyages to Australia*, Kew, 2005

Brooke A. and Brandon, D. *Tyburn, London's Fatal Tree*, Stroud, 2004

Brooks, J.A. *Ghosts of London*, Norwich, 1995

Budworth, G. *The River Beat: The Story of London's River Police since 1798*, London, 1997

Burke, P. *Popular Culture in Early Modern Europe*, Aldershot, 1994

Burke, T. *The Streets of London through the Centuries*, London, 1949

Bushell, P. *London's Secret History*, London, 1983

Butler, I. *Murderers' London*, London, 1992

Cameron, D.K. *London's Pleasures from Restoration to Regency*, Stroud, 2001

Cooper, D.D. *The Lessons of the Scaffold. The Public Execution Controversy in Victorian England*, London, 1974

de Loriol, P. *Famous and Infamous Londoners*, Stroud, 2004

Diehl, D. and Donnelly, M.P. *Tales from the Tower of London*, Stroud, 2004

Emsley, C. *Crime and Society in England 1750–1900*, Harlow, 1987

Evelyn, J. *The Diary of John Evelyn*, London, 1996

Ewen, C. L'Estrange. *Witch Hunting and Witch Trials*, London, 1929

Fido, M. *Murder Guide to London*, London, 1986

Foot, M. *The Politics of Paradise: A Vindication of Byron*, New York, 1988

Forshaw, A. and Bergstrown, T. *Smithfield Past and Present*, London, 1990

Foxe, J. *The Acts and Monuments of John Foxe*, ed. J. Prett, London, 1877

Fraser, A. *The Gunpowder Plot: Terror and Faith in 1605*, London, 1996

Gatrell, V. *The Hanging Tree*, Oxford, 1996

Glanville, P. *London in Maps*, London, 1972

Glinert, E. *The London Compendium*, London 2003

Gomme, L. *Tyburn Gallows*, London, 1909

Griffiths, A. *The Chronicles of Newgate*, London, 1987

Griffiths, P. and Jenner, M.S. *Londonopolis*, Manchester, 2000

Halliday, S. *Newgate: London's Prototype of Hell*, Stroud, 2006

Hay, D., Linebaugh, P. et al. *Albion's Fatal Tree: Crime and Society in Eighteenth-Century England*, Harmondsworth, 1977

Haynes, A. *The Gunpowder Plot*, Stroud, 1994

Heppenstall, R. *Reflections on the Newgate Calendar*, London, 1975

Herber, M. *Criminal London: A Pictorial History from Medieval Times to 1939*, Chichester, 2002

Hibbert, C. *London, The Biography of a City*, London, 1977

—— *The Road to Tyburn*, London, 1957

Hitchcock, T. and Shore, H. (eds) *The Streets of London from the Great Fire to the Great Stink*, London, 2003

Holston, J. *Ehud's Dagger, Class Struggle in the English Revolution*, London, 2000

Honeycombe, G. *The Murders of the Black Museum 1870–1970*, London, 1982

—— *More Murders of the Black Museum, 1835–1985*, London, 1993

Hooper, W. Eden. *History of Newgate and the Old Bailey*, London, 1935

Howell, Thomas Bayley (ed.) *Cobbett's Complete Collection of State Trials*, vol. 2

Huggarde, N. *The Displaying of the Protestants*, London, 1556

Huish, R. *The Life of James Greenacre*, London, 1837

Hutton, R. *The Restoration: A Political and Religious History of England and Wales, 1658–1667*, Oxford, 1985

Ignatieff, M. *A Just Measure of Pain: The Penitentiary in the Industrial Revolution 1750–1850*, London, 1989

Inwood, S. *A History of London*, London, 1998

James, P.D. and Critchley, T.A. *The Maul and the Pear Tree; The Ratcliffe Highway Murders 1811*, London, 1971

Jardine, D. *A Narrative of the Gunpowder Plot*, London, 1857

Jonson, B. *Bartholomew Fair*, ed. S. Gossett, Manchester, 2000

Kent, W. (ed.) *An Encyclopaedia of London*, London, 1937
—— *London Mystery and Mythology*, London, 1952

Kenyon, J.P. *The Popish Plot*, Harmondsworth, 1974

Lake, P. and Questier, M. 'Agency, Appropriation and Rhetoric under the Gallows: Puritans, Romanists and the State in Early Modern England', *Past & Present*, 1996, no. 153

Lane, B. (ed.) *The Murder Club Guide to London*, London, 1988

Latham, R. and Matthews, W. (eds) *The Diary of Samuel Pepys*, vol. I, London, 1971

Linebaugh, P. *The London Hanged: Crime and Civil Society in the Eighteenth Century*, London, 1991

Linnane, F. *The Encyclopaedia of London Crime and Vice*, Stroud, 2003
—— *London, the Wicked City: A Thousand Years of Vice in the Capital*, London, 2003

McAdoo, W. *The Procession to Tyburn: Crime and Punishment in the Eighteenth Century*, New York, 1927

Mackenzie, G. *Great City North of Oxford Street*, London, 1972

McLynn, F. *Crime and Punishment in Eighteenth-Century England*, Oxford, 1989

McMullen, J. *The Canting Crew: London's Criminal Underworld 1550–1750*, New Jersey, 1984

McNiven, P. *Heresy and Politics in the Reign of Henry IV*, London, 1987

Marks, A. *Tyburn Tree: Its History and Annals*, London, 1908

Mingay, G.E. *Georgian London*, London, 1975

Mitchell, R.J. and Leys, M.D. *A History of London Life*, Harmondsworth, 1963

Moore, L. *The Thieves' Opera*, London, 1997

Moore, W. *Lascivious Bodies*, London, 2005

Murphy, T. *The Old Bailey: Eight Centuries of Crime, Cruelty and Corruption*, Edinburgh, 1999

Nichols, J.G. (ed.) *The Diary of Henry Machyn: Citizen and Merchant-Taylor of London, 1550–1653*, London, 1848

Okines, A.W. 'Why was there so little Government Reaction to the Gunpowder Plot?', *Journal of Ecclesiastical History*, 2004, vol. 55

Panton, K. *London: A Historical Companion*, Stroud, 2003

Picard, L. *Dr Johnson's London*, London, 2000

Pierce, P. *Old London Bridge*, London, 2001

Platter, T. *Thomas Platter's Travels in England*, London, 1599

Pollen, J.H. *The English Catholics in the Reign of Queen Elizabeth*, London, 1920

Porter, R. *London: A Social History*, London, 1994

Prebble, J. *Mutiny; Highland Regiments in Revolt 1743–1804*, London, 2001

Purkiss, D. *The Witch in History*, London, 1996

Raleigh, Sir Walter. *The Works of Sir Walter Raleigh*, 8 volumes, 1829

Rowse, A.L. *The Tower of London in the History of the Nation*, London, 1972

Richardson, J. *The Annals of London*, London, 2000

Ridley, J. *Bloody Mary's Martyrs*, London, 2002

Ritchie, J. Ewing. *The Night Side of London*, London, 1857

Rude, G. *Hanoverian London, 1714–1808*, London, 1971

Rumbelow, D. *The Triple Tree: Newgate, Tyburn and Old Bailey*, London, 1982

Saussure, C. de. *A Foreign View of England in 1725–9: The Letters of Monsieur Cesar de Saussure to His Family*, ed. Van Muyden, London, 1995

Sellers, L. *Shot in the Tower: The Story of the Spies executed in the Tower of London during the First World War*, London, 1997

Sharpe, J.A. 'Last Dying Speeches: Religion, Ideology and Public Execution in Seventeenth-Century England', *Past and Present*, 1985, no. 107

Sheppard, F. *London 1808–1870: The Infernal Wen*, London, 1971

Sheppard, F. *London: A History*, London, 1998

Shoemaker, R. *The London Mob: Violence and Disorder in Eighteenth-Century Britain*, London, 2004

Smyth, J. *The Men of Property: Irish Radicals and Popular Politics in the late Eighteenth Century*, London, 1992

Stallybrass, P. and White, A. *The Politics and Poetics of Transgression*, New York, 1986

Stow, J. *A Survey of London Written in the Year 1598*, Stroud, 1999

Tames, R. *City of London Past*, London, 1995

—— *Clerkenwell and Finsbury Past*, London, 1999

—— *Southwark Past*, London, 2001

Thomas, K. *Religion and the Decline of Magic*, Harmondsworth, 1971

Thornbury, W. *Old London: Charterhouse to Holborn*, London, 1987

—— *Old London: Shoreditch to Smithfield*, London, 1987

Underwood, P. *Haunted London*, London, 1973

Wakefield, E.G. *The Hangman and the Judge, or a letter from Jack Ketch to Mr Justice Alderson*, London, 1833

Walford, E. *Old London: Covent Garden and the Thames to Whitehall*, 1987

—— *Old London: Hyde Park to Bloomsbury*, London, 1989

—— *Old London: Strand to Soho*, London, 1987

Waller, M. *1700: Scenes from London Life*, London, 2000

Wedgwood, C.V. *The Trial of Charles I*, Harmondsworth, 1983

Weinreb, B. and Hibbert, C. *The London Encylopaedia*, London, 1983

Wilson, D. *The Tower, 1078–1978*, London, 1978

Wise, S. *The Italian Boy. Murder and Grave Robbery in 1830s London*, London, 2004

Wordsworth, W. *The Prelude*, ed. E. de Selincourt and S. Gill, Oxford, 1970

Index